SAM

REES HOWELLS

A Life of Intercession

The Legacy of Prayer and
Spiritual Warfare of an Intercessor

RICHARD MATON

Samuel Rees Howells, A Life of Intercession: The Legacy of Prayer and Spiritual Warfare of an Intercessor by Richard A. Maton. Arranged and supplemented by Mathew and Paul Backholer, ByFaith Media

As is the nature of the internet, web pages can disappear and ownership of domain names can change. Those stated within this book were valid at the time of first publication in 2012.

ISBN 978-1-907066-13-9 (paperback)
ISBN 978-1-907066-37-5 (hardback)
ISBN 978-1-907066-29-0 (eBook ePub)
British Library Cataloguing In Publication Data. A Record of this Publication is available from the British Library

Richard Alexander Maton: born September 1932
First published in November 2012 by ByFaith Media and updated in 2014, 2016 and August 2017.

- Jesus Christ is Lord -

'Samuel was among those who called upon His name. They called upon the Lord and He answered them' (Psalm 99:6).

Samuel Rees Howells, Director of the Bible College of Wales (BCW) in the grounds of Derwen Fawr Estate August 1963, age 51

Contents

Contents

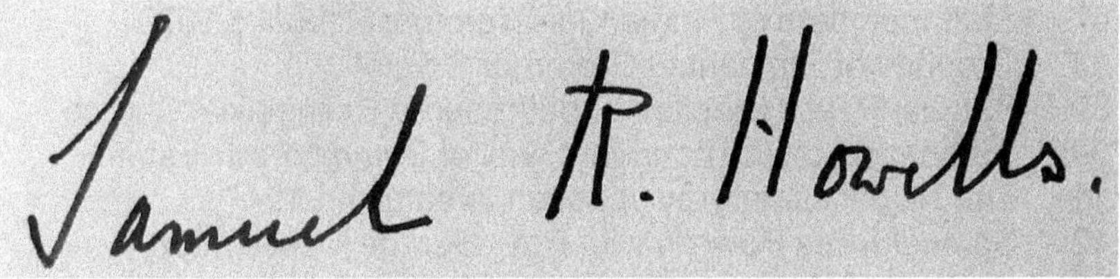

Signature of Samuel Rees Howells

'So I sought for a man among them who would make a wall and stand in the gap on behalf of the land' (Ezekiel 22:30a).

Photos

Page

Foreword

In February 2000, fifty years after Rees Howells' death, his only son Samuel, aged eighty-seven, spoke at the Bible College of Wales (BCW), about the day his father died and the cost of his life of intercession. As young Bible College students, my brother and I sat speechless as the quiet Director decided to share about the enormous burden that he had been shouldering for five decades.

Every Thursday evening at BCW, students would gather in the prayer room and wait for Samuel Rees Howells to enter and begin the meeting. As young students, Samuel seemed to us like an ancient patriarch. This was a man like Abraham, a person of another age, one who had lived through the powerful years of Rees Howells' ministry and was alive as a testimony to them. Those first few months of Bible College life transformed us both, alongside other students. Sitting in front of us in every evening meeting were the remnant intercessors who had 'prayed through' with Rees Howells during the war years. These were the prayer warriors who had left a fingerprint on history and during Samuel's lifetime, they had engaged in spiritual warfare that had influenced world events!

As young students, we longed to be able to sit down with these intercessors and ask them to share their testimonies. They were in their eighties then, but they were once young people when Rees had taught and led them. It took about three years for these frail elderly people to confide in us – we were then staff members. Sixty years had passed since the beginning of the intercessions that led through the war years, yet these intercessors beamed with inner light as they shared experiences as if they had happened yesterday.

Samuel Howells was a very quiet man who confided in few people and he carefully guarded his intercessory burdens and testimonies. Therefore, when Richard Maton told us that he was writing a book about Samuel's life (and was nearing the end of his fourth year of work), and as Alan Scotland, the successor of Samuel Howells as Director of the Bible College asked ByFaith Media to publish it, we were very excited. After receiving the manuscript, our first read deeply moved us. We began to learn much about the hidden path of intercession that Samuel had walked and got to know him as a person, who, though 'being dead still speaks' (Hebrews 11:4). Richard Maton's manuscript also contained precise details about the history of BCW, including many of its staff, students and visitors.

As authors and as the publisher, we also realised that one book could never be enough to tell the full story of the extraordinary life of Samuel Rees Howells. We knew that many people would be very interested in learning the in-depth story of Samuel's intercessions, in line with the panoptic legacy of his father Rees Howells. Samuel's intercessory ministry was very deep and effectual. His prayers had significant impact on world events and therefore we felt an additional book would be able to explore Samuel's intercessions in further detail. With this in mind, we presented to Alan Scotland and Richard Maton the idea of publishing two books about Samuel's life.

Richard Maton's original manuscript would be published first as *Samuel, Son and Successor of Rees Howells*, which also explains the full details concerning the running of BCW, its four estates, school, hospital and aspects of the intercessory ministry alongside the lives of dozens of its staff and students, and their ministries. It also has 110+ photos, including many of Rees Howells.

The second book would be called *Samuel Rees Howells: A Life of Intercession* and would be anchored in Richard Maton's original manuscript. Using Richard's thorough knowledge of Samuel's life of intercession and the BCW archives, this book would be significantly different with a revised layout, additional quotes, testimonies and historical data. The history of BCW, covered extraordinarily in the first book would not need to be repeated, which would give the second book more room to consider the life of prayer, intercession and faith; the legacy of both Samuel and Rees Howells. To aid the chronology of the book, chapters from the original text would need to be broken up and new chapters added. This book would be very different from the first book and would be a collaboration of Richard Maton's original text, with additions. With this in mind, Alan Scotland kindly gave us unlimited access to the Bible College archives to source new material – a task that took us both a long time. Our research took us through records of meetings from the late 1930s up until 2002, newspaper cuttings spanning ninety years, numerous hours of taped sermons and dozens of handwritten notebooks, alongside personal diaries and letters where we found incredible details of Samuel's prayers and the answers he received.

Throughout the re-editing process, Richard and Kristine Maton have given insightful guidance, clarified facts, reworked passages and have also inspired us with their personal memories. Trying to sum up any person's life in one book can never unveil the full complexities of that individual, but the two books concerning Samuel present a fuller picture of him. He was a man of extreme faith and a humble imperfect human being (Acts 15:37-38).

Richard Maton spent fifty-two years of his life at BCW and worked closely alongside Samuel for over twenty years. He was the most loyal ministry friend that Samuel had in the last two decades of his life and Samuel trusted many secrets to no other person. During our combined seven years at Bible College, Richard was the 'face' of

BCW. Throughout those critical final years of Samuel's life, Richard Maton worked unearthly hours, yet remained accessible, patient and practised the presence of Christ, in the fruit of the Spirit.

Richard's wife Kristine joined the College family in 1936, when her parents became staff under the guidance of Rees Howells. Her father's home call came just a year later. Her mother continued teaching mathematics with true distinction in the Grammar School until 1980, and shared in the prayer ministry of the College until her promotion to glory in 1998. Kristine taught in the Preparatory Department and worked in many roles, including head teacher until 1994, when the School closed. She continued working with the College and has given valuable additions to help Richard to record the life of Samuel Rees Howells. Without the Matons' years of research and labour, the story of Samuel Rees Howells could never have been told. We are all deeply indebted to them.

Some biographies glamorise the life of an individual, extenuating their virtues and minimising their flaws turning a work into a hagiography. These types of books can present an untrue reflection of a personality and can demoralise others who seek a deeper walk with God, but often slip-up. Others romanticise the idea of serving the Lord, living a life of faith and intercession, and forget that normal life goes on, as personalities do grate, whilst others clash. Samuel's life was not glamorous; he became the Director of BCW upon the death of his father in 1950 and received monolithic responsibilities, with huge financial liabilities placed upon him at a young age. Like all men and women of faith, he was an imperfect vessel, learning life lessons by trial and error, but the Lord worked through him because of his obedience. This comforting thought helps reassure us, that we too can follow in the Lord's footsteps as we offer our bodies as living sacrifices, fully, totally and unconditionally to Him (Romans 12:1, Galatians 2:20, 2 Corinthians 5:15).

On an editorial note, the financial records in the book are noted in United Kingdom (U.K.) pounds and United States (U.S.) dollars at the rate of £1 to $1.6. The modern equivalent amounts have been calculated by using the official inflation statistics from the Bank of England. The text also contains some Welsh words and phrases, a language rich in consonants. Many quotes are in conversational style which is how they were transmitted; but lamentably the written word cannot reproduce the true personality of the speaker or the atmosphere of the meeting.

Mathew and Paul Backholer
ByFaith Media
www.ByFaith.org

Introduction

This intercessory biography of Samuel Rees Howells carves an unmistakable pathway through twentieth century history and shows what God can do through the life of an individual totally surrendered to Him. The quality and depth of Samuel's ministry as Honorary Director of the Bible College of Wales (BCW) from 1950 to 2002 was greatly shaped and moulded through his years spent under the ministry of his father, Rees Howells. The title 'Honorary Director' was not a position without any responsibilities, quite the contrary. It was initially used to distinguish him from his father, the Director, who founded the College, and the title stuck.

Rees was born in 1879 and lived an extraordinary life of prayer, faith and sacrifice. In 1906, the Lord asked him to lay down all his hopes, dreams and ambitions in an act of full surrender and to invite the Holy Spirit to live His life through him. When he did this, the Lord showed him that the key to a fruitful prayer life, was to pray only the prayers that the Holy Spirit gave him (John 15:7-8).

Intercession was Rees Howells' primary calling and the Holy Spirit demonstrated through him that God has absolute and complete power over the devil, in finances, sickness and deliverance. Throughout his ministry, Rees was always reaching out in the Holy Spirit to raise the standard in the Church to that of the early Church, when the "greater works" (John 14:12) were performed as a clear testimony to the world of that time.

Many of the deepest truths that Rees discovered concerning the work of the Holy Spirit can be found in Jesus' teaching in John's Gospel chapters 14-17. Years could be spent meditating on these, but for Rees, he learnt them as the Holy Spirit made him live them.

In 1924, Rees was led to found a Bible College by faith alone, and ten years later he received the Every Creature Vision from God, accepting personal responsibility to intercede that every person would hear the Gospel. Rees invited everyone at the Bible College to receive the Holy Spirit, and the responsibility for the Every Creature Vision on the same terms that he had accepted them. The entrance fee to this life of faith, he explained, is a full and complete surrender to the Lord. There can be no compromise with God.

This Vision from God placed upon the College staff a personal duty to intercede for the Gospel to go to the world, and to bind any strong man (spiritual power) in the heavenly realms that hindered the progress of the Gospel (Mark 3:27). Rees had learnt that all conflicts on earth are rooted in spiritual battles in the heavenly realms and that intercession has to prevail in this realm for events on earth to be transformed. This was also the experience of the prophets and apostles in the Bible. Paul wrote about it in Ephesians 6:12, 'For we do not wrestle against flesh and blood (against human beings, dictators or failed / evil governments etc.), but against principalities, against powers, against the rulers of the darkness of this age, against the spiritual hosts of wickedness in the heavenly places.' Their call therefore, was to spiritual warfare in the heavenly places as led and guided by the Holy Spirit.

This Vision and the College's personal commitment to it were put to the test during World War II, when in accordance with Ephesians 6:12, Satan raised up Hitler to challenge God's plan for Gospel liberty, freedom and worldwide missionary endeavour. Satan had to be bound and the Holy Spirit led the College staff in a prolonged intercession for the demise of this threat to dominate the world. The believing and faith that the Holy Spirit gave at that time enabled Rees to declare publicly the complete defeat of Hitler. He was confident that Divine power and authority were available to overthrow any spiritual powers restricting the proclamation of the Gospel in every country of the world, for the fulfilment of the Every Creature Vision.

In 1950, Rees was promoted to glory and his son, Samuel, led the College throughout the next fifty-two years of intercessory battles. Samuel always endeavoured to stress the importance of receiving the Person and not just the blessings of the Holy Spirit, in the future of the College. Samuel also oversaw the releasing of Rees' intercessory teaching legacy, through the books, *Rees Howells Intercessor* (1952) by Norman Grubb and *The Intercession of Rees Howells* (1983) by Doris Ruscoe.

Samuel lived for the Lord Jesus Christ and he always stressed the centrality of the cross in history. The victory of all intercessory prayer is established in Christ's triumph on the cross. The central themes of Samuel's life of sacrifice and intercession are summed up in the book of Colossians. Christ's pre-eminence in creation and in spiritual warfare are unfolded within: 'He has delivered us from the power of darkness and conveyed us into the Kingdom of the Son of His love...For by Him all things were created that are in Heaven and that are on earth, visible and invisible, whether thrones or dominions or principalities or powers. All things were created through Him and for Him...Having disarmed principalities and powers, He made a public spectacle of them, triumphing over them in it...If then you were raised with Christ, seek those things which are above where Christ is, sitting at the right hand of God. Set your mind on things above, not on things on the earth. For you died and your life is hidden with Christ in God...Continue earnestly in prayer, being vigilant in it with thanksgiving; meanwhile praying also for us, that

God would open to us a door for the Word, to speak the mystery of Christ…' (Colossians 1:13, 16, 2:15, 3:1-3, 4:2-3). Samuel went to be with the Lord in 2004, having lived according to these principles.

The Howells Family, Rees, Lizzie Hannah and their son, Samuel Rees (age 28) January 1941 outside Derwen Fawr House

Chapter One

A Solemn Occasion

Rees Howells was promoted to glory on 13 February 1950 and an outstanding burden of responsibility crashed down upon the heart of the young introverted, Samuel Rees Howells. There was no time to be swallowed up in grief, for the practical needs of the Bible College were now entirely his personal responsibility. Samuel was now accountable to believe for huge sums of money by faith alone. Like his father, Rees, he was not permitted by the Lord to ask for financial partners, host fundraisers or to make appeals to raise money. Samuel had to go to God alone in prayer, for the College was to continue to be a true ministry of raw faith (Isaiah 36:6, Philippians 4:19). Could Samuel believe God like Rees had?

Fifty years later, on the anniversary of Rees Howells death, his son Samuel, now eighty-seven years of age, was visibly moved with emotion as he testified of the weight of intercession that his earthly father had borne. "He had carried heavy burdens during the war," he said. "Naturally he was a very strong man and could have lived until he was quite aged. But those burdens of the war deeply affected him, particularly the burden that the Lord God laid upon him for the survival of the Jewish people. When he came in one day and told us that the Lord had laid that burden upon him; it affected us profoundly. It's wonderful how the Lord blessed and worked in those days, and although they happened half a century ago, they're still vivid in our minds and memories."

Those present in the meeting testified to the silent atmosphere of respect and awe which pervaded the room. Samuel rarely spoke on a personal level of these costly days of intercession, abiding and faith. For Samuel, every moment was alive and the memory of the struggle and pain was still vivid. Samuel had watched first-hand as his earthly father had entered into a spiritual battle that would cost him his life, the ferocity of which, few could understand. "Mother and I used to discuss the situation," continued Samuel, "and we told one another that his strength had gone and it would be impossible for him to be with us for much longer." There was no sense of regret, for each victory secured through intercession is always worth the price. "But we were not sorry that he had carried those burdens," he said, "but rather we thank the Lord for giving him the grace. I remember it was on a Wednesday evening when he took the last meeting and at the end of that meeting he waved his handkerchief and sang, 'Away Over Jordan With My Blessed Jesus.' Then he left the room and one of the men went up to see if he was alright in his bedroom and there he was in a collapsed state." Lowering his voice and trembling Samuel continued, "He never recovered...never recovered." Only a son could speak in such a manner about one he knew, respected and loved so much.

IT IS WHEN A CRY IS WRUNG FROM THE HEART THAT GOD HEARS AND ANSWERS PRAYER.

Mr Samuel.

A saying from Samuel Rees Howells (known as Mr Samuel to staff and students) as jotted down by an elderly staff member

As Samuel concluded the meeting, smiling, he recalled five decades of answered prayer. "We are so glad for the way that the Lord has been with us. They might have been very, very dark days! The needs were very, very great and we were so weak and insufficient in our own strength. But the Lord was with us. We went to prayer and the Lord dealt with those needs. It took several months of intensive prayer, but it was worth it. When you think, then, of the way the Lord has led us during these past years. The testings have been great, they've been tremendous! But His grace has been more than sufficient and we want to thank Him from the bottom of our hearts for the way that the Lord has been with us for these fifty years. As Joshua was able to say, so we are able to say too, that we have proved, not sometimes, but at all times, His faithfulness and our desire now is to see the work completed" (Joshua 21:45, 23:14, 1 Kings 8:56).

This was Samuel's testimony near the end of a life of faith, testings and intercession. The Lord is faithful. As a young man, Samuel had learnt the principles of intercession – abiding, agony, authority and victory from his father Rees. Samuel had seen the power of intercession, not in theory, but through the intense spiritual battles leading up to and through WWII. He had witnessed intercession in action and world events were altered! In Samuel's lifetime, he himself would prove God's hand in world situations.

Before we consider the intercessions of Samuel Rees Howells, we must first return to those early days of faith, back to 1912, when Rees was a young man and his wife Lizzie was pregnant.

Chapter Two

Samuel, Sacrifice and Submarines

In April 1912, Rees Howells and his young wife Lizzie, now five months pregnant, heard the news that *Titanic* had sunk on its way to New York. Only a few months later, Rees and his wife would be thrust into their own tragic life-and-death crisis. It was the 31 August 1912, and Lizzie Howells was slipping away. The birth of their son in Brynaman had been traumatic and the once glowing face of Rees' wife had been altered into a pale exanimate gaze into death.

Throughout his costly life of intercession, Lizzie had been Rees Howells' loyal friend and now their sacred marriage covenant was in danger of being torn asunder. She was drifting towards eternity and in desperation Rees turned to the Lord seeking guidance. Rees knew the Scriptures and he must have felt identified with the Lord Jesus, 'who in the days of His flesh, had offered up prayers and supplications, with vehement cries and tears' (Hebrews 4:7).

Rees and Lizzie Hannah Howells 1910 (the year of their marriage)

Rees sought the Lord for his place of abiding faith for her healing. At stake was not a stranger he had been called to love, but his beloved wife, the mother of his only child. Rees had seen many people healed in response to believing faith and he consented that medication was a gift from God and should be accepted, unless otherwise directed. But when medication failed, man's extremity would become God's opportunity. Nonetheless, in this private test the Lord led him in an unusual way, telling him that his wife was not to accept any medicine and was to trust wholly in the Lord. "It was a fight of faith for me," said Rees, "and a fight with death for her." Could death be confronted once more and forced to flee by the power of a gained position of intercession?

Rees accepted this position from the Lord and stood his ground, telling his wife in believing faith, "You will not die." The test was severe, but they took courage from the Scriptures and a reading from Mark 11:22 gave them their breakthrough. 'Jesus answered and said to them, "Have faith in God." ' They believed the promise and she began to recover. Faith had triumphed!

Months before this trial, they had sought the Lord for a name for their son and He led them to the story of Hannah, a woman of faith, who had dedicated her son to the Lord after a long trial, calling him Samuel. Rees smiled because his wife's middle name was Hannah and they followed God's leading, calling him Samuel, without knowing that they too would lend their child to the Lord. I "will give him to the Lord all the days of his life," said Hannah, therefore, "as long as he lives he shall be lent to the Lord" (1 Samuel 1:11, 24).

Rees Howells had been taught by the Holy Spirit that he could not ask the Lord to move another to do something which he himself had not done, or had proved willing to do. In 1912, in the same month as Samuel was born, his parents were burdened to pray for more missionaries to be sent to Africa. As they were praying for labourers to be thrust out into the harvest fields the Lord said to them, "I will answer this prayer through you! I will send you both out there!"

A heavy sense of duty fell upon them as they contemplated the cost of the call. Young Samuel could never go to Africa with them, because it would be a sentence of death to expose him to malaria ridden swamps, extreme temperatures and dangerous foreign lands. "It was our first test on the call and the greatest," said Rees.

The words of Jesus shattered their seemingly comfortable faith, "He that loves son or daughter more than Me is not worthy of Me" (Matthew 10:37). This young couple had read this verse many times before, but they never thought the Lord would ask them to live it.

As they brooded over this new call, they began to empathise that God the Father had given up His only Son, because of His interminable love for sinful mankind, and He was now asking them to do what He had already done. Jesus had given His life for every soul in the world, including all Africans and now Rees and Lizzie swallowed their grief to follow Christ to the cross, to lay down their son, and if necessary to die in Africa. With this in mind, foster parents had to be found for Samuel, and after a battle of faith the Lord provided him a home with Uncle Moses Rees and his wife, Elizabeth. In a letter to Samuel in latter years, Rees wrote: 'I am more indebted to them than to any people on the face of the earth.'

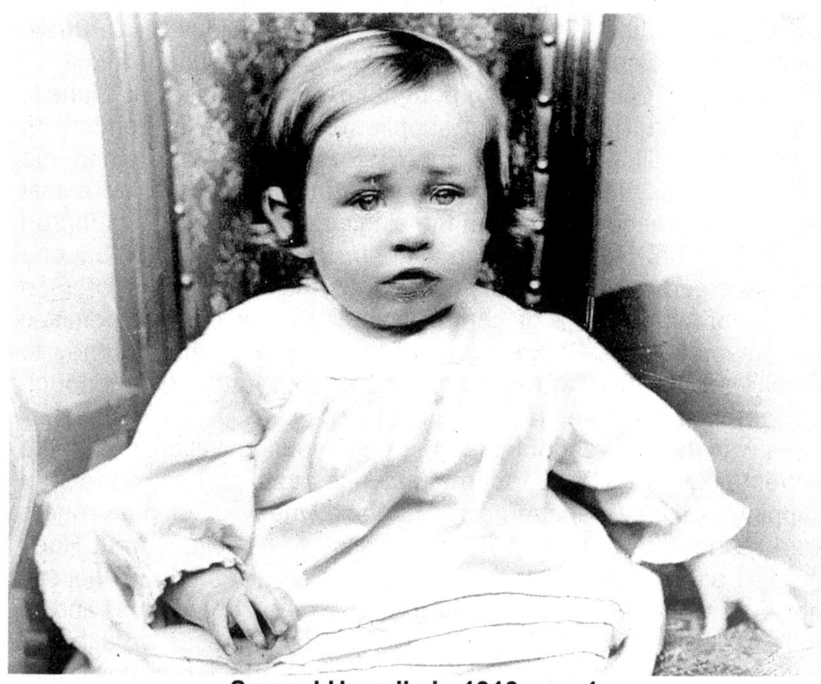

Samuel Howells in 1913, age 1

When the day came to hand young Samuel over, Lizzie's sacrifice proved that she too had made a deep unconditional surrender to God. Folding his baby clothes, she broke her heart. His tiny fingers, gentle eyes and loving smile made her feel it was the end of the world. Rees did all he could to hold himself together for his wife, but she wept the tears of a loving mother. Together they proved that Africa was going to cost. Later, Rees asked his wife how she found the strength to obey the Lord and she told him that the Lord had said, "Measure it with Calvary." If Christ was willing to suffer torture, humiliation, excruciating pain and separation from the Father for her, she too would prove her willingness to follow Him; and the words of the hymn she often sang came to mind: 'But we never can prove the delights of His love, until all on the altar we lay.'

Two months before Rees Howells and his wife set sail for Africa, the RMS *Lusitania* was torpedoed by a German U-20 submarine and sank in just eighteen minutes. 1,198 innocent lives were lost, including 128 American citizens. This act set America on a path that eventually led them to join WWI and it was also a timely reminder that Rees and Lizzie Howells would be sailing into a war zone!

At Samuel's foster parents' home in Garnant, Wales, U.K. at the bottom of the garden and up the embankment ran the local railway line. Samuel could vaguely recall being asked to wave to his parents on 10 July 1915, just before his third birthday, as the train puffed its way along the track, on their journey to Southern Africa.

They had left Garnant having bought tickets only as far as Llanelli; the Lord had not at that point supplied the full fare to London. In Llanelli and still without the money, Rees and Lizzie joined the queue – a real test of obedience and faith, rewarded by a last minute deliverance from one of the singing crowd who had gathered to see them off. This was not an act of bravado to be copied but one that emerged from their experience of the faithfulness of God gained through a walk of complete dependence on His promises over several years. Before they left the station on their journey to London and beyond, they were showered with further gifts, enough to cover their expenses for the whole trip.

This was the first test of many to get the young missionaries to the harvest field. In 1915, German submarines sank 1.3 million tons of shipping. As they departed from England, many other passengers were fearful that their ship would be sunk like *Lusitania*, but Rees assured all who needed it that God would protect them. To believe that God would guard their ship from German submarines, and to publicly declare it to those who were afraid, was a leap of faith that few have taken. Rees was proving the power of intercession. Here was a man of God who had secured a victory in the heavenly realm for himself and his wife. Now he could stand for the protection of all!

Rees was not the first person to attain this intercessory victory. During a storm that eventually wrecked their ship, Paul said, "For there stood by me this night an angel of the God to whom I belong and whom I serve saying, 'Do not be afraid Paul, you must be brought before Caesar and indeed God has granted you all those who sail with you.' Therefore take heart, men, for I believe God that it will be just as it was told me" (Acts 27:1-2, 23-24). God too had granted a safe passage to these two young missionaries and to 'all who sailed with them.' Through experiences like these, the Lord showed Rees and his wife the need of allowing the Holy Spirit to bring their experience up to the level of the Word.

Another test came on the journey when the captain lost his nerve and feared for their safety. But they continued to assure the captain of a safe passage through U-boat infested waters because God was taking them to Africa to serve Him. These profound risks of faith which they undertook were unknown to young Samuel, but they kept in touch and sent postcards to him on their journey.

Many years later, on 27 January 1945, Rees preached on 1 Kings 19:15-16 and 19-21, concerning Elisha being commissioned by Elijah and he recalled his ministry in Africa. "I was called to the ministry and afterwards to Africa," he said, "and those souls in Africa became more to me than my life…Could anything be greater than to go out to the heathen with the risen Christ?" Rees then testified of his intercession for a Welsh village nicknamed Hell-Fire Row, prior to coming to Africa. In this village there was not even one Christian, but he was led by the Holy Spirit to stand in the gap for those people, and he gained a place of intercession for them and revival came. Then, when he went to Africa, the Holy Spirit applied that gained position of intercession for them. The Holy Spirit had taught him to love at home, now he could love the world.

"I knew what He could do in the village – as a proof. That call was the greatest thing, it was greater than Samuel." Rees then explained how Samuel was placed on the altar, just as Isaac was, but in doing so, he was able to claim 10,000 souls for Christ. Rees said, "I went to Africa and oh, the love I had for those natives, and in two months the revival came – I knew I would have 10,000 souls for Samuel."

Whilst in Africa, Rees wrote in a missionary magazine asking for prayer for young Samuel: 'Now we ask you to pray that the Lord will lead little Samuel to walk in the footsteps of the one after whom he is named, and that he shall some day be a prophet of the Lord. Rees Howells' (1 Samuel 1:20). These deep wishes for Samuel were to be fulfilled one day, but there is always the price of obedience to pay. The cost of separation never left Rees and Lizzie Howells in Africa, but in its place the Lord poured His love for the African people into them. Their love for their son is evidenced by a series of poignant postcards sent to Samuel from South Africa.

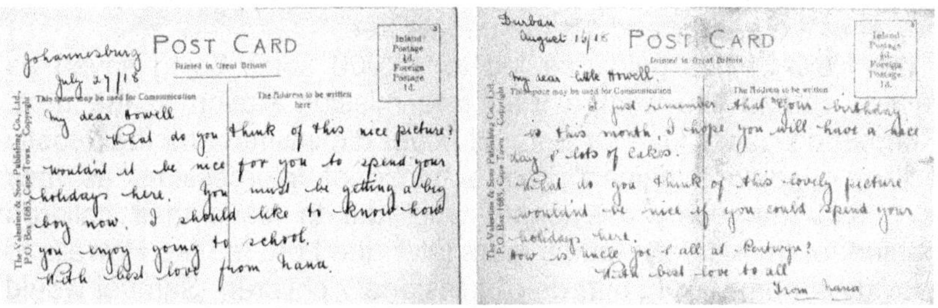

POST CARD

Johannesburg July 27/18

My dear Howell

What do you think of this nice picture? wouldn't it be nice for you to spend your holidays here. You must be getting a big boy now. I should like to know how you enjoy going to school.

With best love from Nana.

POST CARD

Durban August 16/18

My dear Little Howell.

I just remember that your birthday is this month, I hope you will have a nice day & lots of cakes.

What do you think of this lovely picture wouldn't it be nice if you could spend your holidays here.

How is uncle Joe & all at Pentwyn?

With best love to all

From Nana

Two postcards to Samuel from Johannesburg and Durban 1918

Each postcard had its love expressed, which Elizabeth Rees will have read out carefully to her young charge and talked about the typically African pictures on each. One message, dated 16 August 1918 reads: 'My dear little Howell, I just remembered that your birthday is this month (31 August). I hope you will have a nice day and lots of cakes. What do you think of the lovely picture? Wouldn't it be nice if you could spend your holiday here?...With best love to all, from Nana.' Samuel's mother wrote to him as Nana, to help strengthen his bond to his foster parents Mr and Mrs Rees.

These cards were treasured memories for Samuel all his life, as he too felt the enormous pain of this costly obedience by his parents. Out of it, of course, were to emerge waves of revival blessing in Southern Africa, wherever they were to minister.

As an adult, Samuel always spoke with deep reverence and respect for the sacrifice his parents had made by 'lending him to the Lord.' He reminded the College in later years that the Lord promised them 10,000 souls for their obedience. "The Holy Spirit told him (Rees) that every person that he would lay his hands on would enter into life," said Samuel. "He was dealing with souls about eighteen hours a day! That's what happened in Africa. But a price had been paid! When he went out there, the Africans wanted to know everything – where are your respective families? Mother told them that she had an aged father. Father told them that he had an aged mother that was dependant upon him and that they had their little boy of three years of age. The Lord told them to leave them behind and they said, 'We do not know if we shall ever see them again.' It was during the First World War and everything was uncertain." Lizzie told Samuel that they had said to the Africans, "God told us to come out and love you, just as He loved them." Samuel responded, "The Africans never heard anything like it! That was the preparatory measures for the break-up of the strongholds of witchcraft. But he was never afraid of the devil. Did (Rees) express fear of the enemy? Not at all. He knew that the Holy Spirit was far stronger than those spirits that dominated that place. When He came, He broke the power of the enemy and set the people free."

The Holy Spirit's guidance led to 10,000 souls being saved as revival spread like wildfire from one mission station to the next. Rees and Lizzie's love for Samuel never diminished and their costly act of obedience gained them a place of intercession, as they identified with every missionary who had to leave their children behind for their safety. Many years later, the Lord led the Howells to provide a home for hundreds of missionary children. Samuel would take responsibility for the subsidising of this ministry for over forty years. Missionaries had to pay fees for their children to board at school, but at less than cost. Even then, many missionaries still found it hard, especially when two or more children were boarding.

Chapter Three

The Early Years

In Wales, Samuel was safe under the wise protection of his foster parents who renamed him Samuel Rees. Uncle Moses ran a general provisions and newspaper store in the village, called the Piano Stores and Stationery and the family lived over the shop. Elizabeth was head teacher of the local Primary School, so they were well provided for, and Samuel was given the very best of everything.

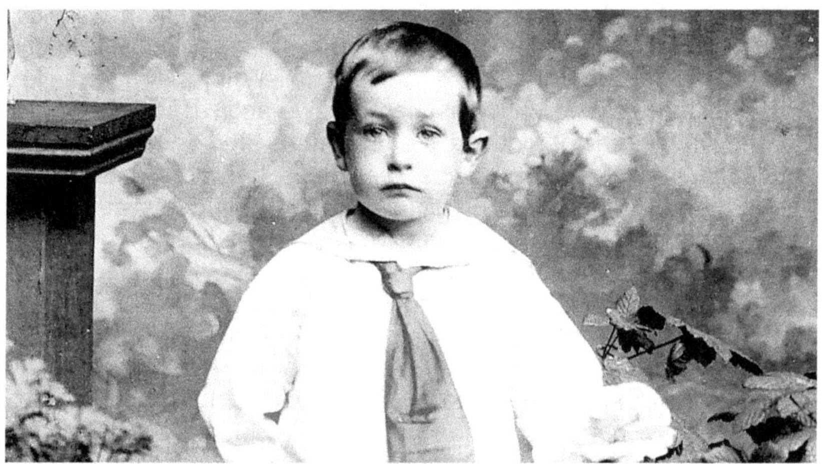

Samuel Rees Howells in 1917, age 5

Samuel was at a very tender age in 1918, when Britain emerged victorious from WWI, but with one million dead and one and a half million wounded, every community and almost every family was impacted by the death or injury of someone they knew. During the war up to 280,000 Welshmen had served in the armed forces and over two hundred official war memorials were erected in the Valleys to recall their sacrifice. The Carmarthen County War Memorial records 2,700 local people who died; some would have been known to the Rees family. Could Uncle Moses recall some of them coming into his shop and did his wife teach any of these young men at school? The devastating impact of the war was compounded in these small towns and villages of Wales; but how could Samuel, age six, understand the grief of his nation?

While Mrs Rees was at school and Uncle Moses tended the store, a young lady, Alice Townsend, watched over Samuel and coached him at home until he was old enough to attend school. He fondly remembered the good days at school and the not so good days. There were times of boyish fun and days of tears, ink-blots on his exercise book, playtimes missed for work not completed, hands on head for being naughty, and in Samuel's case, every misdemeanour was relayed to Elizabeth, followed by the inevitable lecture at home and early to bed! In later years, Samuel always seemed to empathise with young excitable school boys and with a smile! He would often reflect upon those sheltered days cocooned in the religious environment of the Welsh speaking village of Garnant with its neighbouring mining communities of Brynaman and Gwaun-Cae-Gurwen (known locally as GCG), homes of his parents.

Life revolved around the chapels which were always full to capacity on Sundays and the Rees family attended the Welsh Congregational Chapel next door to their store. With its lovingly polished rows of wooden pews and steep gallery for the more agile, the chapel carried its own atmosphere of awe and respect. From an early age, children memorised the Scriptures and Sunday school included adult classes too. It has been described as a nourishing, religious upbringing. The influence of the 1904 Revival, which commenced in Loughor, only twenty miles away under the ministry of Evan Roberts, was still strong. In later years, Samuel would be blessed as Evan would make friendly visits to Rees at the College.

One of Samuel's favourite stories of his childhood was the true story of Welsh girl Mary Jones, who saved for six years and walked barefoot for twenty-five miles to buy her own Bible. When she was told there were none available, she sobbed violently and Thomas Charles was moved to give her a copy which was earmarked to be sold to another. It was that incident which led Thomas Charles to form the British and Foreign Bible Society in 1804. This moving story captured young Samuel's imagination and helped fuel his passion to support all those involved in the printing and distribution of Scriptures throughout the world. 'But these things are written that you may believe that Jesus is the Christ, the Son of God, and that believing you may have life in His name' (John 20:31).

Samuel's childhood memories, gleaned from reliable sources, help to paint the picture of a young man curious to investigate all that life had to offer his generation. On one occasion, Samuel was refused permission by his foster parents to view a film at a local hall. The cinematograph was the up-and-coming form of entertainment, especially for a rural Welsh village. What a temptation! When Samuel was not to be found at home that day as usual, Moses Rees marched straight down and hauled the young offender out of the building and back home, suitably reprimanded. This was possibly the last time that Samuel would ever visit a 'cinema.'

Chapter Four

Rees and Lizzie Howells Return

Samuel was eight years old when his birth parents Rees and Lizzie returned home on furlough from Africa, in time for Christmas 1920. The returning missionaries were expected to rest after years on the mission field, but after just six weeks they could not wait any longer as they beamed with inner light, delighted with the prospect of travelling all over the world to testify how the Holy Spirit had led and guided them in revival.

For the next three years, they ministered non-stop under the auspices of the South Africa General Mission (SAGM) and were swept up in the glories of eternity. Nonetheless, they did take time out of their busy schedule to visit young Samuel, and a few faded photos exist as a memorial to their days out with him and the Rees family. It is also touching to recall that as an adult, Samuel was comfortable to speak of his parents in public using the expressions, "mother" and "father." Considering Samuel grew up in an age when close ties did not always form between parents and children, his use of these terms indicate a deep bond had developed.

Meanwhile, whilst Rees Howells was speaking at the Llandrindod Convention in 1922, an event took place which would shape the rest of his life as well as Samuel's. Rees was preaching and shared how the Lord had asked him to unconditionally surrender his life to the Holy Spirit, and he explained how the Lord had led and guided him in Africa. The question was raised: Who else would follow Rees' example and surrender all to God and obey Him at all costs? The congregation were so moved by his testimony that the chairman felt urged to make an appeal for full surrender and everyone stood. There were so many young people who responded that the ministers felt burdened to pray for a Bible College in Wales to be opened to train them and others. Rees was invited to pray with them and the Holy Spirit said to him, "Be careful how you pray, I am going to build a College, and build it through you!"

As Rees and his wife prayed about this commission, they went to America on a private visit. Among the many personal treasures which Samuel always kept in a drawer in his room, was a postcard of the largest liner of its time, RMS *Majestic*, the ship which had taken Rees and Lizzie Howells to New York in 1922. The postcard carried news of his parents on their way to meetings in the USA. They had asked the Lord to send them a gift the next day as a seal of His call to them to build a College and also to provide their fare. They received a remarkable last minute total deliverance of £138

($220). The postcard reads: 'Here we are within a day's reach to New York. We have had a splendid voyage. We can truly say, 'Fy nhad sydd wrth y llyw.' (My Father's hand is on the rudder and in control). We only wish you were with us especially Uncle Joe, but he prefers running around Pentwyn. We are looking forward to be in New York tomorrow.' Whilst at the Moody Bible Institute in Chicago, the Lord confirmed to Rees that He was to build a similar College through him. This was the beginning of an intense spiritual battle for them to found a Bible College by faith, and Samuel, even as a young lad was to feel the impact of it on his own life.

To build a new Bible College by faith alone, the Holy Spirit had already told Rees Howells that no appeals for money should be made (as had been intended by a group of other interested ministers). Instead, Rees returned to his home town of Brynaman and spent the next ten months in God's presence, waiting for the word of assurance that the money would be forthcoming. This was a fierce conflict for Rees as he stated in one letter: 'I can assure you that I have been through testings of faith before, and have gone through darkness to gain the objectives, but it all seems to have been child's play to compare with this. It seemed that I was fighting with principalities and rulers of darkness, spiritual wickedness in high places. At times it was like Egyptian darkness or, as it was with Abram: 'A horror of great darkness fell upon him' (Genesis 15:12). The battle was so desperate that I was willing to let everything go in order to win the victory over the enemy of souls.' When Samuel grew up and became an intercessor himself, he could understand more of what Rees had experienced, and was encouraged to realise that the Holy Spirit would lead him through to complete victory during his tests of faith and intense intercession.

From the very first direction that the Holy Spirit gave Rees, it took two years of travailing faith for him to intercede for the direction and finances needed to start a Bible College and in 1924, the Bible College of Wales (BCW) was birthed, a living testimony to raw faith. Local reporters were baffled how a poor missionary had bought an estate with prestigious views of Swansea Bay, in an affluent area, without the support of a denomination or even 'a financial partner.' Rees had made no appeals, but as Samuel testified later in life, it was no easy purchase. "At the very beginning he was in very great need for a deliverance in order to complete the purchase of Glynderwen," he said. Although just a twelve-year-old lad at the time, the events leading up to its purchase were carefully related to him by his foster parents Moses and Elizabeth Rees. It was during this time, that Samuel opened his heart to the Lord as his Saviour, while listening to an open-air service conducted by the Salvation

Army in their village. Afterwards he attended all the chapel services with fresh understanding of the rich ministry. Rees Howells would later invite La Maréchele (Catherine 'Katie' Booth-Clibborn), daughter of the founder of the Salvation Army (General William Booth), and Florence Bramwell Booth to speak at the College.

As Samuel's education continued, he was first transferred to Miss Pinkham's school in Oystermouth, just outside Swansea, perhaps to hone his English (his first language was Welsh) and later to Greggs' private preparatory school in Uplands, Swansea. This seemed rather an intense regime as Samuel prepared for the school leaving exam, yet he remained a keen student. During the week he slept in Glynderwen House, the first estate of the Bible College of Wales, giving him an opportunity to get a little closer to his birth parents in a communal setting. Samuel liked this imposing mansion, set in a commanding position overlooking Swansea Bay, on the edge of Blackpill. He was given a large bedroom facing the sea. It took some time for Samuel to get used to his first taste of communal living, as he mingled with the first batch of Bible College students and found a space in the bathroom for his cold early morning wash.

Glynderwen House mid-late 1920s, facing the sea

The influence of these foundational days spent in the Bible College would strengthen Samuel for later years, when he would carry the yoke of responsibility for the College himself, and for furthering the work of the Gospel worldwide in whatever way he could. However, as a child, Glanaman was Samuel's home (the district in which he lived) and it was often with a sigh of relief that he was able to step out of the train at the little station there each Friday. He would time himself as he strode into his familiar territory and he loved to escape into his beloved hills.

Meanwhile at BCW, one of Rees Howells' foundational teachings concerned living a crucified life, death to self. The Holy Spirit desires to show Christ's love to a lost world through His people, but 'the flesh' resists God's purposes and screams, "What about me?" The flesh does not want to give, love or go in response to God's revealed will. Rees showed that the carnal nature is the greatest blockage to the Holy Spirit's purposes being fulfilled in people's lives and must be put to the cross. The flesh cannot be pacified, it must be crucified. Paul expressed it like this: 'I have been crucified with Christ; it is no longer I that live, but Christ lives in me' (Galatians 2:20). The process of full surrender to live a crucified life with Christ enabled Rees to become an 'empty vessel,' because his human desires were no longer able to hinder God's will and thus he could state, "I have been crucified with Christ; He lives in me!"

At a tender age, Samuel proved willing to live the crucified life, when God challenged him to set aside his personal ambition of becoming a doctor to go as a medical missionary. This was the first of many sacrifices that Samuel placed on the 'altar.' The words of Jesus were now bearing fruit in Samuel's young life: 'It is the Spirit who gives life; the flesh profits nothing' (John 6:63).

Aerial view of Glynderwen Estate c.1955 on the Derwen Fawr Road, which runs along the bottom of the photo between the hedgerows. This site was bought by Rees Howells in 1924 and became the first estate of the Bible College of Wales. It was later used for the Bible College School (first located on the Sketty Isaf, Estate in September 1933) which became known as Emmanuel School. Glynderwen House (middle left), El-Shaddai House (far left). Other buildings are classrooms and a vegetable plot (later grassed over) is bottom far right. Half of this site (where all the buildings once stood) is now the Bryn Newyd Estate and consists of 29 two to four bedroom homes.

Chapter Five

Give Us This Day Our Daily Bread

The Lord had revealed to Rees Howells that 'God's College,' as it was called in the newspapers, was to teach the principles of living by faith and intercession. BCW was to be set apart as a unique training ground for students, for theory would never be enough to reach the world with Christ; students needed the Holy Spirit!

These faith values were expressed by Rees Howells in a College pamphlet: 'The great objective of the College is to prove that the work of God can be carried on by trust in God, and that faith and prayer are efficient agents. If this principle is a Scriptural one, God can make it a success in the hands of any of His servants, to whom He gives grace, to have faith and trust in Him. The apostles acted on this principle: 'Be careful for nothing; but in everything by prayer and supplication with thanksgiving let your requests be made known unto God. But my God shall supply all your need according to His riches in glory by Christ Jesus. Because that for His name's sake they went forth, taking nothing of the Gentiles' (Philippians 4:6, 19 and 3 John 7). The College pamphlet continued: 'These principles are not held in living faith by the Church, and every great truth which has been lost through unbelief and carelessness must be regained through deep travail and suffering, and often through great persecution. But the Word the Lord gave to the apostles is true for us: 'My grace is sufficient for thee...therefore I take pleasure in infirmities, in reproaches, in necessities, in persecutions, in distresses for Christ's sake' (2 Corinthians 12:9-10).

'Our desire is to give the very best tuition to young men and women, and also to encourage them to enter the School of Faith. And that all the students who graduate from the College will be able, not only to expound the Word of God, but to give practical demonstrations of it in the same literal sense in which the words, "Give us this day our daily bread," are so often proved in the provision of the temporal needs of the College from day-to-day. We are not aiming to make a new sect, nor to train men and women for any particular denomination, but to give free tuition to men of all denominations who have been called to the home ministry, and to those who are called to be missionaries who are not able to afford university training.' 'Freely you have received...' (Matthew 10:8).

An essential aspect of the College training was to encourage the students to learn the life of faith, which included trusting God when resources were not available, as preparation for pioneering situations that would be encountered in the Lord's service anywhere in the world. Under the ministry of Rees Howells, staff and students were being schooled very thoroughly in this area of Christian experience. "If you fail to move God for yourself in the basic areas of living you are not going to move Him for another person, and it is doubtful if a person knows the Holy Spirit if he can't trust God. You will certainly be building on sand," he would say. Here was another principle of intercession: If you cannot get your own 'small' prayers answered, don't deceive yourself into thinking that your 'big' prayers are changing world events! Prove God in the small things first.

Rees impressed upon everyone that you couldn't pray for other people to give you money, if you had money in your pocket. It always needed to be a full surrender first: use your own resources, then God's unlimited supplies will become available. People soon learnt how difficult it was to part with their own money! These of course, were the initial stages towards living in constant fellowship with God, through the Holy Spirit, to such a degree that the "greater works" referred to by Jesus in John 14:12 would be demonstrated.

Rees always raised the standard of discipleship for all effective ministry and pointed out that the seventy disciples empowered and sent out by Jesus Christ (Luke 10:1), returned with glowing reports but failed to keep their instructions and lost the power. No doubt they learned their lesson and when the Holy Spirit was given after Pentecost, were able to become an important part of the early Church. The life of faith was a vital area of experience for every new student at the College to learn and Samuel was learning too.

Rees Howells never presented the life of faith as an easy exercise and stressed that the entrance fee for the life of faith is a full and complete surrender (1 Kings 19:19-21, Luke 18:22). "If you want to know what a full surrender is, it is this," he said, "You have made a surrender the same as Elisha. Only one thing you know; God has told you to do it, and He will inspire you, and will inspire faith in you. Faith works when you are in a test by choice, not when you cannot get out of it" (Exodus 4). With regard to accepting help from home, Rees' approach was: Never let your parents know your need, but do not refuse family gifts unless specifically guided to do so. God will supply your personal needs, but He will never deliver you while you are not abiding. He will deliver you every time you are abiding.

"You may think you would learn the life and get it to work at once, a thousand times," Rees said. "No. You must start at the bottom. If you need 7s. 6d. (35p / 56¢), get 7s. 6d, not 10 shillings (50p / 80¢). Anything more is a gift and not your gained position of faith. If ever I needed £5 ($8), God would not give me £10 ($16). If you need £10 ($16) and receive £2 ($3.20), you only need to pray for £8 ($12.80). He then warned the students: "You may study many things in the

Bible but be unable to live a life of faith."

There were then presented several laws in the life of faith:

1. No needs are to be made known. (Speak to God, not man).
2. No debt. (Don't borrow your way into a work that is not God's).
3. Do not question a deliverance if you have not attempted to influence the donor and have not made the need known.
4. Natural deliverance (often via somebody you know) before extraordinary, miraculous deliverance.
5. First need, first claim. You use the resources you have to pay all immediate expenses.
6. When essential needs and non-essential needs come at the same time – use any money for the essentials first.
7. You cannot claim deliverance until you have gone to your extremity and used all your own resources.
8. Claim on your abiding. When you are living in obedience to all God has shown you, ask God to fulfil His promise of John 15:7.
9. Claim your wages from God (Luke 10:7, 1 Timothy 5:18).
10. Whatever God asks you to do; you can go back to Him and ask Him to pay for it. (God pays the bills for His ideas; not ours).
11. You must have victory in private before you are tested in the open. Victory is when a particular personal sin no longer has control over your mind or life (Romans 6, 2 Peter 2:19, 1 Peter 1:16).
12. Do not run on the spoil. Do not use finances / materials available for corporate needs (e.g. office supplies) for your own personal needs.

Samuel certainly agreed with all these statements, but it was quite another story to put it into practice in an age that is not of faith; but he did so and many Bible College students also have testimonies of answered prayer, great sacrifice and last minute deliverances from God. There are also some testimonies of students that got carried away and stepped ahead of the Lord and met with failure. These lessons were found to be equally important! A life of faith can never be copied, and only the Holy Spirit can reveal the principles and truths of this life (Psalm 68:19, Luke 22:35, Philippians 4:19).

Samuel would also follow in his father's footsteps and spend his entire life living by faith, going alone in prayer to the Throne. When he became the Director, he had to believe God for the financial needs for the College to be met and for the wider release of money to complete the Great Commission. But his life of faith did not start with big deliverances, but in the small needs that he had as a student at university (Isaiah 28:10). However, these small needs did not appear to be small to Samuel at the time!

Chapter Six

Living By Faith in the Great Depression

The Wall Street Crash of October 1929, set the course for the world economy to sink into the Great Depression. In the next four years, five thousand American banks went bust, U.S. industrial production dropped by almost fifty percent and U.S. unemployment rose to twenty-five percent! Hundreds of thousands of Americans became homeless and moved into shanty towns. America did not truly recover until 1947. In Britain, its knock-on effects led to its largest and most far-reaching economic depression of the twentieth century. Exports halved, unemployment doubled and millions of families were left destitute, surviving with the help of soup kitchens.

South Wales, where the Bible College was located, was one of the worst affected areas. Seventy percent of men were out of work in some areas, with the average percentage being twenty-five in the U.K. Centres of coal mining and steel industries, such as Swansea and Merthyr Tydfil were devastated. This was followed by a series of Hunger Marches in 1932, as the South Wales Miners marched with other impoverished people from the industrial areas of Britain.

As the financial decline spread, Christian ministries were crumbling under the strain, as men who had built a good work by trusting in Christian generosity gave way. Meanwhile, Samuel watched the faith of his father Rees Howells being exercised, as he expanded the College and prayed-in the equivalent of millions to purchase the Derwen Fawr and Sketty Isaf Estates! During the Great Depression Rees Howells wrote: 'These years have been a time of great financial embarrassment in the world; scarcity of money and financial pressure have made men's hearts to fail…but the Lord has proved to us day-by-day that living by faith is above circumstances. The Lord has allowed us to be tested beyond our strength, often pressed out of measure, that we should not trust in ourselves.'

In front of Derwen Fawr House was a large stone plinth with 'Jehovah Jireh' (The Lord will provide, Genesis 22:14) embedded on the front, and 'Faith is Substance' (Hebrews 11:1) on the back. This plinth represented a spiritual landmark, a testament for future generations – that God always fulfils His promises (which are often conditional), and that the faith of God had been gained, not just for a College, but for the fulfilment of the Great Commission.

During this era, the principles of living by faith were being passed from father to son, and now Samuel would have to prove God's promises himself. In the early 1930s, Samuel made preparations, with much persuasion it seems, to take on the challenge of studying for an Oxford University degree in Theology. Final acceptance was received in 1934, enabling Samuel to go to Oxford, England, as an external student. He lived with Herbert Lambourne and his wife, a gentle couple who were very kind and understanding. Herbert actually worked at Brasenose College, Oxford, and won respect by his unashamed loyalty to Christ. "This is my department, sir, and we don't have bad language here," he once told a student.

Samuel had spent the last few years hearing of the testimonies of his father Rees, concerning the Lord's provision for the College, but now Samuel had to step out in faith at Oxford and prove these promises. It is very easy to state that God is able to provide when the trial is someone else's and this young man soon found that before he could have a testimony, he must first have a test!

God established His faithfulness to Samuel and he discovered that living by faith contains a challenge and a promise. The challenge is to abide in the Lord's perfect will, as he sought to meet the conditions for his financial deliverance. 'This is the confidence we have in approaching God, that if we ask anything according to His will, He hears us' (1 John 5:14). Samuel learnt that before he could pray specifically, he must first be close enough to the Holy Spirit to hear God's will, as a prerequisite to answered prayer.

In these early days of living by faith, praying for five shillings (25p / 40¢) must have felt like an unmovable mountain, but with persistence, his prayers were answered. Samuel never minimised the burden of living by faith, but in later years, when he had to believe for hundreds of thousands of pounds for BCW, he must have smiled at the amounts that were once such a struggle to pray-in!

Whilst at university, Samuel received many letters from his parents and others at the College. 'Dear Samuel, we are backing you up in prayer, we miss you very much. The messages in the meetings are wonderful these days. The Director (Rees Howells), has been showing us the way the Holy Ghost took him through his early days in the village, with the tramps and with the little children. No wonder there is the outcome there is today…'

The letters from Rees Howells to his son disclose a warm, honest and trusting relationship. Nonetheless, it must have been hard for Samuel to feel close to him (when he was at the College), because there were so many demands on Rees' time. But in his letters, Rees was mentoring young Samuel, sharing with him the many burdens, answers to prayer and the Vision for the future. Writing to Samuel at university in October and November 1936, Rees noted: 'My dear Samuel, Delighted with your letter yesterday. Yes, the place of intercession over the Treasury has been gained; in a moment the Lord can command the donors to give way, as He commanded the widow woman to sustain Elijah (1 Kings 17:7-16). I am getting wonderful times with the Lord in the mornings. It's like old times when I had no care in the world. The meetings are as good as ever. Cofion goreu (Best regards). Rees.' In another letter: 'My dear Samuel, We are having wonderful times. We are still gazing at the intercession over the Treasury. When you think, after climbing up for two years, putting it all at the feet of the Master, and I am sure it will all come back on its hundredfold (Matthew 19:29, Mark 10:28-31). Every step has been walked so well, first the Vision of Every Creature, then the Every Creature Conference. We have great longings to build colleges in these different countries, or to help those who are building them. It seems that the world has become our parish in a day, there is such a scope in the Vision...At the College here they are all in good form, fighting to the man. They are wonderful people and they revel in the intercession.'

As Samuel was preparing to leave university, the full implications of the Great Depression were beginning to be outworked in mainland Europe. Liberty and democracy were giving way to tyranny, opening the door for Hitler and Mussolini. The tremors of a new war were felt again and Rees Howells was being prepared by world events to give a message to the College which would echo for seventy years in the life of Samuel Howells – "We are on slippery ground," said Rees, "Prayer has failed, only intercession will avail."

Samuel graduated in Theology in late 1936 and with limited financial resources he had lived carefully, and followed his usual disciplined regime that included a very simple diet. The prophet Daniel and his three young friends in Babylon could well have inspired him to do this. With his hard earned MA from Oxford, he considered his future very carefully and followed the Lord's leadings for him to live and work at the Bible College, without pay. (None of the BCW staff received a salary because they all lived by faith). Samuel's foster parents had made provision for him with a newly-built bungalow, but Samuel eventually placed it on the altar and the proceeds were used for the Kingdom. He joined the staff at BCW lecturing in New Testament, Church History and Greek, caring for men students and acting as Assistant Director. Those who sat in his lectures remember him as a gentle encourager, with a keen sense of humour which helped to lift everyone when they were flagging during afternoon sessions (1 Thessalonians 5:11).

Samuel's decision to join the College staff was grounded in his full and unconditional surrender to the Lord, when he invited the Holy Spirit to possess him (Ezekiel 2:2). This transformation in his life took place during the events of the previous year, when Rees Howells had presented the Every Creature Vision to the College.

Chapter Seven

The Every Creature Vision

On December 26, 1934, Rees Howells received a Vision from the Holy Spirit which transformed the College and the lives of everyone who responded to it. In the early hours of the morning the words of Jesus penetrated Rees' heart. "Go ye into all the world and preach the Gospel to every creature" (Mark 16:15). The phrase 'every creature' echoed in his spirit and at 3am he went downstairs in Derwen Fawr House (on the second Estate, Derwen Fawr, bought in December 1929) to spend time with the Lord. That morning, the Lord challenged Rees in a way that would shape the rest of his life.

Samuel Rees Howells, age 23 with his mother, Lizzie, c.1935 with the College car. In November 1935, Samuel crashed the car. He needed a stitch in his head, whilst his passenger, Rees Howells broke his collarbone and his arm was in a sling for two weeks.

Rees was taught by the Holy Spirit that an intercessor can never be free of a prayer, which God gives until it has been fully answered. Now, after 1,900 years of delays and setbacks, the Holy Spirit spoke to Rees and asked him if the Saviour meant His last command to be obeyed? (Mark 16:15-18). Rees knew that the Lord wanted every person to have a chance to hear the Gospel and he responded in the affirmative. Then the Lord said, "Can I be responsible for this through you?"

Rees had proved in Africa that he was willing to go to reach the unsaved, but now was he willing to intercede for others who went and to take personal responsibility to believe that every creature would be reached with the Gospel? If at anytime Satan tried to hinder the spread of the Gospel worldwide, Rees Howells and those who responded with him to the Holy Spirit's leading, would be bond-slaves to intercede until every hindrance to Gospel liberty was restrained and removed. The Holy Spirit already knew Rees' answer, for he had surrendered all many years before and had vowed like Ruth, 'wherever you go, I will go' (Ruth 1:16).

On New Year's Day 1935, Rees presented 'The Every Creature Vision' to the staff and students and asked for them to respond as he had. Every person at the College was challenged 'to give, to pray or to go' in order that every person would have a chance to hear the Gospel. This was no vague inspirational message, for the respondents at the College including Samuel, made a covenant with God that they would dedicate their *entire lives* and lay down every private dream, to do everything possible to get the Gospel to every creature! This Vision consumed the lives of many present, up until the last breath of these intercessors in the twenty-first century!

Rees vividly presented the cost of responding to this call. Whoever decided to follow the Lord would have to make a complete surrender of self to the Holy Spirit. Around one hundred and twenty people accepted the call and laid down all their future plans and hopes, in order to live and work at the College, as intercessors. Rees received no salary and every person who accepted the call would have to live the same, without a wage, trusting in God alone. Their lives were now laid on the altar. In Romans 12:1, Paul refers to this process: 'Therefore, I urge you...to offer your bodies as living sacrifices, holy and pleasing to God.' The 'spiritual' altar was the place where the respondents went to permanently forsake their old lives, never to be owned again. Their lives were symbolically laid down on an altar and the equivalent of death was experienced.

The personal sacrifices of these intercessors would give them great authority in prayer and for at least sixty years, those who remained were available to 'pray through' during any international crisis and for at least ten years, this involved up to five prayer meetings a day. Their intercessory prayers were in addition to their daily work, including teaching at the School, administration, cleaning and various other practical everyday duties.

Doris Ruscoe, one of these intercessors, explains these events in her own words, "The Lord had given to Rees Howells the Vision of giving the Gospel to every creature. This was the last command of the Lord Jesus and the whole College became transformed. The Holy Spirit as it were, passed the Vision on through him to us. I remember the morning he stood before us, having spent the night with God who had challenged him on giving the Gospel to every creature, and as time went on, two things happened. The Holy Spirit visited the College in a very remarkable way at the end of 1936 and the beginning of 1937. For weeks, for days and nights we were in the presence of God. We realised afterward why the Holy Spirit had revealed Himself like that, because Rees Howells became more and more concerned about international events."

Derwen Fawr House, Sketty, Swansea c.1950, a five-minute walk along Derwen Fawr Road from Glynderwen Estate, Blackpill

Rees Howells was taught by the Holy Spirit that any person, government or international situation that hindered the spread of the Gospel would become a legitimate target to be challenged and defeated through intercession. It was the Lord's will for the Gospel to go to every person and anything that got in the way of God's plan had to be confronted. The Lord had been searching for men and women, who would become channels for the Holy Spirit to enforce Christ's victory over all the powers of darkness and he found them in Rees and his team, including Samuel, aged twenty-two.

There were two distinct themes intertwined into every intercession that the Holy Spirit led these warriors to pray through. The first concerned reaching every creature with the Gospel and removing any hindrance to the Great Commission. The second was to protect the Jewish people, so that they could fulfil their end time destiny as outlined in Scripture. These two themes are intimately connected to each other in the end time purposes of God, and both can be traced in the future intercessory ministry of Samuel Rees Howells.

In the 1930s, the greatest threat to world evangelism was the rise of Hitler's Germany, and Japan. Germany had been turned from her Christian heritage and every nation which the Nazis later occupied became closed for evangelism. Concerning Hitler, Doris Ruscoe said, "Before the majority of people, even statesmen, seemed to be aware of the threat that this man posed to the world, the Holy Spirit warned Rees that the devil would use him and that he would aim at dominating the world. Rees began to pray and we prayed with him."

Rees perceived that the spirit which had possessed Haman, in order to annihilate the Jews, was now rising again and had to be challenged (Esther 3:13). At its heart, this was not a physical battle, but a spiritual one. The Holy Spirit was finding His channels to intercede in and through, but Satan too was finding men like Hitler, who would be channels of evil, to terminate world evangelisation, defy liberty, and challenge God's end time plan for the Jews.

The training of students at BCW ceased during WWII (1939-1945) because of call-up, but the School, administration of the four estates, the hospital and the residential children kept the College staff very busy. In addition to their daily responsibilities, Rees called the College to years of intense spiritual battles, consisting of up to five prayer meetings a day. "You can imagine," said Doris, these meetings were "a big slice out of our lives," for they went on "from 7pm to 9, and 10 to 12, and to 1am. They went on all through the weekends, all through the holidays! The only time we ever had a break was when the Holy Spirit brought us through in some wonderful way, and when the presence of God was so manifest. Well, you don't pray then, you rejoice and Rees Howells was never afraid to relax when the Lord gave the word and there was victory. Well, we relaxed the battle, we praised, we worshiped and then in a few days time as the Holy Spirit led we'd go back to the battle."

The stark difference between prayer and intercession was identified at the College on 29 March 1936 when "after weeks of prayer and fasting," said Doris, "Rees Howells came into the Conference Hall, very disturbed in his spirit. He said, 'The Holy Spirit has told me that prayer has failed; only intercession will take us through!' We had never heard anything like that before. Could prayer fail? As the day went on and we had a meeting in the afternoon and another one in the first part of the evening, the Holy Spirit began to make clearer to us what was meant and then in the last meeting between nine o'clock and midnight the Holy Spirit began to call us to become intercessors for the Vision…Intercessors that the Gospel might go out to every creature and that the enemy through the dictators was not to prevent the Gospel going out. The Holy Spirit dealt with every one of us personally and everyone prayed as the Spirit led them..."

On 30 March 1936, the Lord confirmed this new Vision with a wonderful Visitation that continued for some time. "The proof that it was of the Spirit was what happened the next day," said Doris Ruscoe. "When we got down on our knees in the evening meeting we began to sing, it was a chorus welcoming the Holy Spirit and all I can say is the Spirit came on us and we sang for an hour. I can still hear the sound of the singing! Personally, I felt on the steps of the Throne of God Himself. From that day on all through the Easter holidays every time we got on our knees in the meetings, the Holy Spirit came on us and the Lord spoke to us and met us in wonderful ways and from then on we were committed to this battle."

From 1936-45 these warriors prayed day and night. The burdens of the war years affected everyone in Britain, but at the Bible College a dedicated team of intercessors met several times every day, to be responsible to 'pray through' for victory. "I can only say that we were well aware that prayer was being offered by thousands all over the world," said Doris. "But as far as we were concerned, every time events in the war took a vital stage the Holy Spirit always revealed it to Rees Howells and we would pray accordingly."

Reminiscing these years, Samuel Rees Howells said, "I was thinking of the war years, when everything seemed to be against us. If God hadn't intervened at Dunkirk, probably none of us would have been here today. The enemy was gaining on all hands. Rees said, 'This is one of the darkest moments in the history of our country, when we are threatened with invasion and the loss of everything we hold dear.' Humanly speaking all was lost. The enemy was just across the English Channel and the commanders were urging Hitler to invade the country. It was a terrible feeling in those days that we shall be slaves (of Nazi Germany). If Hitler had won, civilisation and freedom as we know it would have gone and Christianity itself would have been mortally threatened." God would not permit this!

The threat to the spread of the Gospel compelled the College to intercession, but they only prayed as the Holy Spirit led them. "Rees Howells, in these situations didn't pray his own thoughts, his own words, he prayed through the Word of God," said Doris Ruscoe. "What he called 'the plots in the Bible' were life to him. In all these instances it was through the Word that the Holy Spirit would bring the victory. In Stalingrad (in Russia), the enemy were fighting in the streets and it was the first time that that had happened and they were driven out. I remember of course particularly El-Alamein; we were on our knees all day while Montgomery was leading the troops in North Africa. We were fighting the battle in the heavenlies. We knew there would be victory and we had proof of all these things because messages were taken down and kept for future reference."

Their commission to spiritual warfare is signalled in Paul's second letter to Timothy. The apostle highlights four prayer responsibilities that the Church maintains in the heavenly realms. 1. Supplications. 2. Prayers. 3. Intercessions. 4. Giving of thanks. These duties are to be made 'for kings and all who are in authority' with the purpose that we may live a 'peaceable life in all godliness and reverence' for God 'desires all men to be saved' (1 Timothy 2:1-6). Whenever the enemy challenged God's purposes in the world, Rees and the College would intercede. To the Ephesians, the Holy Spirit revealed the honour and power of this ministry. 'To the intent that now the manifold wisdom of God might be made known by the Church to the principalities and powers in the heavenly places' (Ephesians 3:10).

The Bible stresses that 'the Word of God is living and powerful, sharper than any two-edged sword' (Hebrews 4:12), and Psalm 149:6-9, explains why this authority has been given to the saints. 'Let the high praises of God be in their mouth and a two-edged sword in their hand. (1.) To execute vengeance on the nations and punishments on the peoples. (2.) To bind their kings with chains and their nobles with fetters of iron. (3.) To execute on them the written judgement.' The passage identifies the process of intercession that Rees and Samuel Howells lived out in their lives. In the context of spiritual warfare, God's prophetic and written Word has been given to the saints to: 1. Execute God's judgement on nations and peoples. 2. Bind and remove dictators / leaders. 3. Fulfil the written and prophetic Word of God in this and every generation.

These were certainly early days and Samuel was conscious of the great challenges that lay ahead, particularly for the generation of young men and women of which he was part, to live solely to reach every nation with the Gospel. In the spiritual environment of faith and prayer at the College, he was ready to play his part. It had been a good beginning, although rugged at times. He was full of confidence still knowing that the Holy Spirit would lead them all through to a glorious victory, but spiritual victories are not gained without travail and intense conflict, which the young generation had to learn. 'Put on the full armour of God so that you can take your stand against the devil's schemes. For our struggle is not against flesh and blood, but against the rulers, against the authorities, against the powers of this dark world and against the spiritual forces of evil in the heavenly realms' (Ephesians 6:10-12).

Chapter Eight

Swansea Blitz

The Every Creature Vision had laid out the principle of the College's responsibility to intercede to remove any hindrance to Gospel liberty worldwide and when WWII broke out, the staff had to put that theory into practice during many tests of intercession.

The College had huddled round the radio on 3 September 1939, as Neville Chamberlain spelt out those fateful words that a state of war existed between Britain and Germany, following the German invasion of Poland. No one in the College anticipated that events would go so far, but the facts were real and everyone, including Samuel, had to face what it would mean to them personally.

Immediately, identity cards were issued and the male population was required to register for military service. Samuel, as a minister of religion, with his pastoral responsibilities at the Bible College and preaching ministry in the locality, stayed in Britain to fight the spiritual battles, although he remained diligent in his fire watching duties and in the disciplines which Rees imposed upon any who remained in the College throughout the ensuing years. These included no holidays and living a vigorously austere lifestyle.

The College staff were redeployed during the war. Some were members of the National Fire Service; others were drafted into the Forestry Commission to act as lumberjacks at the Penllergaer Estate which had been acquired by Rees in late 1938. The ladies too were all involved in serving in one way or another. Several performed vital roles in the Military Services, whilst others served as nurses or taught in Emmanuel School. Others cooked, cleaned or were on fire watching duty. Emmanuel School was opened in Sept. 1933, originally as the Bible College School. It provided a home and education for children of missionaries and home workers, and by the advent of the war had opened its doors to day children. The duties of the College staff gave them the liberty to be free to join Rees in their spare time, to exercise their roles as intercessors.

Gradually the effects of the war impinged on daily life. Food rationing began, allotments sprang up all over the country, and the College found its enclosed kitchen garden very useful. Around Swansea, deprived of its street signs for security reasons, new posters appeared such as 'Dig For Victory' and 'Walls Have Ears.'

Unless a person has lived through a war it is difficult to convey the sense of apprehension and uncertainty that it instils, but gradually the nation adjusted and bonded together, exhibiting its characteristic quiet determination to see the war through.

The stark realities of war would come much closer to Swansea. After the regulation 7pm blackout clothed the town in comparative darkness on the night of 27 June 1940, the chilling wail of sirens filled the still air. This was to be the first of forty-four bombing raids by the German Air Force, the Luftwaffe, including six blitz type attacks. The worst of these lasted for three long nights of concentrated bombing, as Hitler turned his targets away from blitzed London to cities and ports around Britain. As the menacing drone of the Dornier Do 172 and Heinkel 111 engines, a characteristic of German bombers, approached Swansea Bay and was picked up by a searchlight battery, the concentrated barrage of anti-aircraft (ack-ack) guns around the Bay shattered the whole air.

The first of the German parachute flares then descended over strategic targets to assist the aircrews. Showers of incendiary devices and deadly high-explosive bombs brought devastation on the town below. In this prolonged fourteen hours of assault on Swansea, 1,273 high explosive bombs and 56,000 incendiaries rained down on the centre of town, killing 203 people and injuring 409. There was widespread damage to property.

Samuel spent those three nights in prayer while on fire watch duty on the veranda of Derwen Fawr House. "There was no time for sleep," he once said in private, "when people's lives were in mortal danger." With bombs falling nearby and planes flying near the College properties, Rees led the staff in intercession for complete victory against the enemy. "I remember the prayer meetings we had during the war," said Samuel some years later, "when the bombs were falling in Swansea and we were facing death. I shall never forget when we were in the Conference Hall; the whole place was shaking under the impact of those bombs! Do you remember that night when Swansea was ablaze from end to end? I remember standing out on the field between 3 or 4 o'clock in the morning. We didn't think of bed during that time, we didn't think of sleep. Why? Because death was so real!" (Genesis 32:6-11).

On the fields and sand dunes below the Derwen Fawr Estate were batteries of 3.7 inch QFs and the larger 4.5 inch guns. The whole earth trembled and the air was filled with the smell of cordite from the spent cartridges. There was widespread devastation to at least eight of the town centre's main streets. Swansea suffered more air attacks than any other port of Wales and was just two miles from Derwen Fawr. As Samuel walked silently with his father through the rubble past the old gutted market in Swansea, after the bombing, both men were moved to their depths, and renewed their determination to give everything in their cooperation with the Holy Spirit in the intercessions the Lord had laid upon the BCW staff.

Rees had been exercised to believe for complete protection for the properties that he was responsible for, and his reputation was such that people from Swansea sought refuge in the College classrooms overnight. Many bombs fell extremely close to the borders of the College grounds, but not even one landed on them! It was as if the angels themselves blew the falling bombs away from the College to land in the fields nearby! Rees had gained a position of intercession for the protection of the properties he had bought by faith. Now he led the College intercessors to extend this faith victory to believe for protection for the whole nation! Hitler had to be defeated.

Even as College buildings shook from bombs exploding nearby, a deep sense of peace descended over the College and in the prayer meetings taken by Rees some of the greatest revelations were given concerning the last days.

On 25 December 1940, Samuel found a small break from the war to celebrate his ordination, as he became the Rev. Samuel Howells. One great lesson which Samuel learnt during those dark and austere days of the war, which he built into his lifestyle, was that of careful use of the money which the Lord had entrusted to him. Having lived through many winters without heating in his room, his philosophy was to wear adequately warm clothing, which he revelled in even during the summer months. Any waste of water and electricity was anathema to him. This policy did 'ruffle a few feathers' in some staff and visitors, but Samuel could cope with that. He once shared privately, "Some people have called me stubborn, but I am stubborn for the Kingdom" (Luke 12:33, Luke 16:1-31).

The British Prime Minister, Winston Churchill, often visited areas devastated by German bombs to lift morale and made a surprise visit to Swansea on 11 April 1941, saying, "There is a grand spirit in the town. It is standing up to it well. It will be a long pull but we will get there in the end," as he recognised the suffering of "battered Swansea." On several occasions during the war, Winston Churchill was sent letters of faith and encouragement from Rees Howells. They included mention of the unceasing prayers being offered at the College for the final victory over Adolf Hitler and the Nazi regime. One from 1942 states: 'Since you became Prime Minister we have followed you daily with our prayers. We have always had prayer meetings each evening with about one hundred and fifty present. Since the war began we have had two prayer meetings each evening, and for over a year now, without a single break, we have had prayer meetings from 7pm till midnight. As you are the leader of the State, you have a special place in our prayers and what a hero you have been to these young students! They all say you are the only man who could have kept up the courage of the country to lead it to victory after the colossal disaster at Dunkirk. If the country will send a real cry up to God on the National Day of Prayer, we feel sure that the prayers will be answered.'

Hitler was Satan's agent to hinder the spread of the Gospel and intercession had to prevail for his demise. The principle of Satan working through human channels to defy God's will is expressed in Ephesians 2:2. 'The prince of the power of the air (Satan), the spirit who now works in the sons of disobedience.' Satan had to be bound, so that Germany, Europe and the world could be free to hear the Gospel. Samuel's own determination to fight through was sensed in his slow reading of Philippians 3:13-14. 'Forgetting what is behind and straining towards what is ahead, I press on towards the mark for the prize of the high calling of God in Christ Jesus.'

The final air raid on Swansea occurred in 1943, when twenty planes launched a surprise attack on the town centre and included their *more* lethal 'Sprengbrade' (firebombs). One exploded on the entrance of Swansea Hospital, killing thirty-four patients and staff. After that Hitler unleashed his venom on Britain through his V1 and V2 rockets, but by then his grip in the war was weakening, as intercession was prevailing.

Throughout the war years, uninterrupted prayer was maintained at the College, as the Holy Spirit fought spiritual battles one after another through the bodies which had been consecrated for that purpose during the 1930s, and Samuel was totally involved. It shaped and sharpened his future ministry of intercession.

In these intercessory battles, Rees Howells reminded the College that the Holy Spirit was interceding through Samuel and all who welcomed the Spirit in His fullness (Romans 8:26-27). "Samuel has been here from the first," he said in 1943. "He has made a full surrender of everything in this world and of his own person. When we were separated, He entered into Samuel and has taken full possession. It is quite natural and according to Scripture. I shall be able to trust the Holy Ghost in Samuel. The Holy Ghost is using His own intercessions, I walked every inch of this and Samuel will have to walk every inch of it after me." Then Rees reminded the College that the offer of being fully possessed by the Holy Spirit is made to all who will meet the biblical conditions of total abandonment and strict obedience to the Spirit. "On no account are you to limit the Holy Ghost to one body. He is Almighty and He will live in many bodies; but He will not live in you unless you have made that one hundred percent surrender. If the Holy Ghost has gained the intercessions, He can work them through everyone who has gone to death and given his body one hundred percent for the Holy Ghost. It isn't you who uses them, it is the Holy Ghost."

Chapter Nine

Training in Intercession

Rees Howells was reaching the peak of his intercessory ministry during the war, as world events were being bent into the will of God through prevailing prayer. As the strong man was being bound in the heavenly realms, on the earthly battlefield defeats were being turned into victory, great losses were transformed into gains and the invincible enemy, as he had once seemed, was forced to retreat.

Samuel never took a prominent role during these years; instead he soaked in the truths, prayed through with the other intercessors and remained 'in an attitude of believing' as he walked around on Derwen Fawr veranda at night on fire watch duty. The College prayer meetings, which took place several times a day, became Samuel's training ground in intercession. He did not learn by reading a book, but by fighting through the battles in prayer. Many of the victories of these years have been detailed in *Rees Howells Intercessor*, but the College archives overflow with many more. One prayer which transformed history was during the liberation of Italy.

In 1943, Allied troops began their first large invasion of mainland Europe, knowing that the liberation of the Continent depended on their success. After taking the island of Sicily, British Eighth Army's XIII Corps under General Bernard Montgomery's direction landed in Italy on 3 September. Operation Baytown witnessed the surrender of the Italian units almost immediately and plans for a fast victory in Italy looked bright. Soon the Allies hoped to be fighting all the way north towards Germany! Further landings helped to confuse the enemy in preparation for 170,000 troops to land at Salerno.

On 9 September, Operation Avalanche, the main invasion at Salerno by the U.S. 5th Army began with a disaster when a loud speaker on shore announced, "Come in and give up. We have you covered." The battle soon floundered into a mire of defeats and confusion. In the following days, the hope of a fast victory faded and the prospect of a full retreat became credible. All could be lost!

Rees Howells sensed the urgency of the battle and reminded the College that prevailing intercession can transform any crisis as he led the College in prayer for an Allied victory on the beaches. The prayer meeting notes (taken from when Rees Howells preached) tell the story of how they interceded in the many meetings.

13 September 1943: "Judges 7. You leave all now and come back to this battle. Don't allow yourselves to be slack. Every second of the day this is on me. There is not one thing we are doing here tonight that will count much in Italy, only what we are doing by way

of the Throne. When a man fights you know how he fights. Every Nazi tonight fights for his life. It is the most fierce battle that has ever been. You feel tonight that you are afraid of the next news. Don't you put importance now on anything, only on this one. In a fight there are laws where God doesn't feel it right to intervene until a man gets to his extremity (v15). England and America are only fighting for one thing – the end of the Nazis. If you are of value to God in this He will keep you here as an intercessor, otherwise He will put you where you will carry more of a burden. We must pray now as we did when we were nearly invaded (in 1940)."

14 September 1943: "Daniel 5. We are running into a greater test now than ever before – the Spirit witnesses this in me – and there will be no refuge, only in the Holy Spirit. I am not fighting with small or great, only with the enemy over there. I have died to everything the world can offer; I have seen men as men and God as God."

7pm meeting: "1 Kings 20. Hitler and his troops have gained more ground and our troops have been told to prepare to re-embark. Benhadad sent that challenge and God heard it. Are we going to reclaim? Does God hear the challenge tonight? Remember you all have a chance to take part in this battle. The last time we fought like this was for Stalingrad and what a victory that was. We don't want to retreat and we don't want thousands of our young men to be killed. After Alexandria, (in Egypt), and Stalingrad, (In Russia), we can stop the enemy tonight. The next thing is to be the Divine intervention. You must always fight where the Holy Spirit is fighting."

10pm meeting: "1 Samuel 14. The Allied soldiers are fighting for the doom of the Nazis. I would be sorry to find that they have put more time into it there, than I am doing here. The Germans are much stronger but we read in the Scriptures that one man, Jonathan and his armour bearer got through. Tell the Lord tonight, there is no restraint to the Lord to save by many or by few (v6). Have we the faith tonight that this man had? His faith is most perfect."

The next day, news broke in England that the immediate crisis was passing. Defeat was turning into victory as Samuel prayed through with the others. News came on 15 September that the British Royal Navy had succeeded in bombing German strongholds, rendering tanks useless and German divisions were now being driven back. Historians record this as an amazing turn around in what threatened to be 'a near disaster' according to General Mark Wayne Clark, (Commander of the U.S. 5th Army) in his memoirs. The Germans were anticipating a second Dunkirk and it came very close indeed! Who saved them from failure? The Lord mighty in battle! In latter years, Samuel spoke of these wartime battles in private talks – they had made an indelible mark upon his spirit.

Chapter Ten

Intercession for the State of Israel

One of the greatest lessons of faith that Samuel ever witnessed was Rees' intercession for the preservation of the Jewish people during WWII and for the establishment of the State of Israel.

In 1917, after a long campaign by British Christians, the Holy Spirit had secured a victory for the Jews when the Balfour Declaration officially proposed the British Government's support for a Jewish nation in their historical land. A short while after, the Turks were routed by the British during WWI giving the British a mandate to rule and develop the Holy Land. But the future was dark for the Jews.

The burden for the Jews rested heavily upon Rees Howells and in an act of practical identification with them, in 1939, he was prepared to give-up everything to save as many Jews from Hitler as possible. He was ready to sell all three College Estates (Glynderwen, Derwen Fawr and Sketty Isaf, the latter was bought in 1932), and to use the money to rescue Jewish children, housing them on the Penllergaer Estate, which he had purchased in late 1938. Rees had proved to the Lord that he was willing to buy land in Britain and in the Holy Land to save Jewish children and gained a position of authority in intercession, to claim a homeland for the Jews in their historic land. "All I want to know is this. Has the Holy Spirit gained an intercession for the Holy Lands?" said Rees. "If so, we can prevail upon God. If I had the choice today, I'd say to God, 'Take all I have!' "

Samuel recalling these days in later intercessory battles said, "He was prepared for everything to go. It was he who had travailed for these properties and everything. He told the Lord, 'take the whole lot for the sake of the Jewish people.' It cost. That's the point. It wasn't words. It cost him *everything*. I remember him coming into one meeting with us here and he could hardly raise his voice. We could hardly hear him speak and he told us, 'God has made me responsible for the survival of some of the Jewish people.' The burden was so great upon him at that time. He could hardly stand on his feet. That was the price he paid."

On 10 October 1943, the Jewish Day of Atonement, in the course of his 3pm ministry in a College prayer meeting, Rees Howells speaking from Jeremiah 32:27 and 33:3 said, "From today on the Holy Spirit will begin to make intercession for the Jewish people." Thousands of years before, the Jews were in bondage as slaves in Egypt, but God called an intercessor, Moses, who had to believe that God could rescue them. Now Rees and his team had to trust that God could do the same again! "There are millions of Jews all over the earth today crying to God for this to happen," said Rees. "I want God to look down on the Jewish nation and remember these things." These were not just wild declarations plucked out of the air, for Samuel had sat in the back corner seat of the Conference Hall, when his father was fighting through in those intercessions. A whole people group was threatened with extinction during the Holocaust.

Despite the sentiments expressed in the Balfour Declaration of 1917, for self-determination to be granted to Jews, a lasting settlement had never been achieved. President Truman had initiated the Anglo-American Committee of Inquiry in 1946, but by February 1947, the fragile situation had collapsed once more, so it was referred to the United Nations (UN) for their decision.

Samuel remembered how his father watched every move in the Holy Spirit, discerning that God was on the verge of making a significant mark in history. To begin with, even the motion needed acceptance by the UN Assembly, so a vote in its favour was crucial. As the weeks had proceeded, every meeting in the College was charged with the presence of God, and Samuel, with senior staff members, recalled the quality of faith that was being generated by the Holy Spirit through Rees Howells. Here was one individual just reading passages from Daniel 3, Ezra 1, Joshua 5-6, Acts 10 and Exodus 10, interspersed with comments, and each passage seeming as though it was written solely for this situation.

"Faith inspired by the Holy Spirit will bring the same blessing as people received from being with the Lord Jesus," said Rees. "The enemy that attacked Moses when God sent him to be the deliverer is attacking today, when God's will is that the Holy Land should be given back to the Jews." Such precise phrases made an indelible impression upon Samuel at that time. Then, on Monday 24 November 1947, in the 9am meeting after reading Isaiah 59, Jeremiah 33 and sections from Romans 8-11, Rees Howells had declared with typical measured words, "Only the Holy Spirit can really carry a burden and intercede. Paul made a wonderful intercession for the nation and if we make the same intercession today we will be bound to go through."

There were further meetings that day as the motion was being considered. Would it be thrown out even at the start? One young person, Kristine, now the wife of Richard Maton, in the late meeting at the College that night recalls vividly the electric atmosphere as the Holy Spirit lit up the Scriptures afresh to everyone. "In the first prayer meeting that evening we had prayed earnestly and believed that God's will would be done as the motion was being discussed. In the short break after that meeting we fully expected to hear that the motion had been granted, but the radio news was not good. In the second meeting we read 2 Kings 6:8-17. The Syrian king, Benhadad had sent a host of horses and chariots to surround and kill Elisha and his servant, who became distraught with fear. Elisha prayed that the Lord would open his servant's eyes to see God's protection. The Lord did, and he saw that the mountain was full of chariots and horses of fire, which completely protected them. As Rees Howells read this passage under the anointing of the Holy Spirit, we 'saw' the hosts of God's angels surrounding the United Nations building, and knew without a shadow of doubt that God's will would be done when the votes were counted. It was no surprise, though a source of great rejoicing, when we listened to the radio after the meeting and heard that the motion was passed."

Once more the Holy Spirit had triumphed, but there was a further step to come, with a United Nations vote to secure a two-thirds majority in favour of Israel. The voting was postponed for three days, but Rees Howells had always emphasised – and this was another truth that Samuel never forgot – that delays are never denials in the life of prayer. There were further excursions into the Word of God, with great inspiration drawn from Deuteronomy 30, extracts from Jeremiah and Psalm 118:19-23.

"We want to tell the Holy Spirit – You are God. Move that Committee tomorrow, give us that faith," said Rees. "It isn't in man, but it is in God. We want to put this through. We have a chance to believe today." Here was a further lesson which Samuel learnt and later applied to his own ministry. When the Holy Spirit gives a Kingdom prayer it is always essential to be found believing God 'today,' no matter how difficult or impossible the situation may seem.

Dr. Priddy, a senior BCW staff member vividly recalled the prayer meetings that brought God's people back to their land, "We knew God meant this territory to be given to the Jews at this time. It was part of God's purpose for them and we prayed much for this, coming up to this, until the very day when the debate was held in the UN Assembly. We were praying and were really expecting this would come through, then on the late news that night we heard the news, they put it to the vote and they hadn't got the required majority to be able to pass it and they were going to meet again the next day. Rees Howells called us back for a late prayer meeting that night in the Blue Room. He read from Genesis 32 where Jacob was on his way back to his own country and Jacob feeling his vulnerability came to a place where the angels of God met him. He needed a further wrestling with God the next night before he came right through, but in our meeting, we saw the angels of God surrounding the United Nations Assembly in New York. In the Spirit I saw them. Others who were there saw them and Rees Howells saw them. The angels of God were there. They were round about the United Nations Assembly!" (Psalm 103:20).

"Humanly speaking it was nonsense to think that some nations who had argued and made up their minds and had voted against the partition, that they overnight were going to change their minds and vote for it. But we didn't reason it at all. We simply knew that God was there. God was taking it in hand and we saw the angels of God, and because we saw them we believed and faith came into that meeting, we got up and rejoiced and praised God and sang. We knew that the partitioning was going to be granted when they met again the next day. So we had to wait the following evening to get the news, but we had already had the news from Heaven! We saw the invisible, we believed the impossible and God worked."

Midnight on 29 November 1947 brought the news that the United Nations Assembly had voted by thirty-three to thirteen for the partition of the Holy Land, a clear two-thirds majority. A wonderful answer to prayer. Then, at midnight on 14 May 1948, the Provincial Government of Israel proclaimed the new State of Israel! After nearly 1,900 years, the nation was back in its own land and it was one of the greatest days in history, a victory for the Holy Spirit.

This was to prove the last major intercession that Rees Howells was to engage in and it gripped him during the final years of his earthly life. After much travail the State of Israel was established and Rees had assurance concerning the future blessing of the whole world. The outworking of the Vision, for an outpouring of the Holy Spirit on every nation before the Lord's return, also continued.

Nonetheless, this victory came at great personal cost to Samuel aged thirty-six, and to his mother. "The burden that rested upon him (Rees) in those days was really too much for a human frame," said Samuel, "and there were days then that he didn't have the strength to leave his bed. He was there prostrate in the presence of God. But we know that the Lord heard that cry and He worked accordingly and there are millions of them today back in their own country."

Samuel had witnessed the power of God at work in the world at the highest level. He was strengthened to the core of his being in the parallel prayer for the completion of the Vision, the Gospel to be preached to all nations, the Every Creature Commission. As with this prayer, some stiff contests would follow. Through this intercession Samuel learnt an important lesson; prophecies must be believed into manifestation. It is not enough to have a Word from God, a biblical prophecy or a Scripture to quote. There must be human channels on earth who will believe God and intercede for His purposes to come to pass. "What does God want from us today?" Samuel would often ask, "He wants us to believe Him!" (Heb. 4:2).

Chapter Eleven

The Death of Rees Howells

The intercessions of Rees Howells cost him everything, including his life. Speaking many years later, Samuel said, "A real burden descended upon us when we prayed during the war years, and God worked and preserved the Jewish Nation when it was facing annihilation in the gas chambers." He recalled how he would slip quietly into Rees' room at that time and find him slumped and exhausted in his armchair, as pale as death and bathed in perspiration, such was the agony he was experiencing as he carried the intercession. It eventually broke him physically, as up till then he was such a strong person with incredible stamina. Yet, whenever Samuel had asked him if it was worth carrying such a burden, or whether he was all right, his answer was invariably that he was perfectly fine. "Couldn't be better," he would say.

Lizzie Howells with Jewish refugee, Herbert Grunhut of Vienna, Austria, 1939. His parents survived the Nazi concentration camps but forty-two of his relatives did not. On the reverse side of the plinth is "Jehovah Jireh" (God will provide / the Lord my provider).

As his father's health deteriorated, Samuel had not once been free to pray for his recovery for several weeks since his father had spoken personally to him one evening. It followed a memorable 9pm Sunday service in the College prayer room at Derwen Fawr, on 15 January 1950, when Rees had a clear witness that the Holy Spirit in him had finished the work the Lord had given him to do on earth. He had just read the Songs of Moses and David, when Rees declared with such a ring of certainty, "Every Creature will hear the Gospel, the finance of the Vision is safe and the King will come back."

Rees Howells' final services were at 9am on 8 February 1950, when his ministry centred around John 11, and at 7pm when the need for the faith of God was again stressed through Mark 11:22-26 and Luke 12:27-31. All the time he drew from his vast experience of proving the Lord's ability and willingness to operate in the realm of the impossible, in response to faith. "Pray that we will be delivered tomorrow," he said, "as the delay does not put a doubt in us." The service had concluded with the singing of 'Away Over Jordan With My Blessed Jesus,' a popular chorus at that time. Those who were in the late service that night realised that the Holy Spirit was speaking through Rees Howells and it certainly left a deep and lasting impression on everyone.

Several days after the final services in February 1950, Samuel happened to be in his father's room. Rees Howells turned and said, "Samuel, I want to speak to you and I want you to promise in the presence of the Lord that you will do two things after I have been taken." He had never spoken like that before and those words had a shattering effect on Samuel. He knew that moment that the ministry on earth of the Founder (as Rees was often known) was over. Then Rees paused and just looked at Samuel with those piercing eyes of his. That experience would remain with him to the end of his life. Very solemnly, Samuel promised that he would do anything to fulfil his father's desire, despite an overwhelming sense of inadequacy. Then Rees Howells continued, "I want you to promise me solemnly in the name of the Lord, today, that you will carry on the leadership of this work in *exactly* the same way as I have done, and that in the Holy Spirit, you will become responsible for everything and that you will in no sense turn away from the principles, whatever the cost. You will be tested to the hilt as I have been but the Holy Spirit will never fail you if you stand true to Him. I am not asking you to do this because you are my son; although I know that God gave you to me and that is why I gave you back to Him, and as you know, I have had no natural claim on you ever since. I believe it is God Himself who has appointed you to this work, and you will then give me your word that you will carry it on as I have done. If you do this, the Holy Spirit will be with you every step of the way."

Samuel told his father, that although he felt that he was the last person on earth to follow him as Director (and Samuel never lost that personal conviction) yet he believed that it was the Lord's will and he was prepared to accept the commission despite its enormity.

Rees Howells continued, "There is one thing I want you to promise me, that you will see that the £100,000 (£2,700,000 / $4,320,000 in 2012) will be given away to the countries of the world as I have believed and desired to do, because the intercession for world blessing is wrapped up in that sign. You will not let it go, will you?" Samuel reminded his father that he did not have the faith for such a large sum, nor even a much smaller one, but he promised that he would not let it go, whatever happened. With deep emotion, Rees turned and said, "The Lord will bless you, Samuel."

Many years later, Samuel shared other things relating to that event, "I remember just before the Lord took him. I remember him talking to one (Samuel often referred to himself as 'one'), and said, 'Whatever you do, you stand and maintain the intercessions.' But you couldn't do it yourself. Only the Holy Spirit could do it. If anything is precious to us, it is the intercession of the Holy Spirit. It's become a part of us...these intercessions. They are my life."

Samuel was prepared and commissioned, but the days ahead were to prove very difficult. "It was a dark day," quoting from his own words, for Samuel Rees Howells (affectionately known as Mr Samuel to everyone at BCW), when his father Rees Howells died on 13 February 1950. As Samuel prayed, the Holy Spirit then asked him a direct question, "The gap is there. Will you fill it?" Samuel knew that if he took the burden of leadership, he would never be free again. All the pressure would fall directly upon his shoulders. It was a cross that the Lord was offering him and Samuel embraced it, with the knowledge that in death, the resurrection life of Christ would flow through him (Matthew 10:38, Philippians 3:7-10).

Despite the enormity of the task that lay ahead, to continue in the intercessions for the world and also to oversee the ongoing ministry of the Bible College in its training of young men and women for Christian service, Samuel had been well prepared for the task and carried a deep peace which God was giving him. A fresh anointing from God came upon him, evident to all in the College. The severe stammer that had coloured his public speaking for many years, disappeared overnight. His tongue was loosed and he spoke with a fluency to be admired by many an aspiring preacher.

In the past, Rees Howells had trained a team of intercessors ready to intercede for the Gospel to go to every creature, and if at any point in the future the devil attacked the advance of the Kingdom of God around the world, it would be their responsibility to act in intercession. Now Samuel Rees Howells had to lead them!

Chapter Twelve

A Company of Intercessors

Samuel, aged thirty-eight, never expected that the burden of leadership would have fallen upon him so suddenly. To prepare him for the future challenges of intercession, he drew strength and comfort from notes of his father's sermons. In the early days as the new Director, he found himself returning to and meditating on the central themes of his father's life. Samuel recalled that the essential feature of Rees' ministry was that the Holy Spirit is a Person, the Third Person of the Godhead, who had been operating on earth since its foundation. Using these resources gained through the atonement, which also acted retrospectively, He had taken full control of individuals for certain Divine interventions in history, as recorded in the Scriptures (e.g. Othniel, Judges 3:10; Gideon, Judges 6:34; Jephthah, Judges 11:29 and Saul, 1 Samuel 10:6). He witnessed and regulated every facet of Jesus' life and final walk to Jerusalem, culminating in the crucifixion. He empowered Jesus to rise triumphantly from death on the third day and indwelt believers after the ascension (Romans 8:11). The Holy Spirit then became responsible for completing God's work on earth and the fulfilment of all the prophecies concerning the end times (John 16:7-16).

In a short autobiographical booklet, Rees Howells reminded his readers that when the disciples met the risen Saviour, 'they worshipped Him and returned to Jerusalem with great joy' (Luke 24:52). These men had joy before they had power, so joy in that case was not proof of power. They had this joy when they were waiting for the power 'from on high,' the Holy Spirit (Luke 24:49). That had been the state of the Church after the Welsh Revival (1904-1905). They had much joy in the risen Lord, but at the same time they felt the lack of power for service. Unless the Holy Spirit was permitted to deal with an individual's nature and replace it with His Divine Nature (2 Peter 1:3-4) then there would be problems. In Jeremiah 17:9 it states: 'The heart is deceitful above all things and beyond cure. Who can understand it?' (Romans 7:15-18).

Having sat under his father's ministry as an impressionable young man in his early twenties, during those very important years in the College when the Vision was given, Samuel often reflected on the transactions made with God in his own life. On 26 December 1934, the Holy Spirit had placed the responsibility upon Rees of laying the foundation and believing for the fulfilment of the Great Commission. Jesus said, "All authority in Heaven and on earth has been given to Me, therefore *go and make disciples of all nations*, baptising them in the name of the Father and of the Son and of the Holy Spirit, and teaching them to obey everything I have commanded you. And surely I am with you always, to the very end of the age" (Matthew 28:18-20). Although a great spiritual challenge, Rees readily accepted the privilege, believing that God was God and well able to believe through him. After all, Abram had believed for the blessing of the world in his day (Genesis 17-18).

Samuel was also aware of another aspect of the Vision, which the Lord later revealed. The Holy Spirit had offered the little company of believers at BCW the opportunity to be vitally involved in the Divine programme for these last days. In view of God's mercy to them in salvation, they had offered their bodies as living sacrifices, holy and pleasing to God which was their reasonable service (Romans 12:1). It had been clearly pointed out to all those who responded that intercession was required to bring to birth every stage of the Vision, right through to the end times, which is a frequently neglected and overlooked spiritual principle (Daniel 9:3, 17-21, Romans 8:26).

With all this being pondered in his heart, just one day after the death of Rees Howells, Samuel had the unspeakable burden of overcoming his grief and shyness, to encourage the College and prepare them for the Vision to continue. Speaking to the staff and students, he turned to the Scriptures and expounded on the personal tragedy of the disciples, during the trial and death of the Lord. "If we had looked at the disciples that night we wouldn't have thought they could carry on the work," said Samuel. That night "was total darkness to those men." The College felt a similar darkness. "This is a very strange path we have to walk," he said.

In the past, Rees Howells had shouldered the greatest part of the burden, but now Samuel challenged all the young and seasoned intercessors by saying, "Each one of us must carry equal responsibility for the Holy Ghost, for the Vision, for Every Creature."

The next day Samuel led the team towards the future, reigniting the intercessory ministry, teaching them that they were now a company of intercessors. "I don't want to be regarded as His servant's successor," said Samuel. "I feel we are all his successors. This Vision is great. We are coming back as a company to pray through. We are all his successors! Those who are truly in the Vision." During the war years there were up to five prayer meetings a day, plus the duties in the School. "Some have said there are too many prayer meetings," said Samuel. "But I say there won't be one less prayer meeting; if it means coming back day and night we will do it. The burdens are too great – they are beyond a man."

Samuel then counted the cost of intercessory prayer. "The burdens (Rees) carried have been tremendous. During the past few weeks, the burden got so intense that one knew unless something was done he couldn't stand it." Samuel knew the cost, but now he was prepared to pay the same price to be obedient to the Holy Spirit. "I told the Lord today, even if this body is to collapse again, the Vision will go through. The price has been paid...There are these burdens to carry, prayers to be answered and if it costs this life too, I am prepared for it. When you look at the liability, the burdens, you can't face it in the natural way, but the Holy Ghost will carry them. We are one to reach a lost world in intercessory prayer."

The deep spiritual experiences of World War II, when Rees led the staff through those years of intercession, strengthened Samuel often during his later intercessory battles. Rees had been a real role model for Samuel. Pondering the past silent years in his own spiritual journey, and feeling this overwhelming sense of personal inadequacy, Samuel was greatly encouraged by the knowledge that he had the support of a team of staff members who had walked the pathway of the cross through those dark war years and who had also learnt the principles of faith and prayer. They too had given their lives for the Vision for world blessing.

Samuel also expected that the new staff members and students would follow the Lord by receiving Him on the same basis that he had. When the Holy Spirit comes in, He comes in as God to lead, not to follow. He comes to possess, not to be possessed. He comes to intercede, not to cede His right as *the* Intercessor. He comes to live Christ's life, not ours. He wants resurrection life, not the continuation of the old life.

Samuel called for all at the College to receive the Spirit in all His fullness and different translations of 2 Chronicles 24:20 explain the experience. 'The Spirit of God possessed Zechariah.' The apostle Paul knew this process and prayed that the Ephesians 'may be filled with all the fullness of God' (Ephesians 3:19). Peter also states that believers in Christ are, 'a people for His own possession' (1 Peter 2:9). Samuel and senior College staff would only pray the prayers given by the Holy Spirit, because they too had welcomed Him to possess them and pray through them. In College life, Samuel expected that everything was to become subservient to the particular prayers given by the Holy Spirit, just as it had been under Rees Howells' ministry. For those who did not fully appreciate the need for such focused intercessory prayer and failed to recognise the thread of intercession throughout the Scriptures, this became a stumbling block as Samuel developed the ministry. On more than one occasion he stated very clearly, "If intercession is neglected in the College for anything else, then the Lord will bring it to an end."

Chapter Thirteen

The Great Commission

Throughout the 1950s, Samuel continued to focus the intercession of the Bible College towards the fulfilment of the Great Commission. There were many missionaries throughout the world, but how many of them knew the principles of intercession? How many could pray through until the principalities and powers of darkness were bound? The strongholds of Satan in many parts of the world had been entrenched for thousands of years, now these powers of darkness had to be challenged, dislodged and overcome! (1 Thess. 2:18).

If thousands of missionaries were prepared to go to the frontline and sacrifice their lives, then the intercessors at the College would go before them to intercede for victory in the heavenly realms. Samuel had to remind the College once again that our battle is not against flesh and blood. It is the devil who has 'blinded the mind of unbelievers' and only intercession could prevail so they could respond to the Gospel (2 Corinthians 4:4).

On Friday 24 March 1950, Samuel said, "These meetings are to be a cry to God. There is a world to reach and it is only to be reached through prevailing prayer. We are coming tonight to meet God and to cry to Him to fulfil the task. Millions of souls tonight are unsaved and it is only through human channels He can reach them. We are praying these prayers because they are wholly for the Kingdom."

Four years later, with a plethora of messages and prayer meetings behind them, the College were still holding meeting after meeting calling out in intercession. "A prayer meeting should be a place where power is released," said Samuel on 27 September 1954. "Prayers of faith are needed. God has been very gracious to us in the multitude of answers to prayer in these past four years...This prayer for the opening of the world. Think of the prayers God has given us...the evangelisation of the world! Revivals! We heard from Africa last night, God has visited, but the preparation was long and deep." Day-by-day, prayer meetings were held for the peoples and nations of the world. Two months later, Samuel prayed, "Give us liberty and lead us out in prayer for the world. It is through prayer and intercession this work is accomplished. Haggai knew what he wanted, as we do, a million souls, the Continent and Korea!"

10 February 1955. "In the Far East many of the Lord's servants are working there," said Samuel. "From Shanghai to Tibet and from Mongolia to Yuna," and prayer was being answered. "Think of the way God is pouring out His Spirit, where thousands are attending the meetings. This has never taken place before."

20 March 1955. "We believe you have Thy channels prepared for every country," said Samuel in prayer. "There is need for more prayer and intercession. If there is a shade of unreality in us, we pray that Thou will deal with it."

9 April 1955. "If there has been any unwillingness, any disobedience, any hardness, You deal with it. Thou are looking for channels, but only those can be used who have been planted with Thee in the likeness of Thy death."

12 May 1955. "Our prayer is that Thou wilt ever draw us nearer to Thee. The world needs another Pentecost! We are looking forward to witnessing millions turning to Thee. We are one with all Thy servants striving to extend Thy Kingdom. Keep us all in prayer and intercession until we see these things coming right through."

5 June 1955. "We have a burden that these millions may taste again the riches of Thy grace. Through the Holy Spirit, help us again in our prayers and intercessions. We believe Thy heart is yearning to reach these millions. Thou hast said Thou art going to 'pour out Thy Spirit on all flesh.' We believe we have a contribution to make; maybe the intercession is not complete. May we forget our own need and be drawn-out in prayer for a lost world."

Over the years, prayers were offered for the nations of the world. Special prayers were also made for many evangelistic outreaches including Billy Graham's to the U.K. "The first meeting was very cold in Glasgow," said Samuel, "unless the Lord works there will be no results." The next night they received news of answered prayer. "When the appeal was made, four hundred came forward!"

Three months later, the burdens still continued. "There are millions and millions outside of the fold," prayed Samuel. "We feel we can do much more; help us again Lord. We thank Thee the Holy Spirit has come! Apart from the Holy Spirit we can do nothing." The following month Samuel prayed, "It is for a lost world that prayer is made."

The chronicles of Samuel's meetings from the 1950s stir the heart with the adrenalin of prayer, faith, intercession and anticipation documented on every page. Samuel in his preaching from the 1950s frequently mentioned revival: in Korea, Congo, Argentina, and the centenary of the 1859 Revival. A number of revivalists also spoke at BCW (notably during the Every Creature Conferences or during a long weekend of ministry), men such as Duncan Campbell, Andrew Gih and James A. Stewart. Nonetheless, Satan was not going to let the Kingdom's advance go unchecked. Just as the Lord had His channels who prayed and interceded, Satan also had his channels that he used to drag the world into conflict and oppression. During the 1950s, there were many special prayers for the Lord's will to prevail in various conflicts and the first was in Korea.

Chapter Fourteen

War in Korea

The intercessory battle against the hosts of darkness working through Communism became a continual thread of intercession in the life of Samuel. This battle began with Rees, when he called the College to intercede for the anguished German people as they were being freed from the Nazi regime. Rees saw the threat of Russian domination in all of Germany and called the College to prayer. Wherever Communism took hold of a nation, the demonic powers working through the leadership would crush the Christian witness and outreach. The Gospel was being hindered and prayer warriors needed to engage the enemy on every front and force him back.

Rees Howells with his son, Samuel, c.1932 on Derwen Fawr lawns

In the 1950s, Samuel did not know that the Lord would one day call him to intercede for the demise of Communism worldwide, but in his early intercessory battles the Lord was preparing him, as he was led to gain positions of grace by challenging and binding various principalities and powers during Communist conflicts.

It was no secret that the West regarded Communism as a threat to liberty worldwide, but Samuel was not led to pray for the fall of Communist regimes because of Western hostility to this system. Samuel was never led to pray political prayers. Every intercession that the Holy Spirit laid upon him was always a Kingdom prayer. Whenever a situation or conflict was placed in Samuel's spirit, his greatest concern was to know the will of the Lord. God's purposes, as revealed by the Holy Spirit to him, would always concern the Kingdom of God. He was never led to pray for his nation's overseas interests (unless it was in accordance with God's will), because the intercessor cannot have a national, political or a denominational bias. They may indeed love their country and vote, but their intercessions can never be influenced by the foreign policy of their nation or the politics they hold. All these have to be put to the cross and cannot bear down on the intercession. "There cannot be a cross-current," Rees had taught his son.

Samuel's prayer battles to bind the spiritual hosts working through Communism were far-reaching all around the world. Nonetheless, whenever progress seemed to be made, the threat from the demonic powers often switched to another theatre of war. Samuel would spend most of his life interceding for Gospel liberty around the world and just as the College was focusing prayer for world evangelisation, a battle began in Korea that threatened the whole of Asia. At 4am on 25 January 1950, the army of the Communists of North Korea opened fire on all fronts on the South Korean positions south of the 39th Parallel. By 11am, North Korea had officially declared war on its southern neighbour. In a land where revival fires had swept and blessed whole communities since 1903, this was an attempt to engulf the whole peninsula in virtual slavery to a godless ideology. Fighting was very vicious, often hand-to-hand, and the defending U.S. forces, later backed by other UN countries, entered into a fierce battle. For Samuel Rees Howells and the College staff, intercession would have to prevail once again.

As Samuel interceded for the Korean people, he had to ask himself if he would embrace the call, if it came, to evangelise a free Korea. Would Samuel be prepared to go to Korea and identify with them in hunger and thirst? Would he be willing to go to the post-war Korea and preach the Gospel? Korea was not a wealthy nation in the 1950s and war was devastating the country. This practical identification was real to Samuel and he would only find victory after a long battle. "It may not be our work but the Holy Spirit is so keen," he said. "If I had not prayed for Korea last night I would not have been able to go to bed. There would have been a cross-examination with the Holy Spirit. He would ask, "Don't you live for the Kingdom?" We are dealing with a Divine Person who knows everything within us. But I can say I have prayed for these people with the same feeling as if they were our people. He tries to get us to be as concerned about other people's work as with our own."

Without identification, there can be no intercession. The purpose of identification is to make the intercession real. How can you prevail upon God, weeping for the cause, if you have not been made one with it? Jeremiah had to remain single (Jeremiah 16:1-13), Ezekiel had to lie on his side and take food and water by measure (Ezekiel 4:4-17), Hosea had to marry a prostitute and gave his children names that reminded him of the backslidings of God's people (Hosea 1:2-11). Every time Hosea saw his wife and children, he recalled the unfaithfulness of God's people and his intercession became 'living' (Hosea 2:1-4, Hosea 3:1-5). Doris Ruscoe said, "The path of intercession binds you to the will of God in every detail of your life, until the prayer is 'prayed through,' until the Holy Spirit gives the witness that the prayer is through."

As the prayer warrior abides in his or her identification with the subject of intercession, the Holy Spirit transfers identification from the subject to the intercessor. "If we are disposed to abide in Christ, the enablement is there," said Samuel. "We know that from experience. Abide in Him, His words abide in us. What a relationship!"

In the process of identification, the intercessor embraces the agony of the burden and somewhere in the mystery of the spiritual battle, faith has to be found which is equal to the task. It is not faith in man, but the faith that the Holy Spirit plants as a seed in the heart of the intercessor. When the intercessor prays, he or she must allow God's faith to take over and he or she will find that it is not the intercessor that believes, but the Holy Spirit within them. As the process of identification progresses, the intercessor finds him or herself entering into a realm far beyond prayer, and the empty vessel discovers a depth of spiritual reality previously unknown. Suddenly the account of Moses' prayers (Exodus 32:11-14, Numbers 14:1-20, Deuteronomy 9), Daniel's intercession (Daniel 9-10) and Paul's identification (Romans 9-10) comes alive in ways impossible to explain. The intercessor 'knows' from experience, what these people of faith experienced. For Samuel these principles were applied in his life many times, as he interceded for many peoples and nations, but now his focus was Korea.

The first few months of the Korean War were a complete disaster as the North swept down the peninsula, forcing those fighting for liberty into a small corner on the east of the country. By September 1950, the victory of the North was almost complete. During dark and trying days, Samuel was often encouraged by the words and experiences of Rees Howells in his intercessions. During one intercession the Lord told Rees, "Don't expect Me to intervene, until you get to your extremity." When Britain was on the verge of invasion in 1940, Rees made a declaration of faith, "The enemy will not invade Christian England." Now Korea was in its extremity. Could God intervene again? Prayer warriors around the world lifted their voices to God and UN forces prepared for the counterattack, which broke them out of the southern Pusan Perimeter. Two months later, the UN forces took back almost the entire nation and the North was ready to collapse, but in response, the Chinese Communists invaded to support the North Koreans.

While complete victory was close, the principalities and powers had transformed the battle by dragging the 'Red' Chinese into the war. This meant that the intercessory battle was now on two fronts. Daniel experienced this same scenario in the Spirit, when the Prince of Persia was defeated and the Prince of Greece came into battle (Daniel 10:20-21). On the military front by January 1951, with almost one million Chinese soldiers ready as pawns to be sacrificed by their leaders, the UN troops fell back to the south of Seoul. The situation was bleak and prayer was desperately needed.

The Welsh Revival (1904-1905) had a great impact on Korea leading to the Pyongyang Great Revival (1907-1910), and if the nation was to be free again for the spread of the Gospel, the College would need to travail in prayer. "Evan Roberts had gone through deep travail and deep exercise of soul," explained Samuel. "He went to Loughor and revival broke out! There is a quality in that travail, this man prayed through. That is what I want to see! Let us see that the Lord will defeat the enemy not only in a negation sense, but in a positive sense by bringing revival. Let us believe Him again." Then in prayer Samuel encouraged all to believe, "Thou did say if two of Thy children agree on anything Thou wilt answer. Thou art calling on every one of us to believe."

In the physical battle, the British Government joined the Americans and called upon the Far East Fleet of the British Empire to move along the Korean coast. British troops stationed in Hong Kong were sent and reinforcements were also sent from Britain. These young people were fighting the war on the ground and the College were called to the frontlines of intercession on the spiritual front. All over the world people were praying and intercession at the College continued long and hard. Prayer was being answered and the allies pushed north again to liberate the nation.

When discouraging news was heard from the battlefield in many conflicts, the College would be reminded of one of Samuel's sayings concerning fixing our eyes on Jesus and not on circumstances. "The men of the Bible were dwelling on the Person of Christ, not on their misfortunes...The emphasis all the time was 'Walk in Christ.' "

Over the months, the American and British fleet torpedoed North Korea's navy and blockaded the nation achieving total naval supremacy. On land, America sent almost 500,000 soldiers into the theatre of war and the British called upon 100,000. By July 1951, the British Government and Commonwealth nations sent their first Commonwealth Division, consisting of 27,000 Canadians, 17,000 Australians and 1,400 from New Zealand. But by mid 1951, there was stalemate on the ground and negotiations began as the front stabilised on the 38th parallel. For the following two years, talks continued but the spiritual and physical conflict in Korea did not cease until 27 July 1953, when an Armistice was agreed.

Prayer had been answered and now that agony in intercession was complete, Samuel had the authority to declare that a wonderful move of God would sweep South Korea. Samuel often bore the cost of intercession in a private manner, but the internal strength of his identification with the Koreans was expressed publicly in a prayer meeting on 27 September 1954, as his inner feelings burst through in an impassioned declaration, "God is opening up the world. He has men in all the countries. I have told the Lord that I will go to Korea. I am exercised about it. There are things I have to finish here now. If someone could go, tens of thousands could be reached with the Gospel. Are we alive to these things? Korea is ready and God is going to give the offer of the Gospel to them!"

God answered the prayers of Samuel in an abundant way. The Church in South Korea grew and is now the second largest missionary sending nation in the world. What a victory of intercession! South Korea has approximately 13,000 missionaries in 160 countries with a vision for 48,501 missionaries by the year 2030. Even though Samuel never went to Korea, he was blessed as Korea came to him! In the following years, sometimes seventy percent of BCW students were Korean!

Intercession had prevailed for the South, but the burden for the demise of Communism worldwide, which had not yet been fully introduced to Samuel, was only just beginning. The North was still bound because of Chinese strength. For the North to be free, the demonic hosts operating through hard-lined Communism in China would have to be dealt with, but that was not the prayer this time.

The intercessor, whose prayers are directed by the Holy Spirit, cannot choose his battles. In addition, 'failures' in any intercession are a reoccurring theme at the commencement of any great prayer, where a new position of faith and grace is to be gained. In these great intercessions, the Lord will not allow human flesh to glory in His presence. The intercessor must have first 'died' to his new position of grace, otherwise God will not be free to use that gained position again. The first-born and the first-fruits of any intercession belong to the Lord and must be laid on the altar of sacrifice. Even though Samuel had gained a position for Korea, he had to walk parts of it as a failure, embracing the sentence of death to the flesh. With this in mind, all future intercessory victories would bring no glory to any personality or ministry (2 Corinthians 12:7).

Graduation Day, July 2002 in the Prayer Room, Derwen Fawr House. A section of first and second year students singing. Students were from Korea, Wales, England, USA, Brazil, Nigeria and Tunisia.

Samuel never forgot his identification with the Korean people and continued praying for them, particularly those suffering under the oppressive North Korean regime, right till the end of his life. "Think of those believers in North Korea," said Samuel in 1982. "Who has kept them? Who has maintained them and sustained them down these years? It is the Spirit of God. When these dear ones meet together, don't you believe that there are deep cries ascending from their hearts? They are reaching the Throne of God. How wonderful will it be when that country again is open for the Gospel! That will be an answer, to the intercessory walk and cry of these dear folk."

Chapter Fifteen

Persistent Prayer

During the days of Rees Howells and then under Samuel, the College partook of *intercessory prayers* during its prayer meetings, with each individual present assuming a measure of responsibility to believe for victory. The spiritual identification with those being prayed for proved heavy to carry. Some days it was difficult to continue and staff attended the prayer meetings feeling physically tired or exhausted; but their intercessions had a worldwide impact.

The profound premise that shaped Samuel's life was his belief that intercession could alter international events. In history, when God found an intercessor (such as Moses), the Lord often intervened miraculously in impossible situations. In Samuel's ministry, he also was willing to be led by the Holy Spirit into the forge of intercession, enabling God to metamorphose any situation for His purposes. With the Sword of the Spirit in his hand, he embraced a life of spiritual warfare, and as he prayed, God's will was brought to bear upon world events (Ephesians 6:7, Hebrews 4:12).

In the early decades, when Samuel called the College to pray, they always went down on their knees on the bare wooden floorboards, often for over an hour at a time. Long hours were spent each week seeking the face of God for world situations, but these would always be preceded by anointed ministry from the Scriptures, when the lives of the heroes of faith were studied carefully. In his ministry Samuel stressed the intense and powerful awareness of the need for importunate prayer to soak into every fibre of his life and into the lives of all those concerned for, and committed to seeing God's Kingdom penetrate the far corners of the earth (Luke 11:2).

God's presence was very real in these sessions. It was in one such evening session in the 1950s when Samuel opened his heart to the College staff and students. "These dealings you have with the Holy Spirit – it is very difficult to put them into words. It seems that He has been speaking to me all day long and one has felt within oneself (Samuel often referred to himself as 'one') the travail of the Holy Spirit for a lost world. One doesn't want to bring a message but to go back to God. The pressure upon us must be increased if anything. One believes that the Holy Spirit has been searching for a hundred years to find a man to take this Commission (Matthew 28:18-20, Mark 16:15-18). Is it right that millions should be lost? He did find one man who was willing to take it up and we all know what it cost him." Samuel was referring to Rees Howells. "What has come to one today, even if prayers are answered, is that there is a world to reach and it is only to be reached by prevailing prayer. We are coming tonight to meet God, to cry to Him to fulfil the task."

Samuel read and then referred to Jesus' parables of the Unjust Judge (Luke 18:1-8) and the Friend at Midnight (Luke 11:5-10). "When He gave these parables it wasn't only teaching but from the depth of His experience," he said. "We believe that He knew what it was to be importunate and persistent in prayer. Probably there were hundreds of times when the Saviour went alone and spent nights with His Father. What was He doing? Didn't He have prayers we know nothing about? He had a commission to put through, a ministry to fulfil. You might think the Saviour could have chosen twelve disciples without prayer and communion with His Father, but He spent the whole night in prayer (Luke 6:12-16)."

Samuel held no illusions about what would be required of him in the 1950s, to pray through his challenges of faith. It would require many hours spent in the Divine Presence. Sometimes he would make startling pronouncements in his pulpit ministry during the evening prayer meetings, such as, "Don't think you can pray like Moses and see God's purposes fulfilled unless you spend the time Moses did in God's presence. If you think you can pray like him without spending the time he spent – you are shallow."

Little did staff and students know what he was really facing which produced such passionate words. It was mainly through reading and meditating upon the Scriptures in the Lord's presence that Samuel now drew his real strength. After the restoration of the Jews from seventy years of captivity in Babylon (through the intercessions of Ezekiel and Daniel), Samuel saw afresh, through reading Ezra 4:1-25, that the work of rebuilding the Temple in Jerusalem was suddenly brought to a halt. These satanic onslaughts on God's work often bring progress to a standstill even today. However, as a result of the persistent prevailing prayers of Haggai and Zechariah over a fourteen year period, the Holy Spirit came upon the prophets in a powerful way, enabling their work to proceed. The prophecy of Zechariah brought great encouragement to Samuel. 'This is the word of the Lord to Zerubbabel saying, "Not by might nor by power, but by My Spirit," says the Lord of hosts' (Zechariah 4:6).

There were many trials for Samuel as he took the College forward, but the Lord brought great relief to him, and led eventually to many of his early prayer objectives being achieved. The Holy Spirit was teaching Samuel the vital place of prevailing prayer in the progress and development of God's work. He was proving the truth of the Lord's promise in John 15:7. "If you abide in Me, and My Words abide in you, you will ask what you desire, and it shall be done for you." He had learnt that abiding in Christ was the key.

Chapter Sixteen

The Heart of Kenya

When Samuel led the College through an intercession, he never sought to raise the prayers of the College to an emotional high of self-propelled excitement and sound. Instead, he would invite the staff and students to believe God with him, and enter into the quiet life of abiding. The things that students and staff members 'confessed' outside of the meetings had the same spiritual impact as what they prayed publicly. In every minute and hour of the day, they were to be believing God and whenever the prayer was laid on their hearts, they were to continue to trust in God (John 15:10).

The heavenly realm does not reverberate when human effort produces a deafening disturbance on earth, but rather when the faith of God is operating in and through His people. An intense noise during an official prayer meeting can never substitute for true believing faith. One famous visitor to the College, the revivalist Duncan Campbell, once told the story of a rousing prayer meeting, as many believers made a rumpus commotion, stirring each other up in shouts of praise and victory. Enjoying the experience, Duncan looked to an elderly prayer warrior and asked his thoughts. "It's beautiful to hear these folk praising God," the man said to Duncan, "but it's a shame that all the steam is going out of the whistle instead of to the piston!" Immediately Duncan Campbell understood the analogy of a steam train, where pressure is built up, only to be carefully released to produce maximum results to move the train forward; but in this meeting, all that was produced was noise. Consistency of faith is always more important than noise.

Boisterous prayer is not to be forbidden in church, for the people of Israel were told by God to make a thunderous shout before the walls of Jericho fell down, and Samuel recalled how after months of intercession during WWII, people at the College would shout and sing rejoicing in victory. But this was the exception, not the rule; and these events took place at the end of a prolonged period of trudging intercession, as the intercessors entered into the grace of faith.

Samuel was also careful concerning whom he prayed with at the College. Moses had to pray outside the camp (Exodus 33:7), when the multitudes were not in faith. Inviting untested strangers into 'an intercessory prayer meeting,' to pray with those who had surrendered all seemed to be inconsistent with the principles of full surrender and the life of abiding. How could they have the faith of God operating through them, if they had never surrendered and invited the Holy Spirit to believe through them? How could visitors only pray the prayers of the Holy Spirit, if they had never met Him personally? How could an unholy or compromised believer become one with a prayer of the Holy Spirit?

We must recall that Paul called himself a slave of Jesus Christ (Romans 1:1). In modern translations he is called a 'servant,' but this rendering does not paint an accurate picture of Paul's original expression. Everyone whom Paul wrote to knew that Roman slaves had no rights. They went where they were told; they did what they were asked and therefore identifying with them, Paul called himself a slave of Jesus Christ. This is Paul's expression of full surrender and total consecration. This will always be the price to be paid to have intimate fellowship with Christ. For Samuel, full surrender rendered one's heart suitable to enter into a life of intercession and in 1952, a great prayer came on all who had made this sacrifice.

In October 1952, the British declared a state of emergency in Kenya, as Mau Mau fighters intensified a brutal campaign of terror against political opponents, white settlers and farming communities. The College was called to prayer, but they were not led to intercede for the furtherance of British rule in Kenya, but rather for the binding of the demonic forces operating through the Mau Mau (Matthew 12:22-29, Matthew 16:19, Matthew 18:18-20). The effectual process of peaceful reform leading to independence from Britain had already begun before these troubles, but the Mau Mau sought to highjack this transition for their own political advantage, and demonic spirits were working through them.

In the spiritual realm, where intercession operates, the forces of darkness had found their channels in the Mau Mau who had taken demonic oaths, calling upon ancient spirits to possess them to fight against the British and the Christian God. The brutality of their oaths and practices was shocking. They covenanted that they would be cut off "from all hope, outside Mau Mau, in this world and the next." Their spiritual rituals involved digging up human corpses and eating the flesh, drinking human blood and many other unspeakable acts. Their vows became a renunciation of all Christian belief and morals. 'The things which the Gentiles sacrifice, they sacrifice to demons' (1 Corinthians 10:20).

This conflict began with acts of terrorism, but metamorphosed into an all out guerrilla war, with British and Kenyan political leaders on one side and the Mau Mau on the other. Both sides were seeking to win the hearts and minds of the decent Kenyan people. British missionaries had brought Christianity into Kenya during British rule and Satan was seeking to use this to turn Kenyans away from Christ. If the Mau Mau won, the principalities and powers operating through them would use force and manipulation to turn the people of Kenya away from Christianity and back to worshiping the former gods, who would be credited with their liberation.

As Samuel found many times in his intercessions, he was not called to pray for Britain's interests, but for Kingdom concerns. He saw this as a battle for the spread of the Gospel and for the souls of the people of Kenya. It was never a case of taking sides in these prayers. People of every nationality and persuasion are all precious to the Lord, whose atoning death was for all of mankind. "I have no pleasure in the death of the wicked, but that the wicked turn from his way and live" (Ezekiel 33:11). God 'desires all men to be saved and to come to the knowledge of the truth' (1 Timothy 2:4). As the Holy Spirit was establishing Christ's Kingdom in Kenya, so Satan would stir hatred into human hearts and conflicts ensued and erupted.

The key prayer was for the Mau Mau to lose all support and credibility, as the enemy working through them would be exposed. Only intercession would lead to this taking place. "We feel a great deal is dependent upon our prayer and intercession," said Samuel, now aged forty. "The weapons of our warfare are mighty to the pulling down of strongholds. There are many strongholds before us, but they can all be dealt with."

Through visits from Ken Terhoven, the College was given reports of the testimonies of those who had courageously survived the fanatical Mau Mau attacks, but also of the sound of Christians returning home through the bush singing, 'Onward Christian Soldiers' gradually growing less and less, as one by one, they were slaughtered. Those dear martyrs paid the supreme price for freedom and blessing. "Who drove the people to their fury?" asked Samuel. "It was the enemy." Samuel was reminding the College that their battle was not against human warriors, but against the principalities working through them. Speaking about the violence, Samuel said, "How little we know of that. Not one of us is in fear of physical danger. The circumstances at the College are like paradise compared with the mission field. We have everything here."

This war became one of the bloodiest of the British Empire, as the African Home Guard, recruited by the British sought to defeat the Mau Mau and in response, the rebels would raid Kenyan villages. On 25 March 1953, the rebels herded one hundred and twenty villagers into huts in Lari and set fire to them. In another attack, the Mau Mau, killed over seventy people, mostly women and children. The one who came 'to kill, steal and destroy' was operating, turning brother against brother and the Mau Mau made no distinction between civilians and soldiers. Everyone was a potential victim.

Deeply exercised about the situation Samuel wrote: 'Affairs in Africa too are in a most critical state. Satan is undoubtedly exploiting the present upsurge of nationalism and seeking to destroy the missionary efforts of the last one hundred years. Will anything less than an outpouring of God's Holy Spirit on these people, prove to be sufficient? Without another great Divine awakening the situation seems practically lost, but we firmly believe that God will again intervene. However, in order to pray and intercede for such a visitation we need the faith of God. In praying for a worldwide revival we are doing something that is in accordance with the will of God.'

THE BIBLE COLLEGE OF WALES
DERWEN FAWR, SWANSEA.
ANNUAL MISSIONARY
CONFERENCE
July 24th to August 1st

An advertisement in *The Christian*, 18 June 1954

Many historians tend to dismiss the brutality of the Mau Mau, favouring them as freedom fighters, but this was a civil war led by followers of a bewitching cult. There were many legitimate Kenyan leaders seeking peaceful reform and some of these were targeted by the Mau Mau. During the eight year conflict, only thirty-two white settlers were murdered, but many thousands of Kenyans were slaughtered by the rebels. As a direct result of this brutality, the evil working through the Mau Mau was eventually exposed and they lost support of the population. Prayer was being answered as the Kenyan people rejected the Mau Mau and their non-Christian vision for the future of the nation. Kenya would remain a Christian nation!

Wrongdoings took place in the conflict, subjecting decent Kenyans to violence and in London, leaders in the Church spoke out against atrocities. On 21 October 1956, the rebel leader Dedan Kimathi was captured, leading to the ultimate defeat of the uprising by 1960.

In the spiritual realm, the demonic powers who sought to use the Mau Mau to take over the nation and turn it away from Christianity were defeated. Kenya found independence from Britain in 1963 and became a member of the British Commonwealth. Today eighty percent of their population state they are Christian, with fifty percent calling themselves evangelical and there is an explosion of growth in Pentecostal and Charismatic churches. The College had the privilege of remembering the whole nation, and having a small part in this Kingdom prayer. Kenya was God's and the future of Christianity in the nation was safe. What a victory!

Chapter Seventeen

Emergency in Malaysia

At the heart of Communism are spiritual realities that despise the faith of the God of Abraham, Isaac and Jacob. During Samuel's life, whenever Communism took control of a nation, churches were closed, evangelism was stopped and Christians were imprisoned. In a spiritual sense, Communism is not a political ideology, but a principality whose primary aim is to derail the spread of the Gospel and to challenge the Kingdom of God on earth. In the physical realm, men and women embrace the Communist ideology, but in the spiritual realm, it is the powers of darkness that are working through them to defy God's purposes in the nations.

The forgotten war in Malaysia (Malaya) from 1948 until 1960 was Britain's successful Vietnam War, when Communist elements attempted to take control of the nation. Malaysia has a large Chinese population and the Malaysian Communist Party (MCP) was essentially a Chinese organisation. With half a million supporters, the MCP was a formidable organisation. After failing to institute a Communist government in the nation, the MCP changed tactics to engage their military arm to carry out guerrilla operations and terrorist attacks. In response the British Government trained ethnic Malaysians to fight the enemy and sent in 35,000 men. After five years of battles, the war slowed to a stalemate.

At the College, the 1950s were an intense time of resurgent prayer and intercession. Samuel led his team of intercessors into many prayer battles, for many nations, calling them out and asking for God's will to be done. "If we persevere in these prayers they are answered," said Samuel in prayer. "But the tendency is when You give us a prayer, we let it go before it is answered." It was a warning to the intercessors, that all must persevere to pray through. "It may be at this time there is opposition, but we thank Thee that with intercession we can penetrate the powers of darkness."

In 1953, elements of the British fleet came into port in Malaysia, with the 848 Naval Air Squadron and S-55 helicopters. With these helicopters, soldiers were able to penetrate deep into the jungle, set up bases behind enemy camps and fight on every front. However, as we learnt in Vietnam, military might is not enough in these spiritual battles, where 'we do not fight against flesh and blood' (Ephesians. 6:12).

The war for Malaysia was not a political struggle, but a spiritual one. If the MCP could gain control of the nation, the large Malaysian Christian community, itself the fruit of British missionaries under

British rule, would be driven underground and could collapse. Missionaries had made major inroads inside this predominantly Muslim population, but all this was in jeopardy. "Undoubtedly during this time God is expecting us to believe Him in the impossible," said Samuel. "When He speaks to us He expects us to believe Him implicitly; however impossible the prayer may be. It's impossible to us, but it's not impossible to Him!" (Matthew 17:20-21).

Samuel Howells (left) preaching in The Gospel House (Maison de l'Evangile) at Bois de Boulogne, Paris, France in 1962, age 50. The property was bought by Rees Howells in 1937. Frank Nixon, a former BCW student (pre WWII) is interpreting.

Samuel would often preach on the prophets of the Bible and the challenges they embraced. He would never allow the College to forget that these people were ordinary men and women, just like us, who had to believe God in the worst of circumstances (James 5:17-18). Elijah had to believe that an entire nation could be turned back to God, when Jezebel and Ahab had all the power and used it to turn the nation to false gods. There were many other examples that Samuel cited of identification, agony and the gained position of intercession that leads to authority. "Daniel believed Him," said Samuel. "There wasn't a shade of doubt and there was no need then for Daniel to proceed with that prayer. He caused the people to go back to their land, wasn't that impossible? (Daniel 9). The Holy Spirit is with us and He is giving us an opportunity of believing Him."

Samuel told the College that there is much prayer in parts of the Church, but little believing. Samuel was looking for people to believe with him that God would intervene in international events, just like He did in the Old Testament in response to the faith of the prophets. Doubt is the currency of the flesh, but believing is the currency of the Spirit and the Bible warns that without faith, it is impossible to please God (Hebrews 11:6). "There's hardly any believing in the Church today," said Samuel. "What does He want from us today? It is to believe Him in the impossible! We need to go back to these things. It's a different world all together" (Luke 1:37, Luke 18:27).

These were the challenges Samuel presented to all. Think of Esther and Mordecai. Those two people were entirely responsible to believe for every Jew in the world's largest empire to be saved. Could we do the same? Now in Malaysia an entire nation was at stake. Who would intercede? Who would believe?

Aerial view of Sketty Isaf Estate (front) and Derwen Fawr Estate (back), c.1950. The Derwen Fawr Road divides the estates running approximately from top left corner (of photo) to bottom right, but above the house on bottom right. The bottom field where the two cows are grazing (and far top left) now have homes built on them, whilst bungalows have been built on the top right field. From this aerial view, the Glynderwen Estate was a five minutes walk to the right in the direction of Blackpill.

The Bible states that 'the king's heart is in the hand of the Lord,' (Proverbs 21:1), and as prayer was answered, God's influence upon leaders on all sides in the conflict began to be felt. The British were given wisdom on how to defeat the Communist insurgents and the MCP were making tactical errors which led to military failings. As Christians in Malaysia prayed, the true nature of the enemy working through the MCP was exposed and public support collapsed. The MCP killed every soldier that they captured and routinely stripped villages of their earthly goods. In response the British Government introduced a 'hearts and minds' initiative providing medical care, food and protection from the MCP. The helicopters enabled them to reach out to remote tribes and this strategy instilled confidence in the British, although great mistakes were made.

When Christian doubters questioned why the various wars that the College prayed for had gone on for some time and why they had to experience setbacks in prayer, Samuel often reminded the College of Hezekiah. This man put his trust in the Lord, but he saw major defeats in Judah when the Assyrians attacked the nation. "We know Hezekiah found it difficult to believe to the end," said Samuel. "The test ran to such a height. Very often the Lord goes beyond, just to prove the test of faith. If He was going to preserve Jerusalem why didn't He preserve Judah as a whole? There was hardly a city standing except Jerusalem. It was the same in WWII and in Abyssinia. We fought every step to stop Satan and the Lord gave the victory. The purposes of God were fulfilled, but it was a struggle. Isaiah had been very faithful to the Lord and said in the height of the test that the Lord would turn this man back, 'I will put a hook in thy nose and turn thee back.' We can use these words lightly today, but we couldn't in 1940. Isaiah and Hezekiah had to cry to the Lord then the Lord spoke to Isaiah, and Sennacherib was humiliated outside of the walls of Jerusalem."

In Malaysia, the terrorist attacks of the MCP alienated them from its Chinese supporters and the British were now gaining the upper hand. The 'hearts and minds' initiative was very successful and many ethnic Chinese, Indians and Malaysians joined in peaceful talks for the future. The Communist threat was defeated and independence came to Malaysia in 1957, in a democratic form, with official freedom for Christians to worship. Today almost ten percent of the Malaysian population are Christian, with mega-churches and outreach. There are challenges in this Muslim nation with Islamic extremism, but their prayers were wonderfully answered.

Chapter Eighteen

Intercession for China

Rees Howells had led the College in prayer for China on many occasions and in 1936, he sold land for the modern equivalent of £54,000 ($86,400), and gave it to evangelise one thousand villages in China. Meanwhile, after WWII, whilst the West was occupied with threats from the Union of Soviet Socialist Republics (USSR), a small group of revolutionaries swept themselves into power in China, as Satan sought to capture the souls of one fifth of humanity!

The College notes for 29 January 1948 record: 'Prayer for missionaries and Christians who are being persecuted by the Reds.' Ten months later the concern needed to be engaged at a deeper level as Rees Howells called them to 'the beginning of prayer for China.' The burden continued for years and after Samuel became Director, the intercession proceeded to a further untapped level.

10 February 1955. "We were thinking of Abraham pleading with the Lord for the cities of the plain," said Samuel. "Concerning Isaac God said, 'Is anything too hard for the Lord?' We believe He spoke those words to us too. In the Far East...we are believing for revival."

11 Feb. 1955. "There are countless millions outside of the fold" prayed Samuel, "we ask Thee to lay their burden upon us. We thank Thee for the prayer Thou hast given us this week for the millions in the Far East. We thank Thee for the many parts Thou hast already visited with revival and Thou wilt (will) visit these places again!"

After a month of prayer, Samuel challenged the College to prepare for the battle ahead. "Paul stood out for the Gentiles. Christianity was dependent on the revelation of this man. They were coming out of heathenism. He had seen the atonement and he knew there was enough power to keep these converts without any outward restraints." Just as Paul had stood for the Gentiles, the College had to stand for China. "Special meetings are starting tomorrow for prayer," said Samuel. "As we pray these things we want Him to inspire those servants of His who are praying for revival in China. If there is a release of the Spirit in one place, He can be released in other places." Samuel was speaking of the principle of a gained intercession. Once a position of intercession has been gained, the Lord can apply it again for any other situation that He chooses.

Another month of prayer passed, calling out for many nations, and Samuel reminded the College how the principle of death and resurrection in intercession had worked in the lives of the early British missionaries to China. "Hudson Taylor, founder of the China Inland Mission was at his extremity. How could the millions of China be reached? Their burden had come upon him and he felt helpless and broken. God spoke to him. He was going to raise that mission and he believed the Lord's word. His wife sensed he was a new man. It was a meeting with God, like Jacob at Peniel. In China, he had periods of disappointment and setbacks and unless the Lord would meet him afresh he could not go on. He entered into that realm of full surrender and faith in the God of the impossible." God had worked in the past through intercession, would He work again?

As was often the case in the College, whilst they were engaged in one burden, the enemy tried to distract them by introducing another conflict. The First Taiwan Strait Crisis of 1954-1955, was an armed conflict between China and Taiwan. China was an increasing problem for the West for its support of Communist dictatorships and some asked, "Why don't we use *the bomb?*" In the West, the hardliners thought that using a nuclear weapon on China would finally solve the problem of Communism in Asia, and secret documents now released state that the U.S. Joint Chiefs of Staff recommended its use during this conflict! In addition, Admiral Robert Carney publicly stated that Eisenhower is planning "to destroy Red China's military potential." These were serious days indeed!

Samuel sensed this in the Spirit and was deeply concerned calling the College to prayer. In a 7pm meeting Samuel said, "Tonight, let us pray for the Far East. The position seems explosive. We want the Lord to restrain these powers (the West). Think of what will happen now if these new weapons are let loose on China. China has not had the Gospel yet. Leave politics aside. We must be impartial, where God is." Samuel loved Britain and in his lifetime he knew that God was using America to hold back the Communist tide, protect Israel and send forth missionaries. But in this crisis, Samuel had to pray for the West to be restrained. "There has been such blessing in these countries (of Asia) and they would all be closed again if there was war." In the 10pm meeting Samuel said to the College, "You are essentially intercessors, though you do other important work. Think of the situation in the East. Is anything too hard for the Lord?"

In many conflicts Samuel prayed for Western victory, because their triumph was often aligned with God's greater purposes. But in this conflict, he prayed for a restraining hand because he believed the West was out of alignment with God's ultimate purposes for China. If the 'Christian West' had used a nuclear bomb on China, the moral authority would have been lost and the Chinese may have rejected Christianity for this reason. Their prayers were answered, when President Eisenhower sensed that history would judge him harshly if he used *the bomb*. The immediate crisis was solved, but the College would return in later years to serious prayer for China.

Chapter Nineteen

A Biblical Foundation

To fully appreciate the depth and far-reaching effects of Samuel's hidden ministry, it is important to have a clear understanding of the legacy of ministry that had been revealed through his father, Rees Howells. The main elements of these foundations of truth emphasised by Samuel, are:

1. The cross stands central in history. The vicarious death of Christ to atone for mankind's sin was complete. Christ rose triumphantly from the grave and returned to His Father in Heaven (1 Corinthians 15:3-8, Acts 1:9-11).

2. It is essential for the new birth to be established in the life of an individual before God takes him any further into a true personal walk with Himself. To be born of God is a wonderful miracle, not just a hackneyed phrase. So many disappointments in so called Christian lives are the result of neglecting this initial step into the Kingdom of God (John 3:3-8). Purging repentance (and pure faith in Christ) cannot be avoided, or omitted from the Gospel (Job 42:6, Matthew 4:17, Mark 6:12, Acts 16:31, Revelation 2:5). Saying, "Sorry," is not repentance, but forsaking sin to live a transformed life is. Jesus' Great Commission is to preach the Gospel of repentance. If there is no repentance, it is not the whole Gospel (Mark 2:17, Luke 24:47).

3. God's Holy Spirit will then seek to lead the individual to the point of being totally yielded to His leading and direction. It is then possible for the Holy Spirit to endue that individual with Divine power and authority to use him as a clear witness of His character.

4. There are only two Intercessors. The first is Jesus Christ who, as our great High Priest, is interceding for the Church. The second is the Holy Spirit on earth, commissioned to complete God's purposes in the world (Hebrews 7:24-27, John 16:7-14).

5. The Holy Spirit on earth must have 'bodies' through whom He can intercede in the world (Romans 8:27, 1 Corinthians 6:19). He uses the bodies of believers cleansed through the application of the blood of Christ (Hebrews 9:14, Revelation 1:5).

6. As the cross stands central in history, the Holy Spirit has always been able to minister the cleansing power of the blood of Christ to prepare His channels. In the Old Testament, this process was used retrospectively in the lives of certain individuals raised up for specific ministries, i.e. the Patriarchs and Prophets (Hebrews 11).

7. Today the means of grace are available for all believers. All can be totally cleansed to become temples for God to live in (1 Corinthians 3:16-17, 6:19-20). The NCV translation of James 4:5

expresses this truth clearly. 'Do you think the Scripture means nothing that says that the Spirit whom God made to live in us wants us for Himself alone?'

8. The apostles were the selected few in their day who turned the world upside down, because they were totally filled (or possessed) by the Holy Spirit and made pliable for service (Acts 1:8). In these last days, the Great Commission, with the total fulfilment of Joel's prophecy will only be completed through channels of this calibre; able to deal effectively with the spiritual powers of darkness that rule the world (Ephesians 1:21-22, 3:10-11). "Even on My servants, both men and women, I will pour out My Spirit in those days" (Joel 2:29).

9. God has always used these means. There is no other way (Acts 2:17-21, Ephesians 6:12). The eleven disciples were stripped of their confidence and were truly baptised into the death of Christ before He met them on the resurrection side and later revealed their position in glory to them. Any individual aspiring to these spiritual heights will be asked to pay a great price (Acts 9:16).

The illustration of purchasing a chocolate bar from a machine on a railway station was often used by Rees Howells. You must pay the full price before the machine will release the chocolate (candy). So it is in spiritual matters. There are no short cuts, no easy roads. Resurrection life is only obtained when the old nature is completely put to death in any given part in our lives. The Holy Spirit deals systematically with our old nature. Some of what we hear today, even in conservative, evangelical and charismatic circles, is a religious counterfeit which carries no authority in Christ.

10. Intercessory prayer means becoming responsible for a particular situation, individual or group of individuals, as the Holy Spirit gives a burden, and continuing to carry that burden until it is lifted (having 'prayed through'). Christ's teaching on the need for importunate prayer is found in Luke 11:5-10 and Luke 18:1-8.

11. Death is the route to victory. Death to self and to reputation is essential for intercessors to abide in Christ. To be an intercessor, one must expect to be misunderstood and maligned. We must first be united in Christ's death and then in His resurrection (Romans 6:5). 'For to you it has been granted on behalf of Christ, not only to believe in Him, but also to suffer for His sake' (Philippians 1:29). There can be no room for human pride. Humility, with absolute reliance on God, leads to triumph (Proverbs 29:23, Matthew 23:12).

We can trace this foundation weaving its way through every stage, as Samuel's ministry unfolds through the years. To complete it in triumph, Samuel would be torn to shreds by metaphorical lions, hardly able to take a further step at times. Any victories would be totally those of the Holy Spirit.

Chapter Twenty

Sending Out Missionaries

Ever since God had met with Rees Howells on 26 December 1934, and placed a special responsibility upon him to see the fulfilment of the Great Commission, there was a deep desire in him to see new countries reached with the Gospel. From its earliest years, young men and women had left the College and pioneered new works. More than 1,100 students trained at the Bible College of Wales, have come from or gone to at least eighty-five countries of the world and this process of training labourers for the nations was renewed and encouraged under Samuel's ministry. There were many who have entered strategic ministries throughout the world and became vital cogs in advancing the Kingdom of God.

Every year, Samuel and his leadership team had the joy of 'sending forth labourers into the harvest fields' (Matthew 9:38), but before students went out from the College, staff would always prepare them with special messages. "We feel that during this time it is Thy will for us to follow Thee to the utmost of our capacity," prayed Samuel as he opened a meeting. "We can only do so in the Holy Spirit. If the disciples failed, we shall fail too, apart from the Holy Spirit. If Thou wilt come upon us, as Thou didst on the apostles, we shall be able to witness. May these days be days of deep dealings. Open the Word this evening. Speak to us again."

The messages during these periods were designed to prepare students for life after graduation. Samuel and other members of staff would encourage students to abide in prayer, trust in the Holy Spirit's leading and follow Christ wherever He led them. First students need to continue in the life of faith. "Don't let go," said Samuel. "I believe at the end of your training you will be able to look back and say the Lord has supplied all your needs. Continue now." This life was only possible when students had given themselves unconditionally to the Holy Spirit. "Our prayer is that you may be fully possessed of the Holy Spirit," said Samuel. "Then He will be your Teacher. The disciples did not fully understand what the Master said, but the Holy Spirit taught them everything after He left them. Let the Holy Spirit deal with you inwardly. The Lord is not able to work unless you place yourselves in the position for Him to do so. The secret is to learn the art of prevailing – so the Lord can lead you to some of those hard fields. It all depends on prayer and intercession. Men have spent years in the secret place. It does not come cheaply or easily." Samuel then explained that the characters of the Bible were normal men and women like us. "Gideon was very ordinary and insignificant, but he was God's vessel through the strength God would supply. The Midianites were innumerable and the Israelites were helpless, but Gideon was made strong by the Spirit." Many of these students over the years seemed weak and insufficient like Gideon, but this man of faith trusted in God and saved a nation. Could these young people do the same? "Are we losing touch at this time?" asked Samuel. "We need to meet the Holy Spirit. He wants to clear you out. He wants clean vessels. In prayer now, do you feel the Spirit coming on you?"

All the students had received theological training, but had they allowed the Holy Spirit to come into their lives and transform them? Had they applied this teaching? "We have seen everything in theory," said Samuel, "but how much has become part of our experience?" In the life of faith and intercession, these biblical principles that the students had been taught must be applied one by one, in case after case. "You will not do the spectacular unless you have done the ordinary small things," said Samuel. "The Spirit is supposed to possess us now! Has each one of you determined not to let God go until He blesses you? There are hundreds and thousands of ministers today, but they have not touched it. It takes time to get accustomed to His presence. After you have been in His presence for some time, He draws near and then you touch Him with that touch of faith. The days ahead are important."

If these students were to see any fruit on the mission field, they needed to surrender to Christ and abide in the position Christ has made available. "Undoubtedly the Lord has offered to each one of us a new position in Christ," said Samuel. "Let us not miss this. We must dwell on these things outside the meetings. He lived the resurrection life. This is something revolutionary. If we have become one with Him, His life is ours! In that realm, whatever we shall ask the Father in His name it will be done. We shall only believe the things we need to believe now when we are in that relationship. He spoke of Himself as the Vine and His life was to flow through them. It is the same position with us" (John 15:4-10).

Every year, young students from the College were preparing to go to the ends of the earth, but missionaries like all Christians can be overcome with selfishness and doubt. "We can spend so much time on our frets and worries," said Samuel. "But if we have seen God, we are transformed into another world altogether. It is not lip service that God desires but life service." After all the miracles students had witnessed at the College, Samuel warned them not to trust in themselves and go back to ordinary human ministry. "If we live limited lives again...It would be pharisaical after seeing Christ with all authority – in that place of power! This resurrection power must be released in the world and we believe we are to be some of God's instruments." The Holy Spirit was searching for empty vessels, but not all the students wanted to pay the price to follow the Lord. Those who did surrender all paid a price. Was it worth the cost? "The devil would have us to think that this life of abiding is bondage," said Samuel. "It is the old life that is bondage."

The College always began and ended meetings in prayer. "Help us to pray effectively, earnestly and constantly for these lost millions," prayed Samuel. "Draw us nearer to the cross and deal with everything that is not worthy of Thee." Every student that obeyed the Lord went out in prayer and many felt the intercessory blessing follow them. Meanwhile the battles of intercession continued at the College. "Prayers that have been prayed for years, intercession that has been made for years, the time has come to press the battle to the gates," challenged Samuel. "We thank Thee for the revelation we have had again of the risen Lord in these past days."

Samuel invited each batch of students to live in the impossible realm, to believe for the inconceivable and to surrender all to the Lord. "Have you been transformed? Do you live for the things of this world? Can you honestly say today that you have left everything and that you are following God?" These were the deep questions that Samuel asked students. "There's no compromise. There's only one condition, it's a full and unqualified surrender." Dr. Priddy often reminded students that the Lord does not want us to build a work for Him, but He wants to build a work in and through us. He does not want our help in ministry, but our empty vessels for Him to live His life through. He once explained how the Holy Spirit had shown him. "There is all the difference in the world between your surrendered life in My hands and I living My life in your body."

Ten years later in another message to students, Samuel said, "We know that we can't take one step further without the help and aid of God." Was it wrong for the students to feel weak and insufficient for the unimaginable tasks ahead? "If we didn't recognise our need, we wouldn't be dependent on the Holy Spirit," said Samuel. "We've been called to live a life that is impossible to do of ourselves. It is only the Holy Spirit who can do it. It's all right to say this, but it's another to do it! What we need is a meeting with the Holy Ghost, nothing else will do. This is not theory, its reality. Don't withhold whatever price He will ask of you. It's worth paying the whole price, for His possession. Not that He would merely influence you, but that He would indwell you. You look to Him and whatever He asks of you, comply with Him so that He can take absolute control of your life and your possessions. Then you won't be going out in your own strength, but in His strength."

Chapter Twenty-One

The Bible School of Living Faith

In many countries today there are Christian leaders who passed through the 'school of faith' and are now exercising, or have exercised fruitful ministries. To each generation of students, Samuel would give a challenge, "The life of faith is most intelligent because God is in it, but faith must become substance before it becomes evidence." Then Samuel warned the students that living by faith is not easy and will always come at a cost, with heavenly conditions. "In every promise, there is a condition! Unless you can prove God to answer in an emergency and in a test case, it is nothing but talk in a very big way. The 'old man' can sound very convincing but he does not see his folly. You can never exercise real faith for £100 ($160) unless you've had £50 ($80), nor for £50 unless you've proved God for £20 ($32), nor for £10 ($16) unless you've proved God for £5 ($8). You only give mental assent and imagine these things, unless you have had an experience with God in the impossible. Man's extremity is God's opportunity."

Samuel never asked the students to make any sacrifices that he himself had not made and he taught by experience. "There are some very important things to pray through," he said. "There are two or three other prayers amounting in their thousands and we feel they must be put through before we can go on to the bigger things."

In the trials of the life of faith, Samuel often shared with the students the financial burdens and liability that he carried. With no physical means of support, Samuel continued like his father Rees to go to the Throne alone and pray in the daily needs of the College. He was often tested to the extreme, but he said, "I know there are these testings but there is no need to dwell on the testings but rather on Christ; that's a miracle in itself, isn't it?" He was always inspired by the thought of being One with the Lord in this life of faith. "What privileges the Lord has conferred upon us!" The burden was heavy, but the impact of Samuel's faith would only be known later.

In 1959, Samuel received another batch of new students into the school of faith and one of them was a young Reinhard Bonnke. Not everyone in Reinhard's Pentecostal home church could understand why a German student, with no English language skills wanted to study in Britain, in a non-denominational College that did not have an emphasis on the gifts of the Spirit; but Reinhard explained that the Holy Spirit had revealed to him, "This is the College." Reinhard already spoke in tongues, so he must have been sent to learn something additional to his personal experiences – the life of faith.

After stepping out in faith, he was surprised that his application was refused, due to the language barrier. But a family friend wrote to Samuel and Reinhard was accepted on the condition that he spent the first few months with Dr. Symonds learning English and within three months he was preaching in English!

In those days of austerity, Reinhard shared a room with Bryn Jones, a future Charismatic pioneer in Britain, who also mentored the successor of Samuel Rees Howells, Alan Scotland. In his first term, Reinhard learnt that every staff member, from the cooks to the preachers, received no salary and lived by faith, and the students were encouraged to do the same. 'The glory of Swansea Bible College was that it forced us to live by faith,' wrote Reinhard on the Christ for all Nations (CfaN) website. 'We prayed for everything. For the huge supply of winter coal necessary to heat our buildings, to the bus fare to take us street preaching at the weekend. The school supplied only food and lodging for us. We were instructed to 'pray in' all the extras. And always, we were required to pray in secret without publicly mentioning our needs. This had been George Müller's legacy and the legacy of Rees Howells as well. Now Rees' son Samuel followed the faith path. I learned to embrace it. Whenever a student or staff member saw their need met by the Lord they would testify about it. These stories were meant to encourage the other students to live in complete dependence upon God. The phrase that was used when God met a need was "I've been delivered." ' (Psalm 23:1, Mark 6:7-9, Luke 22:35).

Many prayer meetings had been given to prayer for specific College needs, including finance for College fuel bills and for supplies for the wood burning boiler, and these early days of faith were special to Reinhard. 'Samuel Howells joined us in a student prayer meeting one morning not long after I arrived. Winter was knocking at the door. Night-time temperatures were plunging toward the freezing mark. He asked us to pray for several hundred pounds to buy coal to heat the classrooms and dormitories. This amount was needed by the end of the week. To me this seemed like a huge sum. I had never faced a need so large. Nor had I been forced to come up with such an amount so quickly. I joined my prayers with the others and waited to see what God would do. At the end of the week Samuel returned to our prayer meeting. His eyes were bright and his face beaming. "Praise God! We've been delivered," he said. Right then, I prayed in my heart, "Lord, I also want to be a man of faith. I want to see your way of providing for needs." '

Reinhard's life of faith began in a tiny shared room at BCW when he was challenged by the Holy Spirit to give away all his money to a visiting missionary. After a struggle he obeyed, and his first faith test was to believe for a postage stamp. After purchasing the properties by faith, Rees Howells had the phrase, "Faith is Substance" (Hebrews 11:1) prominently displayed on a plinth in front of Derwen Fawr House; now Reinhard had to prove it himself. Could faith alone provide a postage stamp! After a battle, this prayer was answered. Later he was tested to believe God for a bus ticket. In 1915, Rees Howells had stood in a queue at a train station with empty pockets believing that God would give him the money for the journey, now after preaching in the local area, Reinhard was standing at a bus stop in the same predicament. After praying in German, English and tongues, God came through and with many other tests behind him; his enrolment in the life of faith was evident.

Reinhard graduated from the College and became a missionary to Africa. On the mission field he found remarkable favour with God and in obedience to the Lord began to witness the birth and growth of an enormous soul-winning ministry. Samuel loved to hear from former students and as a young missionary Reinhard wrote back to Samuel from Maseru, Lesotho stating: 'Thank you very much for your wonderful and inspiring letter – your gift will help pay for a consignment of over five metric tons of paper for our Gospel Press. We shall print one million tracts to be dropped by aeroplane in April...In our conference at Maseru the power of God was mightily real among us. A totally blind man received his sight in front of all the people. In Pretoria, miracles happened by the score. I had never intended to pray for the sick – it was just the Spirit of God taking over. My prayer is that His Spirit shall be poured upon all flesh.' Yours in His service, RWG Bonnke (Reinhard).'

A couple of years later, Samuel received another special letter: 'There is only one passion left in my heart, namely that my whole being will be a channel through which the healing waters of the Redeemer will flow unhindered to people who are in such desperate need. We are simply amazed at all that has been accomplished through the Holy Spirit. I think we can reach millions of souls with the Gospel! This is the hour of opportunity; please pray that in every detail God's will shall be done.' Reinhard went on to win tens of millions of souls for Christ and in 1999, he returned with his team to the College to film the remarkable journey of faith that he had been on. *The Life of Fire: The Calling* and the *Full Flame* presentations contain many of the testimonies from those early days.

Reinhard's life of faith began in the small things, as he believed God for a postage stamp at BCW. Decades on, he was praying for the millions needed to reach the millions of Africa. In 2001, he emailed one young staff member at BCW stating: 'Right now we are still praying for the funds for our crusade in November this year in

Ibadan / Nigeria, where we expect another batch of millions of souls for Christ. Great blessing requires great resources and that exponentially. But God is on the Throne, as we have all learned at the BCW. Yours in His service, Reinhard Bonnke.' 120 million people have heard the Gospel through Reinhard's outreaches, with more than 55 million people responding; also 185 million Gospel books and booklets have been released through the ministry!

Over the decades Samuel Rees Howells received many reports from former students and encouraged them with gifts, both small and large. The College archives contain a plastic folder filled with names of former students and missionaries, to whom he sent gifts. The calculation from this file, finds that in one year Samuel gave over £260,000 ($416,000) to support missionaries on the field, which is a large sum for such a small organisation as the College. In response, Samuel received many letters of appreciation for prayer and practical support, as the ministry of giving grew. Many were from former students. Extracts from these letters tell their own story as he encouraged others with news he received.

One former student wrote: 'The Spirit is moving in many places, despite the relentless attacks from the evil one. There is much blessing here in Indonesia at this time. Hundreds are turning to the Lord. This is remarkable when you consider that just a while back the Communists made a determined attack to engulf the whole of this area of South East Asia.'

Another wrote: 'South America is undoubtedly a fruitful field these days. Hardly a week passes without many entering into the experience of salvation. It has not always been like this, for we have laboured for many years (actually about thirty years with only one furlough) with very few results. God has wonderfully fulfilled Psalm 126:6 to us. Now our principal work is to guide these new believers that by the power of the Holy Spirit they may become victorious and that their zeal may be guided into the right and most useful channels for Him. It is important to place the Word of God in the hands of these young converts and really that has been the secret of blessing. They are eagerly reading the Word and they love it.'

From Africa came: 'The other day a missionary and an African believer visited us at our compound. This African was truly a Spirit-filled man and through his ministry the Saviour was revealed in every meeting in a most wonderful way. It turned out that he was brought into a real relationship with God and into the fullness of the Holy Spirit at the time when Rees Howells visited our missionary station at Natal in 1917.'

Samuel was also encouraged when the fruit of his previous intercessions ripened in the lives of young people. In reflecting upon his years at the College, one former Korean student wrote: 'God sent me to the College for missionary training. I had a language barrier problem and found difficulties adapting to the strict regulations of the College. It was at that time that Rev. S. Howells taught me about a life of prayer. I learnt that he slept few hours and spent day and night praying for the whole world. I was surprised when he told me that he had been praying for North Korea for many years. Even though I was a Korean I had never prayed for North Korea. His life of prayer inspired me. I woke up every morning at 4 o'clock and left the dormitories to pray for all parts of the globe as well as North Korea. Since that time I have always prayed early in the mornings for the work of God.'

After leaving the College, this Korean student left for Africa as an independent missionary without any support. 'When I came to Malawi, Africa in 1985, I was one of the poorest missionaries. God sent me to an area where poor people lived. My life became very difficult to live but I couldn't run away from the calling of God. I had to practise what I learnt from Samuel Howells so I started to pray and fast. God touched Samuel Howells' heart and he often sent me letters of encouragement and money. Even though I never spoke to him about my lack of support, God communicated with him showing him my need when I was praying to God. Howells' prayers are bearing much fruit in Africa and I'm sure in other parts of the world as well. The Lord has established over five hundred churches through us in seven countries in Africa and used us to establish kindergartens, primary schools, middle and high schools, a Bible College, a mission farm, a prayer mountain, one medical centre, two clinics, and we are still building an orphanage in Swaziland. We are also establishing a university. Samuel lived a simple and humble life but inspired and motivated many throughout the world. He taught me to think big and therefore pray big. Because of him I do not pray only for local ministries but for ministries all around the globe.'

That testimony alone indicates the impact Samuel's tireless ministry was to have upon the whole world and the emphasis placed upon young people learning, not only men's theories about the Scriptures, but to experience the challenges of a life of prayer and faith. Samuel prayed for all his former students who served the Lord and made it his responsibility, in the Lord, to correspond with, and send gifts to all those whom the Holy Spirit laid on his heart. Some of the intercessors, who also lived at the College, kept a detailed account of former students and regularly prayed for them on the mission field. When one of these intercessors died in 2004, an enormous list of names was found on a long roll of worn paper. Students who graduated years before were still being prayed for.

Chapter Twenty-Two

Supplying the Living Bread

Samuel encouraged all his students to surrender their lives *fully* to the Lord, but he warned them not to pray superficial prayers. When a believer goes to the spiritual altar to lay down his or her life in full surrender, the Holy Spirit may test the sincerity of his or her prayer. The Lord will often ask that person to lay something down that will cost very dearly. If he or she retreats, that person will have failed the first test of surrender. If repentance and obedience follows, a fresh phase in Christ will start. This was what happened to the biblical intercessors when their ministries began (1 Kings 19:19-21, Luke 14:33, Acts 9:6, 16, 1 Corinthians 4:9-16).

In his teaching, Samuel always treated the men and women of the Bible with great respect. Leaning over the podium and pointing his slender index finger in everyone's direction he would challenge them by saying, "Could you do what Abraham, Isaac, Jacob, Moses and Daniel did? And if you can't do it, then be careful what you say about these men." Sound advice for budding preachers! It was these men and women who had preserved the whole thread of salvation through the Scriptures by their faith. This emphasised the essential need to cultivate true faith and believing in our Christian walk with God. "What has your faith produced?" was his question.

Samuel observed that the men and women of faith in the Bible took personal responsibility in their intercessions. Moses had to trust God for the daily provisions for more than two million people in a desert for forty years and his faith was equal to the task. Now could Samuel's faith be equal to the call that had come upon him?

It was during the early 1960s that the Lord spoke to Samuel in a very personal way concerning enlarging his support of worldwide missionary endeavours. In addition, to share the news of the worldwide mission movement that he was receiving from his own correspondence. This calling came upon him as the Holy Spirit began to lay a personal responsibility on him to provide the 'living bread' to countless numbers of people around the world. The challenges ahead would be formidable and Samuel took it very seriously. This was another act in his living intercession for the world, which would consume his life and shape his decisions for the next forty years. In these latter years, Samuel would even be prepared to lay down the entire College on the altar to fulfil this commission from the Lord!

The strategy in this new ministry was for the Lord to link Samuel with an individual or agency working in as many countries of the world as possible, preferably nationals. These would become 'points of intercession' representing the nation. Samuel was to pray for and provide practical help to everyone in the name of the Lord. The Vision was for the world and all should have the Bread of Life.

In accordance with Rees Howells' teaching to give first out of one's own substance, the release of finance through the eventual sale of Penllergaer Estate would contribute significantly to this new development in his ministry. He referred to this as a "new thrust forward" in response to the Holy Spirit's instructions, "Give ye them to eat." These were words that Jesus Himself spoke to His disciples, as recorded in Luke 9:13, when they asked Him to send the crowd of five thousand men, plus women and children, back home empty-handed. To trace these new developments the following entries are from Samuel's personal diary of 1962:

- 3 January: Opened the Foreign Missionary Fund in the bank.
- 12 January: Matthew 9:2, great liberty in prayer regarding the new commission.
- 15 January: Drew out a list of societies and individuals to be assisted by the Missionary Fund. About twenty-five countries included and a sum of over £1,000 (£17,505 / $28,000 in 2012) involved. This is only the initial list – more will be added in the course of the next weeks.
- 17 January: Received a gift of £2,000 ($3,200). This is a seal on the new step and timely, especially after the last meeting.
- 13 February: Spoke on the preparation of Joshua. Special prayer for Portugal, Lebanon and Algiers. Good liberty. Paid out £1,000 ($1,600) in gifts and transferred another £1,000.
- 14 February: We are desirous of doing everything possible to place the Word of God in the homes of the people.
- 21 February: Received a gift of £1,000. Another sacred token and a further confirmation to proceed with the new ministry.

As the months went on, new entries continued on a daily basis, all with the greater purpose of getting the Word of God preached and distributed all over the world. By the end of the year, he stated: 'Prepared the last number of letters for this year with relief to missionaries abroad. It has proved to be a wonderful year in giving to others' (28 December). In glancing through Samuel's 1962 diary, it names over thirty countries being prayed for, and some of the organisations. Over £10,000 ($16,000) was received that year in gifts committed for the ministry alone (this is worth £166,400 / $266,200 in 2012). This was a very substantial amount for such a small ministry and represents a significant percentage of the overall income of the College for that year. Samuel always gave away far more than a tithe; he made sacrificial offerings.

Chapter Twenty-Three

First Missionary Journey

Samuel had learnt always to respond to the prayers that the Holy Spirit gave, which involved the outworking of God's covenant purposes in the world. Central to Rees Howells' Vision during the final years of his ministry was the establishment of Christian centres around the world. In April 1938, Rees and Samuel went to France to view one such centre. On his return Rees wrote: 'My son and I went over to Paris and we hope to open a College there. We have students who are going out after this term to work there. In this way we hope to reach the Continent through that College in Paris.' As Director, Samuel now carried many burdens in order to develop the ministry overseas as his father had wished and the first phase of this expansion began with Samuel's first mission journey back in 1951. With the exception of the outreach in France, Rees was not able to expand the work overseas as he had desired, because of the intercessions of WWII, and the liability of the 270 acre Penllergaer Estate (on the other side of the Swansea district).

When living by faith, Rees taught students not to go into debt because 'the hand of the flesh' could always borrow money for a work which the Lord had not called into being. His exception to this rule was practised in his intercession to purchase Penllergaer, which involved Rees taking personal liability to save Jews from the Nazis. In this context, his liability was part of his living intercession. Samuel could vividly remember a prayer meeting at the Bible College on 8 September 1949, when Rees Howells was free and had declared, "I have looked forward for ten years to the day I would recover all, and this is the day. There is not a penny owing on one of the properties. I took £20,000 (£1,049,900 / $1,678,800 in 2012) liability in the bank for Penllergaer, our fourth property, to take in the Jewish children and the Lord said then, 'You will recover all,' and this is the day. Tonight I begin to pray for the establishment of Christian centres for the Bible Lands in earnest – I step on it now."

Samuel was taking up this prayer, so through contacts already made by Lizzie Howells in a previous visit to Israel, he planned a visit to the Middle East with a view to setting up a Christian centre near Jerusalem. With the preparations complete, Samuel commenced his first of several missionary journeys to the Middle East in May 1951, calling first to encourage the members of the College family in 'The Gospel House' in France. From Marseilles the journey was by sea, calling in at Alexandria, Egypt. On 10 May, Samuel wrote to his loyal friend Tommy Howells (no relation), who had stood with Rees Howells throughout his ministry from the early days in Brynaman where they were both coal miners: 'I am looking forward very much also to visiting these sacred places such as Bethlehem, Nazareth, Bethany and Jerusalem which were so dear to our Master when He was on earth. I shall especially remember you when I get to the top of Mt. Carmel and stand on the spot where Elijah challenged the prophets of Baal and called down fire from Heaven. Pray that the Lord will fulfil all His purposes regarding Lebanon and Israel. Surely He will, after all the travail and intercession of the Director (Rees Howells). As the Holy Spirit has prospered the work in Swansea, He will do the same in the Bible Lands again.'

The negotiations on the trip were successful and laid the ground to establish a Home and School for girls in Ramallah (meaning Hill of God), north of Jerusalem in March 1954. Many from the College left by faith to teach and witness in this School and the work was hard at first, with few funds coming in to support it, but, as with Joseph, the Word of the Lord tried them (Psalm 105:19), and a solid foundation was laid. Samuel remained acutely aware of these single ladies who had gone out to pioneer a new work in a land where women played a different role in society from those in the West. He was therefore thrilled to receive a letter from one of them, and read it out in the Tuesday evening service on 16 August 1955. "We can again raise our Ebenezer and tell you of two wonderful answers to prayer." The letter contained news of God's miraculous provision for the work. Here was proof that God was finding others who would step out and live by faith, no matter what sacrifices had to be made!

Samuel was always pleased to hear testimonies like this of the Lord's deliverance in answer to prayer as it enhanced the life that Rees Howells had introduced into the lifestyle of the College. Samuel wished these principles to be retained in the training programme, lessons which could not be learnt in the classroom, only in the school of life in fellowship with the Lord. Samuel then continued by reading the second answer to prayer from the letter, and explained that he had been hindered from sending them money but the Lord had intervened Himself, "The needs here (at the College) are great but God has supplied," he said. "We have spent much time in prayer and that is the only way, wrestling through like the Director (Rees Howells) and George Müller. We could easily slacken but what would God say? He would say, 'You are a hireling and not the shepherd.' The world is heavy upon us and we do not know what God is going to do; we are waiting upon Him...God will never let His children down," Samuel concluded.

Whilst abroad, Samuel also visited a Christian school and outreach in Beirut, Lebanon, giving them his support. Later, two of the College family went to teach there and he prayed for God's blessing. The school in Lebanon was subsequently blessed through the persistent prayers of the staff, as a letter dated 29 March 1954 indicates: 'You will have heard how the Lord was in the school convicting and converting. Last week was a week of preparation and we saw many children coming through for salvation. The Xth class was really facing surrendering their lives to the Lord. Previously there had been much weeping and brokenness but when I went into the room the presence of God was so real that I hardly dared step forward. Each head was down on the desk. When challenged if they were ready to give their lives completely into the hands of God the whole class, as if some invisible hand were lifting them, rose – en bloc – without a sound. One by one, in a little room alone, they dedicated their lives to God; what a solemn time it was! I do wish you could have heard the testimony meeting on Friday.' Emerging from that blessing in Lebanon was a student who came to study at the Bible College and for many years exercised a very fruitful outreach ministry throughout the Arab and Islamic world.

As Samuel travelled overseas, he sowed a seed of intercession for revival in the Middle East, and as he did so the Lord blessed the work at home. Dr. Priddy wrote to Samuel about developments in the Bible College's Emmanuel School: 'There has been such a burden for the School and now He has begun to do a new thing. He has given us the key to leading the children into a keen life of practical walking in the light with the Saviour, and that in a way which will not be a 'flash in the pan' revival, but will do what we have prayed much for, to raise the normal level of their Christian living to one of fullness of victory and joy in the Saviour. Without excitement and emotion He has broken right through in the lives of many of the boarders and some day children, and they are quite transformed. He is beginning to revive the fellowship groups throughout the School, which meet in Wednesday dinner hour. There has been a marvellous move among the home staff too, many barriers swept away, many reconciliations and much brokenness before the Lord.'

God was really at work in the College and as Samuel returned to BCW, preparations were already in hand for the Every Creature Conference, which became a well attended annual event up until they ceased in August 1964. Missionaries and Christian workers from across the world, many former students, would share their news and students would testify of God's special call upon their lives. The College also welcomed many prominent ministers and preachers from around the world, including Duncan Campbell, who was to make significant contributions in these conferences, following his experience in the Hebridean Revival (1949-1952). While he was preaching in 1955, the presence of the Holy Spirit was so manifest that the strong stone walls of the Conference Hall trembled! During this conference, Samuel spoke to Campbell about his burden for global revival. On 7 August he told the College: "Duncan Campbell told me he believed it is God's will to visit us again with an awakening. When people meet God in revival, they do not go back again," said Samuel. "I asked Duncan Campbell if there was any backsliding in the Hebrides; he said there was not one instance. This is what we need in Wales and everywhere" (Psalm 85, Isaiah 32:15, 44:3, 45:8, 64:1, Acts 2:17-18, 4:27-33, 10:44-48).

Brian Halliwell and his wife Stella were students and then staff during the years 1964-71 and never forgot when Duncan Campbell, on a regular visit to BCW, preached over a long weekend. After five meetings when Campbell preached, the students came to another service on Monday morning and a move of the Holy Spirit broke out. Students fell on their knees crying under conviction of sin. In the past, Campbell had learnt to the let the Holy Spirit do His work, and with other commitments in the nation, he left the students on their knees weeping, to catch his bus home. On another occasion, Campbell McKalpine preached on a Sunday evening and what can best be described as a mini-revival broke out. McKalpine counselled some of the students from Sunday night through to the early hours of Monday morning, and this move of God went on for a week as many of the students were being baptised in the Holy Spirit.

Throughout his life, Samuel's worldwide intercessory ministry was being confirmed, not only by the moves of the Spirit at the College, nor by the news reports that proved prayers were being answered, but also in the practical down-to-earth provisions that were needed on a daily basis. His deep life of faith was a source of continual encouragement to all. By now, Samuel, having experienced God's mantle of spiritual authority coming upon him had settled into his pulpit ministry. Ending a long exposition from Luke 2, back in the 1950s, he said, "This is the realm where God is. Let Him find us in the right relationship with Himself, humble and at His feet. As we seek His Kingdom He will answer other needs. This week we have spent about £500 (£11,000 / $17,600 in 2012) but the Lord is gracious. We have received sums to cover – £100 ($160), £250 ($400) and another £100. Surely He will deliver what is required. Do not neglect this life of faith. If you have not been delivered spend the weekend in prayer. It is a hard school, but a glorious school. We know God is real. He answers prayer every day." These years were to be the prelude to many glorious victories in the decades that lay ahead, and some fierce conflicts; but God was on the move!

Chapter Twenty-Four

Second Missionary Journey

On 7 May 1962, Samuel left the College on his second missionary journey stating in his diary: 'Left the College at 12:15pm on the start of the long journey to the Continent and the Middle East...believing for great blessing in the different places.' The purpose of the journey was to visit the College's extended work in these regions. On an intercessory level and with historical hindsight, the journey also suggests that he was 'spying out the land' and 'claiming the ground' for future intercessions (Joshua 2:1).

Samuel was joined on the road journey by Toby Bergin, his co-worker and friend. Toby was very pleased with a gift of a large, Armstrong Siddley car capable of managing the roads across Europe and beyond, and stops were planned with friends, mostly former students to survey the work. They visited the College's ministry in Paris, France, then on to Switzerland and Austria. There were opportunities to minister in Austria before the breathtaking drive up through the Austrian Alps and crossing into Yugoslavia. They arrived as strangers from the West in a Communist country at the peak of the Cold War. It was important that they made absolutely no mistakes in their directions, so Samuel read through them carefully. No-one wanted to drive to a military zone by accident and end up in a Soviet prison!

Samuel and Toby arrived safely and spoke in a Church in Zagreb, now the capital of Croatia, where the hall was packed with people. The great respect for God's Word was shown by the congregation standing for the reading of the Scriptures. This was now Communist territory, yet the hunger for the Gospel was very evident. There were further opportunities for Samuel to minister in Belgrade and in Bulgaria, where the Soviet Premier Khrushchev was visiting. Red flags were flying everywhere. Khrushchev represented the power of the Soviet Union, Samuel represented the Holy Spirit's ability to send His people behind enemy lines to intercede, witness and claim the ground. Outwardly the former seemed stronger, but history records another story! Speaking in Bulgaria, Khrushchev said, "Now it is the atomic age. Whoever has atomic energy, whoever has missiles, they have power!" On his return to Russia, he pushed forward with the plan to place missiles in Cuba; something which would later grip Samuel in intercessory prayer.

Meanwhile, Samuel's mission continued to Ediner, for a night stop just inside the Turkish border and finally to historic Istanbul, where they met a dear friend who had arranged a rally. Toby and Samuel shared the platform with the Director of Youth For Christ, a unique meeting for Turkey. From Istanbul, after their 2,400 miles (3,840 kilometres) road journey, they flew to Beirut, Lebanon, where they encouraged friends there, and then proceeded by air to Jordan to stay at Ramallah for a week. Besides attending to official business, Samuel was able to visit the biblical sites of Jerusalem.

The return run from Istanbul was via Greece, staying at Philippi, Amphipolis, Thessalonica, Berea and Katerini, with opportunities to encourage the brethren – following in Paul's footsteps. At each planned stop Samuel had a congregation waiting for ministry from the Word, and the anointing of God was on him. The journey followed the River Varder into landlocked Macedonia, stopping at Skopji, then the capital; Belgrade, Zagreb and Villach, to meet former students and on to Munich in Germany. Although still in the process of being rebuilt after the devastation of WWII, Munich with its Marienplatz still commanded their attention.

In Germany, a visit to the Nazi Dachau Concentration Camp was a solemn occasion and reminded Samuel of past intercessions. They stayed with former students there, before crossing the Rhine at Strasbourg and driving through the countryside to the College's outreach in Paris, where Samuel spoke to the Russian believers.

The College missionaries had established a vibrant French congregation as well as a fellowship of Russian believers on the same site, emigrants from the Russian Revolution. Eventually this ministry became independent of the College. This was a very forward way of thinking, when many other ministries may have been tempted to build 'empires' around the world. Samuel's missionaries had learnt that their purpose was to work themselves out of a job!

On 28 June 1962, they arrived back in Swansea about 8pm to a very warm welcome. The second missionary journey was complete and the Lord had blessed all the way. Speaking to the College of the mission trip, Samuel reminded them of the need for continual intercession to break down the spiritual strongholds that had been gaining ground through Communism as well as the hosts of spiritual wickedness in the Middle East. Samuel recalled that the apostles also had to undertake this challenge. "Is it harder today than in the days of the apostles?" he asked. "The enemy had full sway then but he was broken down." But then he warned, intercession had been neglected: "When people are on a verge of a blessing and they do not come through in prayer, these places get harder and harder. While I was out there, the place was charged with the power of darkness. The missionaries were bitterly attacked, some were put out. Paul was attacked and left for dead, think of that experience! When I came back from the Middle East the oppression ceased."

Chapter Twenty-Five

The Cold War

Samuel's second missionary journey of seven and a half weeks from May to June 1962 had served to deepen a growing conviction that, in order to break the rapid spread of Communistic ideology which was gripping the world, intercessory prayer must be focused upon this need. He was under no illusions that if he responded to this new leading from the Holy Spirit, both he and the College would be plunged into an intense spiritual conflict resulting in many misunderstandings and 'casualties.' His personal reputation would be shattered and outwardly there would be the inevitable pathway of failure in the eyes of the world, even the Christian world.

Two BCW staff members with the Howells family & Haile Selassie, Emperor of Ethiopia, at the Penllergaer Estate, November 1939

Samuel had seen these aspects of intercession enacted at a very deep level in his father's life when World War II had broken out in September 1939. Rees Howells had known the threats posed by Adolf Hitler and the Nazi Movement, but, being fully convinced that the Holy Spirit had complete mastery over all powers of darkness in the world, he was totally confident in making a prediction that there would be no general war in Europe. When war broke out, at that crucial point, the Lord had shown Rees that it was necessary that he should experience this failure in the world's eyes so that full focus and attention could be given to the spiritual conflicts which were to ensue. No explanation should be given by way of justification. Death to reputation is an essential ingredient for all intercessors to follow. In spiritual warfare, Christians take delight in the concept of fast and decisive victories, but this was not the case with the prophets, nor is it often the case in the Church. 'What you sow is not made alive unless it dies' (1 Corinthians 15:36).

Samuel remembered very vividly how Rees' prediction, and all his father's plans to assist the Jewish refugees and eventually settle them in properties purchased in the Holy Land (modern day Israel), had come crashing down; all publicised widely in local and national newspapers. He had lived every minute of those dark days, when even his own personal faith was tested to the limit. He had endeavoured, as best he could, to stand alongside his father and was inclined to agree, that had the whole nation turned to God for His help, the story might have been different. However, Rees had not wavered in his total conviction that the doom of the Nazis and other dictators would one day be realised throughout the world.

The Penllergaer Mansion (the Big House) c.1938 on the 270-acre Penllergaer Estate. The estate was bought by Rees Howells to house a minimum of 1,000 Jewish refugee children. During World War II, the British Government requisitioned the House and parts of the estate. The Big House was sold in 1950 and on its site now stands buildings for the Glamorgan County Council.

The whole question of failure is one which every intercessor has to face at some point in his or her ministry and Samuel had faced it alongside his father in 1939. The war did proceed and the bitter struggle lasted for six years. Samuel recalled the ignominy of those days when even the Christian world kept them at arm's length, so he himself would not flinch in later years when he was plunged into further depths to see the development of God's covenant plans for the blessing of the world in his day (Proverbs 15:33b).

Now twenty-three years later, Samuel was challenged by God, through looking at a photograph of five Russian pastors who were imprisoned for their faith, to intercede for them and others suffering under brutal Communist regimes. Immediately after World War II, the Soviet authorities imposed tight security on all borders between the Eastern European countries which they had occupied and the West. Their aim was to make them Satellite Communist States in which true vibrant Christianity was marginalised, driven underground and defeated. The Bible was outlawed and influencing children on Christian truths forbidden. Persecution was very real.

Berlin itself, which was isolated in the Eastern section of Germany, was zoned off between the four major Allied nations to oversee, due to the Potsdam Agreement, signed in 1945. To prevent too many defections into West Berlin from the East, the Russians tightened their grip and prevented vital daily supplies, even of water, reaching the West, forcing the Allies to launch the famous 'Berlin Airlift' from June 1948 to May 1949. A continuous convoy of planes ferried in everything required by the beleaguered population. Changing tactics, the Russians created the German Democratic Republic (GDR) of East Germany with its one candidate voting system, strongly supported and controlled by its 'mother state' with its much feared Stasi (GDR Security Police) arresting any suspected dissenters. The situation intensified when a complex barbed wire barricade between East and West was erected in 1961. By 1969, the infamous concrete Berlin Wall completely isolated the inhabitants of West Berlin. An iron curtain had truly descended!

The Cold War between East and West was fully established. It was a bleak era, especially for Christians, so many of whom were transferred to slave in the harsh corrective camps known as 'gulags' in the frozen wastes of Siberia. Endless numbers were to die there.

In one evening meeting, holding up the photograph of the imprisoned pastors, Samuel explained to the congregation its special significance for him. The Lord had spoken to him asking if he would intercede for these pastors. Fully understanding the cost of intercession, Samuel did not give an immediate response, but in the Lord's presence there was no other response he could make than say in the words of Jesus, "Not My will, but Thine be done" (Luke 22:42). This intercession was to grip Samuel and the College for the next twenty-five years and proved to be very costly.

One of the chief ingredients of intercession is identification with the situation or people being prayed for, with the Holy Spirit exercising His right to baptise the individual into death. It is always important to understand fully that death and resurrection are one process. As death to the old nature operates in the life of the intercessor, so the resurrection life of Christ can be appropriated. Paul sums the process up in the words of 2 Corinthians 4:10-12, 'Always carrying about in the body the dying of Jesus, so that the life of Jesus also may be manifested in our body. For we who live are constantly being delivered over to death for Jesus' sake, so that the life of Jesus also may be manifested in our mortal flesh. So death works in us, but life in you.' Being baptised into the death of Christ, means that all of our self-life, the good things and the bad, will be subject to the same process of death if the Holy Spirit is to have room in our lives to express the true nature of Christ. We are reminded of the quality of the carnal nature in Jeremiah 17:9, 'The heart is deceitful above all things and desperately wicked; who can know it?'

The principle of death and resurrection would therefore take place in different ways and be at work in the College as identification with the Russian believers. But for the believers in the Eastern bloc countries, it would mean life and true spiritual growth. Samuel built links with ministries working 'behind enemy lines' and identified with each one, as the Spirit made him able. He was disturbed by reports of the prison camps in Siberia and of tortured prisoners, who were abused because of their faith in Christ. Based on reports of these prisoners, a poster in the West stated: 'If you were put on trial for being a Christian, would there be enough evidence to convict you?'

Those early lessons of intercession, learnt thoroughly during the World War II conflict, now enabled Samuel to persevere through twenty-five difficult years. "There's need for prayer of great intensity in these days," said Samuel. "Think of the Russian armies poised in East Germany and in Poland and in some of the other countries. God will honour us. He will answer prayer."

There will always be death in intercession, but the Lord does honour His servants who obey Him unconditionally; and one true story indicates how Samuel gained a reputation as a powerful man of prayer. In Britain, Samuel always sought the Lord's mind when controversial laws were being debated in Parliament and on one occasion, received a strong letter of disapproval from a well known Honorary Member of Parliament (MP) who had heard that Samuel was praying for an election victory for the opposite party. God was honouring Samuel's faith, as this influential man certainly feared his prayers!

Chapter Twenty-Six

The Cuban Missile Crisis

In Samuel's fiftieth year, the demonic hosts in the heavenly realms once again challenged the commission to give the Gospel to every creature, by attempting to drag millions of souls into a lost eternity and to simultaneously destroy the largest mission sending nations (America and Britain in 1962), and other countries in an apocalypse.

Samuel took courage from his past decade of answered prayer, where he had been led deeper into specific intercessions on an international level. Each case stretched his faith further, as he gained positions of grace in one nation or crisis at a time. There had been setbacks, deaths and discouragements, but the Holy Spirit had been preparing him for his new intercession which would reach around the world and impact every nation. In 1962, the Holy Spirit laid upon Samuel a long intercession to pray for the demise of Communism worldwide; yet this burden had hardly been laid upon him when Satan challenged his new intercession by manipulating the Soviet leadership to a menacing precipice.

The world was brought to the verge of a nuclear holocaust in 1962 when a United States U2 spy plane reported a build up of Russian SAM missile sites being set up in Cuba and aimed towards the United States. Beginning in early 1962, the Soviet Union began shipments of arms to Cuba, deceitfully hiding them in cargo ships. When challenged they followed a deliberate campaign of elaborate deceptions and denials. This led to the largest seaborne operation in Soviet history, transferring 40,000 men and nuclear missiles to Cuba, which prompted the U.S. to move the American military to Defcon 2, just one step away from all-out nuclear war!

'Some months ago the Russians exploded a bomb, which we are told, had twenty-five times the combined force of all bombs dropped throughout the Second World War,' wrote Samuel three months before the crisis. 'In view of these grim facts the question which naturally comes to everyone is this; by what means can such trends of evil and destruction be adequately dealt with? By nothing but a Divine intervention!' Samuel was citing the Tsar bomb, the most powerful nuclear bomb detonated in history, with a mushroom cloud reaching sixty-four miles into the air, almost seven times the height of Mount Everest! The bomb sent an undeniable message to the West; the USSR has the ability to wipe you off the map.

On 14 October 1962, an American spy plane brought back photos detailing Soviet SS-4 medium range ballistic missiles with nuclear warheads on the ground in Cuba. These had a range of 2,000 miles

(3,200 kilometres). Two days later the President was briefed. The situation prompted a red-alert with 125,000 U.S. troops being marshalled ready for a possible invasion of Cuba. President Kennedy held emergency meetings to decide on which option to take. Immediate action to bomb Cuba was likely, as spy planes reported Russian ships carrying more nuclear missiles to Cuba. Samuel therefore sensed the urgency and resorted to prayer.

Samuel's leadership and personal involvement in these world situations was already evident in his pulpit ministry at the time, as he drew strength from the life of Elisha. Samuel never divorced the prophets of the Bible from their real-life dangers and national crises that they lived through. Their faith had to be equal to the challenge, and now the faith of the College had to be equal to today's threat. Could faith save the world from a nuclear apocalypse?

When faced with the prospect of war, Samuel was always honest about the seriousness of the conflict. "We are living in the day of crisis," he said. "At this time there is a succession of crises. Once we are out of one, we find ourselves engrossed in another and it is only the Holy Spirit that can fortify us. Think tonight of all the threats abroad. Threats of war! If we be like other people, we would tend to be dismayed and we'd expect war to break out. If war broke out, everything here would come to an end. The College would come to an end. We are on the verge of disaster, humanly speaking, but God is with us and God can preserve us. We're not asking the Lord to preserve us. No, we are not bringing a prayer of that kind (self-centred) to Him. We are asking Him to preserve the millions, for them to have an opportunity of meeting their Redeemer."

In the White House, President Kennedy was advised to strike first and hard. But this would be a war without a winner. If America struck Cuba, the USSR would respond and before long one third of humanity could be dead. Could the Bible be a guide to the intercessors to know what and how to pray? Thousands of years ago, Elisha and his servant were trapped in the city of Dothan, with the Syrian army besieging it. Now the Lord led Samuel to consider the ministry of Elisha and how the prophet had learnt the secrets of prayer in their conflicts. Quoting from a Saturday evening service we find Samuel at full stretch, "Elisha and the prophets didn't do these things in their stride. He had entered into the realm of God. In the case of Dothan (2 Kings 6:8-18) was he perturbed? Not in the least, but his servant was. This realm is so delicate. One man was living in the spiritual realm and the other in the natural realm. A life of faith has a very sobering effect. It is a real gauge of our spiritual life. Unless we are in victory here we are not going to be in victory in these greater prayers. His dealings and guidance are all orderly.

When the eyes of the young man were opened he saw the hosts of God and then he was as strong as the prophet. God has visited us. His presence can be felt brooding over the whole place. These revelations are given to us so that we can be more effective in our service and believing prayer."

President Kennedy was under pressure to mount a strike on the bases in Cuba before any missiles became active. The need of the hour was heavenly wisdom and the USSR had to be restrained from within, but who could prevail with God in such a matter? How could this situation be solved in a way that would pacify the USSR and protect America's interests? Only intercession could prevail to bring peace and the real battle was in the spiritual realm.

"Forget everything else now and concentrate on these battles," said Samuel. Everything was at stake. The combined nuclear weapons arsenal of the U.S. and the USSR was over 35,000 and President Kennedy's predecessor had calculated that all humans in the northern hemisphere could perish if either side began to fire. How could the world be reached with the Gospel if annihilation took place? Millions would be lost for eternity and the work of world evangelisation would cease. Satan was working, manipulating the USSR to drag millions into eternity without Christ (1 Timothy 2:4).

On 18 October, the crisis deepened when the Soviet Foreign Minister, Andrei Gromyko assured the President that no offensive weapons were in Cuba. This wilful perversion of truth convinced the Joint Chiefs of Staff that air strikes followed by an invasion were the only option. However, the Secretary of State, George Ball warned that a surprise bombing attack "is not conduct that one expects of the United States," and Dean Rusk, the Secretary of State recalled the Bible, stating that 'the mark of Cain' is born by those who attack first. 'What have you done? The voice of your brother's blood cries out to Me from the ground' (Genesis 4:10). President Kennedy received wisdom and postponed the bombing strategy. In its place he chose a naval quarantine. (This was essentially a blockade without using the word 'blockade,' which denotes an act of war). It was strength with restraint. Wisdom had prevailed! Decades later we learnt that on 20 October, the first missile sites in Cuba were operational. If the U.S. troops had been sent in, it would have been to a nuclear battlefield! God had saved the troops!

Two days later the U.S. quarantine began and Kennedy addressed the public. In the days that followed, the world edged closer to the abyss. One rogue captain or error could lead to the beginning of a catastrophe. Three days later an urgent meeting was called at the UN and the Soviets were given opportunity to be honest. They refused and secret intelligence proved their aggression. The threat of war consumed many hearts, and around the clock sixty American aircraft loaded with nuclear weapons were airborne and at sea and on land, the world's superpowers prepared for war. Very dark days!

The College held its nerve in believing, but then on 26 October, prayer was visibly answered, when the irrational Soviet leadership ordered ships to respect the quarantine. Intercession was gaining ground, but the Soviets were still in a position of strength, for there were 134 nuclear warheads already in Cuba and all three missile regiments were now operational. One false move could lead to the first missile being fired. Who could forget that forty-eight years previously, the death of one man led to World War I and the loss of 35 million lives. A great test came on 27 October when a Soviet anti-aircraft missile in Cuba shot down a U2 plane killing an American pilot. The first combat fatality meant war was inevitable within 24 hours. The U.S. informed Britain: "The United States may find it necessary within a very short time...to take whatever military action may be necessary." The British knew their alliance with their American friends would lead them to stand side-by-side with them to attack the Soviets in a pact of mutual destruction. There were sixty-four nuclear weapons ready to strike the USSR on British soil.

Unless a settlement was reached within the next few hours war would begin. Anatolia Burnov, a Soviet officer of the SS-4 Missile Regiment in Cuba said, "The whole of mankind was on the verge of a nuclear abyss." M. G. Kuzevanov, a Soviet Missile Commander in Cuba said, "We were two hours away from the end. Two hours!" Could peace still prevail for the sake of the advance of the Gospel?

In 2 Kings 7, the historical account of the siege of Samaria is told. Elisha would have prevented the siege if he could, but he could not. He had to wait for the word of the Lord. Samuel knew the same for this situation. It was entirely in God's hands. The College was learning that God can take a crisis to the limits to prove that all things are possible for Him. Sometimes it's only in the deepest test that we learn to appreciate the meaning of the word 'testimony.' The word of the Lord came at the last minute, in Elisha's case, just as his servants were holding the door against the King of Israel's henchmen sent to kill. The immortal words, "Hear ye the word of the Lord," reversed the situation in a flash (2 Kings 7:1). The College meeting went well into the night but the word came from the Lord: "Tomorrow about this time..." A compromise by the leaders was reached in secret; but it wasn't diplomacy that saved the world from nuclear annihilation; it was Holy Spirit led intercession. The USSR would vacate the missiles out of Cuba and the Russian Missile ships left. The crisis was averted; God had worked! 'Come, behold the works of the Lord...He makes wars to cease...' (Psalm 46:8-9a).

Chapter Twenty-Seven

India, Yemen, Jordan and the Nations

As the world was focused on the Cuban Missile Crisis, a war broke out between India and China that caught Samuel's attention. On 20 October 1962, a month long war took place in the Himalayas called the Sino-Indian War. Fought in harsh conditions at 14,000 feet, India with around 10,000 troops in the area was overwhelmed as 80,000 Communist troops began overrunning their borders.

India was proving to be a very fruitful harvest field for the Gospel's advancement and if an all-out war broke out between China and India, the stability of the region was in doubt and the missionary endeavour could be forced to cease. Prayer had to be effectual.

Samuel began to pray, but as the war intensified India was losing. It was essential that the war should cease quickly, but if China decided to take advantage of their military strength the conflict could be prolonged. Five days later, Samuel had to lay aside the prayers for other nations, to focus intercessory prayer on this crisis alone. Samuel's diary for 20 November states: '7:30pm, 1 Kings 21, 22. Special prayer for India in her hour of crisis.'

Samuel would often turn to the prophets of the Bible for inspiration, for they believed that God could intervene in world events; therefore the intercessors of the Church who are led by the Holy Spirit can follow their precedent. In Micaiah's time, when war broke out between Israel, Judah and Syria, the Lord showed the prophet that Israel would be defeated. The leaders of Israel and Syria believed they were in charge, but the Lord showed Micaiah that it was God who was influencing them. Samuel believed in the modern world that God could influence the leaders of China and India too.

Samuel turned to the College staff and students to read Micaiah's testimony of seeing into the heavenly realm during the conflict. 'I saw the Lord sitting on His Throne and all the host of Heaven standing on His right hand and His left. And the Lord said, "Who will persuade Ahab King of Israel to go up that he may fall at Ramoth Gilead?" So one spoke in this manner and another spoke in that manner. Then a spirit came forward and stood before the Lord and said, "I will persuade him." The Lord said to him, "In what way?" So he said, "I will be a lying spirit in the mouth of all his prophets." And the Lord said, "You shall persuade him and also prevail; go out and do so" ' (1 Kings 22:19-22). "It is wonderful," said Samuel on another occasion, "when we think of what Micaiah told those two monarchs. He had been lifted up to the heavenlies and he had witnessed what was going on there."

Samuel too was seeing into the heavenly realm and perceived that God's ultimate plan was for the conflict to cease so that the greater works of the Kingdom could continue. But who would persuade the Red Chinese to cease fighting in a war which they were winning? As in Micaiah's time, the Lord Himself would intervene! The Indian troops were like Israel's army 'scattered on the mountains as sheep that have no shepherd' (1 Kings 22:17), but as the College came back to special prayer in the 10:30pm meeting and Samuel spoke on 2 Kings 6-7, he wrote in his private notes: 'Assured that God is intervening in the situation.' China was winning the war, but suddenly on that very day, the College received news that their prayers had been answered. The Chinese had backed off and declared a ceasefire. The crisis was over.

In the same month that India was fighting in the Himalayas, a huge war in the Middle East was also burgeoning! In Samuel's lifetime, when a fuse was ignited in the Middle East, the entire region was soon ready to explode into war. The conflict began when an Egyptian supported coup in North Yemen led to a bitter insurgency in Southern Arabia, with Egyptian forces enabling the new regime to stay in power. Saudi Arabia and Jordan showed support for the royalist side and Egypt bitterly opposed them. Would it all explode?

Samuel watched closely as the countdown to a regional war began and intercessory prayer was focused at the College. Politics were rife in the news media with various players offering political support, but Samuel had to move beyond the natural to find the Kingdom prayer in the crisis. If an all-out war in the Middle East began, Israel would be in grave threat and the strength of Egypt, now at an all time high, would bear down upon the Jews challenging God's end time purposes for Israel. Additionally, the Christian outreach in the School north of Jerusalem, would be under severe strain. If the Kingdom purposes were to be fulfilled in the region, Egypt must be weakened and angry Jordan must be kept out of the war.

On Sunday 4 November, in the 9:45am meeting, Samuel spoke on Daniel 4, stating how Nebuchadnezzar, a biblical Middle Eastern dictator was brought down and humbled; God would do the same again! Samuel then urged prayer for Jordan and other nations. On 8 November the crisis deepened and Samuel spoke on 1 Kings 20, stressing how Syria's mighty army was defeated. 'Special prayer for Jordan in view of the acute situation arising there,' he wrote.

War clouds were gathering as Saudi Arabia and Jordan prepared for possible air raids in Yemen, and the new government supported by Egypt warned that an all-out Middle Eastern war would ensue. In Jordan, political tension and instability increased. On 12 November a Jordanian pilot of a military transport plane defected, followed the next day by two Jordanian pilots in fighter jets. These defections, a serious life-changing decision for the pilots and their families, reflect how ordinary Jordanians were discontented and angry.

13 November: 'Much prayer for India and Jordan!' Samuel was still focusing prayer on India, but he was also called to believe for God's purposes in Jordan as well. Having secured one victory at a time in conflicts in the past, Samuel was now holding several prayers in his heart together. 15 Nov: 'Continued prayer for India and Jordan!"

The sharp internal conflict at home drained the will of Jordan to join in the war in Yemen and by the end of the year, Jordan had retreated from its aggressive role and a wider Middle Eastern war was avoided. Egypt flooded troops into Yemen in the next few years, sending up to 70,000 and found themselves bogged down in another nation's civil war that vigorously weakened their military capacity. Egyptian military historians refer to their engagement in Yemen as Egypt's Vietnam. This war downgraded Egypt's military strength which helped Israel's victory in 1967. God was at work!

The College must have been relieved by the end of 1962 as their prayers were answered, but during these years, in addition to the prayers for various conflicts, the central theme of intercession remained for the Gospel to go to every creature. At the end of 1962, Samuel wrote of answered prayer: 'We hear of movements of God's Spirit in the most unlikely places these days. There have been spiritual awakenings among the tribes of New Guinea, with thousands burning their fetishes and turning to God. Even among the Indians, who live on the banks of the Amazon there has been such an awakening that they rise at dawn to pray.' On another continent, 'the people there were so unresponsive to the Gospel that missionaries called it the cement area.' But after prevailing intercession, 'the Holy Ghost has worked wondrously among them, the result that nearly four thousand of them have been converted.'

Samuel often spoke of prayer burdens for many nations – China, Congo, Angola etc. They prayed for stability, Christian revival and for finances for the distribution of Christian literature, especially Bibles. 'The need for Christian literature in such countries as India, Austria, Yugoslavia, Greece and Turkey is desperate in the extreme,' he wrote. The following year Samuel reported: 'The Lord has wonderfully answered prayer during the past twelve months. Last year, He enabled us to send more gifts to people serving Him abroad than in any other year since the foundation of the work.'

During these years of prayer, the College was also fortunate to hear first-hand reports from former students, who could share accurate accounts of what needed to be prayed through, from Africa to Asia, and from South America to Europe and beyond.

Chapter Twenty-Eight

Congo in Crisis

During 1953, the Belgian Congo experienced a powerful spiritual revival and two former College students, who had studied under Rees Howells, Ivor and David Davies (brothers), were Worldwide Evangelisation Crusade (WEC) field leaders at the time. They gave graphic accounts of their experiences and the effects on the Church when they spoke in services on their return. Satan did not let this sudden growth in the Church go unnoticed and he replied by unleashing anarchy in the nation, with a very vicious wave of persecution, directed against the native Christians and the supporting missionaries.

Congo gained independence from Belgium in 1960 and for six years there was a prolonged period of turmoil leading to the death of over 100,000 people. Politically the whole country was in turmoil as drug-crazed gangs of men swept through the villages and mission stations, rooting out any semblance of colonialism and subjected their victims to horrific deaths. The heroic tales of those twentieth century martyrs are documented in Christian literature, as a permanent tribute to their devotion to Christ.

The Director of a mission supported by the College wrote to Samuel: 'There is nothing in the whole world that can save Africa except prayer. It is only prevailing prayer that can prevent the nation from sure destruction. It is impossible for you to imagine what it means for us to know that so many at the College are pleading for this Dark Continent. It is not too late yet for the Lord to save the land provided He finds us faithful as intercessors.'

The years 1964-1965 saw a vicious new wave of persecution, known as the 'Simba Uprising' / 'Simba Rebellion' directed against the native Christians and the supporting missionaries. Samuel set everything to one side and called the College back to prayer, with each morning and evening session in the prayer room devoted to the subject, particularly as three former students were there. In these Kingdom prayers an amazing unity pervaded the College meetings, which included extra voluntary sessions from 10pm to midnight, and sometimes another till 2am. It was a real-life training ground for the students, as they experienced the Spirit's ways in these conflicts.

The strength of the prayer lay in the believing, or faith, that the Spirit was able to generate through the anointed reading and exposition of the Scriptures. Samuel would be led to read from certain passages which threw particular light on the current problems. One such passage was in Acts 8, when the Jerusalem Church experienced its first wave of intense persecution and was scattered abroad. This seeming tragedy resulted in the expansion of the Church and the fulfilment of the Lord's words that they would be witnesses in Judea, Samaria – to the ends of the world (Acts 1:8). The prayer continued for weeks and heightened when news reached the College that two former students, David Davies and Brian Cripps were in rebel hands. News of their whereabouts was scant and the College was tempted to fear the worst. The ordeal continued for nine long weeks from late July to September 1964. At one point, held captive in one room with other hostages, they watched each day as one was taken to the next room and hacked to pieces, and their numbers decreased. As they later testified, it was not the fear of death that troubled them, but the fear of pain.

It was then that the Lord told Dr. Kenneth Symonds, an intercessor at the College, following a night of prayer (and despite other reports to the contrary), that the captured missionary Brian Cripps was alive. There was a shout of praise, especially among the students, and later the news confirmed what the Lord had already revealed!

David Davies also survived and returned with his wife to his Mission Station in Nala, but their lives were soon in deep danger. The Simbas had a system of telling their next victims the exact time when they would arrive to massacre. David and Anne received their notice and waited. The Lord brought them into a position of peace knowing that the perfect will of God for their lives was the pathway of joy. Quoting from David and Anne's own description of their situation: 'Nala Mission compound, where we were stationed, is a cul-de-sac two hundred yards off a secondary road. At the entrance to the Mission there was a large metal sign, painted white with black letters 'Mission Protestante, HAM Nala.' No one could miss seeing the sign. The rebels passed along that road almost every day and often several times a day. For three and a half months we were moment-by-moment in danger. You can imagine the tension. The Africans brought us news of the slaughter and torturing of blacks and whites. We looked death in the face and gave ourselves over to the will of God, happy to die for Him if He wished it. But each time we returned to prayer (and we had several sessions of prayer each day), we were led to pray for deliverance. Oh the preciousness of the Word of God! Oh what a wonderful Book! What great assurance and strength we gained from such verses as, 'Call upon Me in the day of trouble. I will deliver thee and thou shalt glorify Me' (Psalm 50:15).' Each day, at 2pm they joined with their African Christian brothers and sisters 'for a special period of prayer,' and David continues: 'They knew our danger. Often during the prayers we could hear the rebels pass the entrance; we would sometimes stop, thinking the cars were coming in. Their prayers were intelligent. How they marshalled their arguments before God. 'O Lord, You put a hedge round about Job; now put a hedge around the Mission, then the rebels will not be able to come in.' This was a great challenge when the rebels could see some of our houses from the entrance.

The Africans reminded the Lord of the cherubims and the flaming sword that guarded the way to the Garden of Eden; of the enemies of Lot who were struck blind and could not find the door of the house; of the Israelites in Egypt who had light in all their dwellings whereas the Egyptians were in darkness, and so on. They argued, 'Jesus Christ is the same yesterday, today and forever' (Heb. 13:8).

At the College, Samuel ministered on the life of Jephthah in one late meeting (Judges 11). Jephthah had vowed a very costly vow before the Lord which would unlock the situation before him and Samuel was led to make a private costly vow, though he never divulged the details. After this, Samuel sensed in his spirit the victory of the grace of faith and brought the special services to a seemingly abrupt end. With a developing ministry he was learning to discern the word of the Lord for a given situation. As with the true prophets in the Scriptures there was always a personal involvement, a point of real identification and responsibility, the hallmark of intercession. Similarly, the conflict was subdued and the prayer was through, and Samuel continued his quiet walk with God alone. The Bible College missionaries had finally escaped with their lives when paratroopers rescued them, whilst other missionaries had already been martyred. Their lives were seeds, buried in Christ.

Satan has constantly fought for the souls of Africa. The human answers to the root of the conflicts in Africa could be explained as colonial abuse, government mismanagement, corruption, political infighting, struggles for power and many others. But these are all matters of the natural realm and the true battles are fought in the heavenly realms. God's eternal concern is for the souls of the people, and as we have witnessed in the West, wealth does not lead to saving faith. In the Congo, God has reached out to save a multitude of people, but Satan has sought his channels too, people who are filled with demonic powers, to kill as many as possible before salvation can reach them. But Satan has failed. In the year 1900, only one percent of the population of Congo were believers, but today that percentage is over ninety! Satan had fought viciously for Africa, but the King and His Kingdom cannot be contained and the victory was Christ's! Africa is being saved!

Chapter Twenty-Nine

The Darkest Hour in China

Samuel Howells carried a burden for China throughout his life and the intercession was all uphill. Mao Zedong, who had become the President in 1949, commenced his reign of terror with the disastrous Great Leap Forward. Even before the full extent of the fatal events that were to follow, the Holy Spirit was revealing where the spiritual battle lay and the final victory that would be realised. By 1966, Mao had organised his Red Guards and the Cultural Revolution soon gained momentum, with terrible consequences for any semblance of the West. The horrific reports of children betraying parents and witnessing their barbaric executions, of church leaders being publicly humiliated, of intense daily indoctrination classes for the people and of families being separated for life, shocked the College family who resorted to prolonged periods of intercession.

Middle section of Hudson Taylor's headstone (1832-1905) which was smashed into seven pieces during the Cultural Revolution, but preserved by the Church in China. Rees and Samuel Howells were greatly inspired by Hudson Taylor's life of faith and ministry.

The hard-lined Communists blamed all their problems on the West and introduced calamitous policies which led to forty million Chinese deaths and mass starvation. China had never suffered to this extent in all history; but the Communists' anger was directed towards local Christians and churches, because of their connections to foreigners. Missionaries had already been expelled from China and their fine buildings were confiscated for government purposes or demolished. The situation seemed to strike a heavy death blow for the Church. In history, Christianity had tried to gain a hold in China, but each time it was persecuted until Chinese Christians were almost wiped out. Would this happen again? Samuel had to believe that for the first time in Chinese history, the Church would not collapse and disintegrate; but how could it survive such a savage mauling?

Intercession was long, hard and continuous. Ten years had passed since Samuel had led the College to pray in the 1950s, but the burden continued. 'During the past year the Lord has definitely led us in the College to spend long sessions in prayer for some of the countries that at present are in a state of affliction and upheaval, such as China and Tibet,' reported Samuel. Deeply burdened about the spread of Communism worldwide, Samuel stated: 'Today the Communists are flooding the different countries with propaganda. Millions of people…have nothing to read but this atheistic material. Everything possible should be done to get the Scriptures to these peoples before it is too late. Millions of people are living in these lands without ever having seen a Bible or even a portion of the New Testament. We are deeply exercised about this crying need.'

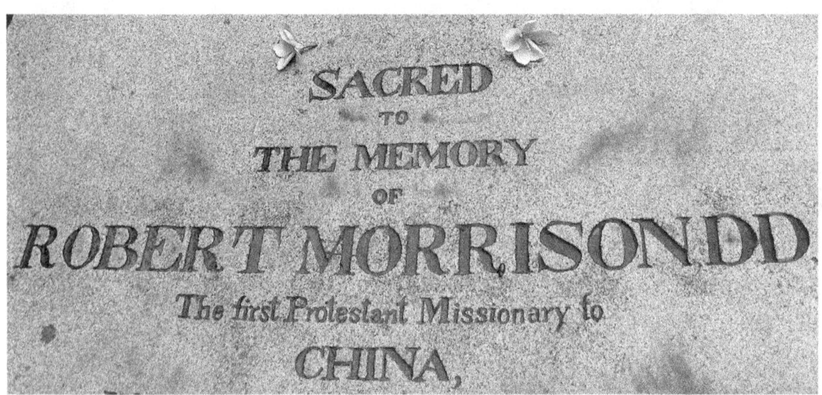

Section of Robert Morrison's tomb (1782-1834) in the Protestant Cemetery at Macau. Morrison was the first Protestant missionary to China (1807) sent by the London Missionary Society in employ of the East India Company. He translated the Bible into Chinese.

It was during the darkest of days in China that Samuel welcomed Gladys Aylward, the then-famous missionary to visit the College to preach. Gladys had commenced her missionary career in Swansea, at the Gospel Mission and had then made her own way across Siberia to China after being declared unsuitable for mission work by a society! Now this diminutive figure, her face barely visible above the lectern of the platform of the Conference Hall, pronounced with a resounding declaration of faith, "China WILL open again."

Outwardly, the Communist takeover of China was the greatest spiritual failure, but in God's eternal Kingdom, the first-fruits and the first-born always belong to the Lord. The first-fruits of the intercession for China and of the missionary work were publicly dying and placed on the altar. As the Church went through the fire, they were purified like a precious metal and the resurrection power of Christ was released amongst them. Even the dictatorial leadership found themselves as Cyrus, being mere instruments in the hands of God. Little did people realise then how Mao's determined efforts to create one language throughout China to improve communications, and to drive the true Church underground, would one day turn for the furtherance of the Gospel within that awakening giant. Mao's violent policies brought a spiritual vacuum into the nation, which Christianity began to fill; whilst the cruelty and catastrophe of the Cultural Revolution cured many of the Chinese of any hope in Communist theory.

Samuel continued in his intercessory ministry for China; supporting Chinese radio broadcasts into the nation in 1966, and constantly brought this great land before the College. Into the 1970s, Samuel rejoiced as their prayers were being answered. "We prayed for China constantly with no results," he said. "But now millions are responding!" Throughout the next few decades Samuel and the College staff continued to intercede and correspondence confirms how Samuel sought to support agencies and individuals who were engaged in providing Bibles and New Testaments for the greatly oppressed, but growing, company of believers.

"There's a man in Hong Kong that is ministering in a large scale in mainland China," said Samuel in 1982. "It a great privilege to be behind these people" (in intercession and with financial assistance). A few years later Samuel presented another report from several Chinese Christian leaders and explained how these men and women were living lives of sacrificial faith. "They are expecting another Church growth explosion," he said. "Why don't they fold their arms and say everything is over? This is the word of faith in the midst of the storm and clouds, declaring that God is going to fulfil His purposes. Don't you think that this brings great glory to God? They are looking to God. God has heard the word of faith and will fulfil it. Are you inspired tonight? Are you entering into this? If we are entering into it, we will be identified with it" (Matthew 16:18).

In 1989, the Communist government of China shocked the world by massacring their own people in Tiananmen Square; but Christian revival continued and Chinese Christian leaders now testify that God has used this harsh system to purify the Church, to protect them from the Laodicean spirit that has gripped the West (Revelation 3:13-18). "Reports we are getting from China are astonishing," said Samuel in 1989. "After the massacre many students who were very hardened proclaimed that they would turn to Christ as the only hope for China. The brutal killing of the students has pushed them to despair, disillusionment and grief. They know that politics are not the answer to China's many problems. They have seen the total corruption of human nature and see Christ as their only hope."

"We have letters (and gifts) ready for mainland China," said Samuel in 1991. "The people in China are yearning for the Word of God. There are restrictions still in mainland China, but now the dear people are taking as many copies of the Bible and the New Testament as is practical to do in these difficult days. Isn't a ministry like that worth supporting? The Word means everything to us. In the New Testament we read of what our Saviour did for us. It's all in the Word and when the Holy Spirit quickens that Word we appreciate it. Well these people are in the same situation. It's our desire for the Lord to enlarge (our ministry of giving). God will open China again."

As the years went on, Samuel rejoiced as their prayers and that of many other believers around the world were being answered. "In China, when the missionaries were expelled from the country, there were hardly one million believers in China," said Samuel. "Now they say nearly 100 million! Isn't this the work of God? God has been exalted. The Holy Spirit, undoubtedly in fulfilment of the words of the Master, has taken possession of some of these Chinese believers. He's clothing Himself with them. They are just His garments. What about Peter and Paul, they were just garments of the Spirit."

The intercessions of those days were contributing to the overall plan for the blessing of China and the results today are a vibrant expanding Church of millions, still experiencing persecution in many provinces, with evidence of the power of the resurrection and the reality of Christ living among His people. In every area of China today there is testimony of a Christian witness. Prayer and the Word of God are prominent, signs following the preaching of the Word are common and a strong and healthy missionary zeal to share Christ with the world exists. The thousands of Chinese Christians who paid the ultimate price or who spent long years of imprisonment for their faith, were true seeds sown into the ground and through that process, once more, resurrection life has been poured out.

Chapter Thirty

Behind Enemy Lines

A most memorable experience touched Samuel deeply in 1966, when he attended the ten day World Congress on Evangelism hosted by Dr. Billy Graham in a divided Germany. The theme was 'One Race, One Gospel, One Task.' There were 1,200 invited guests from all over the world and Samuel had great fellowship. On one occasion Samuel was driven through Checkpoint Charlie, one of the crossings between East and West Berlin. How many guards at the border realised that before them the fifty-four year old man, 'spying out the land' behind enemy lines was a grave threat to Communism! Samuel was able to meet several evangelical pastors, subject to constant harassment and to tell them of his intercessory prayers with the assurance that their day of deliverance would come. He often spoke of those precious moments.

A few times in his life, Samuel travelled behind enemy lines when he found 'points of intercession,' as he crossed borders and stood, like a watchman with his eyes transfixed at the barbed wire which marked the separation between the free world and the bound. Few knew this, but Samuel lived most of his life on the other side of that wire, identifying with the suffering Christians under Communist dictatorship. "I believe that some of the men God is going to use are in these labour camps today," said Samuel. "He's going to bring them out again. There are people today in prison in Siberia, in parts of Russia, in Romania and in these other countries, North Korea and China. God is going to bring some of them out again."

These surreptitious undercover missions reminded Samuel of the severe persecution Christians were experiencing and strengthened his conviction to identify with them. "If we neglect the burdens for the countries, what would the Lord think of us?"

One of Samuel's places of abiding for various intercessions was to limit the food he consumed. If believers in prisons camps could not indulge their human appetite, how could he claim he was identifying with them if he yielded to overeating? Even in his elderly years, the cooks were given instructions to provide him with a pitifully small plate of food. In Samuel's latter years, when the College had fish and chips (every Monday), instructions to the kitchen were for a maximum of eight chips only and two small spoonfuls of peas (no fish), however the cooks ensured that the longest possible chips were selected. Rees Howells' mother used to fill his soup with extras when he was fasting a few meals (and still working down the mines) and now the cooks were simply following her precedent!

In Samuel's intercessions, his aim was to pray for measures which promoted the liberty of the Gospel in the nations. He firmly believed that all governments were in the hands of a sovereign God who works all things according to His purposes (Romans 8:28).

True to the promises he initially made to his father, Samuel was resolute in the course that he and the College should steer into the pathway of intercession. He had seen very clearly that throughout the whole Bible, God's purposes were only moved forward through men and women who became clean, anointed channels for intercession. At the pulpit during long ministry sessions, when time seemed to disappear, the Patriarchs became living characters, something which many students vividly recall. The long and painful periods of preparation in their lives over many years, became necessary as God emptied them to fill them with Himself.

Moses was convinced after forty years in Pharaoh's court that he was the deliverer for the Israelite slaves, since no doubt his mother had told him of his miraculous rescue by Pharaoh's daughter. Knowing that the four hundred years promised to Abraham were complete (Genesis 15:13), he came crashing down as a failure when he was discovered to have killed and buried an Egyptian, and fled to Midian. After a further forty years of tending someone else's sheep in the backside of the desert, his attitude changed to, "Who am I?" when God met him at the burning bush. A somebody had to become a nobody before God could use him. Who could feel sufficient to deliver a whole nation from slavery? However, the burden for the emancipation of the Hebrew slaves had gripped Moses more and more during those silent years, knowing that it was within the covenant purposes of God. God had promised that He would come down to effect the deliverance, but Moses had relinquished all thoughts that he was to be that one. Only when Moses had come to the end of self, was the Lord able to use him. The carnal nature wants to be seen and honoured by men. It wants to be recognised, but the true intercessor only wants to be close to God. They don't want to be known; they have seen the emptiness of man's honour (John 2:24-25, 7:4-6). Moses was called into the hidden life and he didn't want to emerge from it; and only those who don't want the ministry, are fit for it. Then, at the burning bush, God took full possession of his empty channel and the work began.

Every character in the developing story in the Scriptures was different, but in each case the principles remained the same. It was the spiritual calibre of these men and women of God that challenged Samuel, as he realised that in every corner of the world the Holy Spirit was looking for a similar response from His people in order to further God's purposes today. That had been the reason why the

Holy Spirit had brought Rees Howells back from a powerful revival ministry in Southern Africa, to be buried as a seed in Swansea, all those years previously. A single buried seed would one day produce a rich harvest in the lives of many young men and women in the last days. Samuel could see the principle very clearly and now he could see the harvest of that seed bearing fruit in many lives of former students around the world, who were winning souls for Christ.

The prophets, too, all exercised powerful ministries. With their fingers on the spiritual pulse of their day, they carried burdens for the nations around them and were able to declare the word of the Lord for each one. Yet they had that unique initial experience which lifted them into God's realm where they lived and saw Him at work. Ezekiel's deep experience exemplifies the process that the Lord is seeking: 'As He spoke to me the Spirit entered me...' (Ezekiel 2:2).

In the New Testament the lives of the apostles, including Paul, the apostle to the Gentiles, were studied carefully by Samuel under the searchlight of the Holy Spirit, as they touched the Jewish and Gentile world of their day. The Lord often led Samuel back to consider in-depth the life and ministry of the Saviour, and the sacred scenes of the trial, crucifixion and resurrection of the Lord came alive in the services. You could hear a pin drop, and folk just wanted to return to their own rooms quietly afterwards. Samuel always brought the presence of the Lord into the services. There was a quiet reverence and awe, with no cheap talk; how could there be when the Christians in the Soviet bloc and throughout China were experiencing such terrible suffering and when intercession was called for at a very deep level. "Shall we let these passages touch us to the depth of our souls?" he would say, and "in the light of these passages shall we tell the Lord again that we do not want to go part of the way but all the way in our service for Him?"

"There is an ocean before us," he once declared, quietly closing his well-worn black leather Authorised Version of the Bible, filled with white slips of paper poking out from various pages for quick reference, "but we are still just paddling in the shallow waters."

Words spoken by his father in a meeting often echoed in Samuel's mind as he spent long hours alone considering these deep truths. "Don't think you are ever going to be true leaders unless you are one hundred percent the Holy Spirit's." The compass was set and the helmsman had a tight grip on the tiller as the vessel ploughed its way into deeper waters (Ezekiel 47:4-5, Luke 5:4).

Chapter Thirty-One

The Six-Day War

Samuel often carried an intercessory burden for the Jews. Though Israel's politicians and their decisions are not always aligned with God's will, Samuel understood that the Bible foretells Israel's role in the end times. Therefore the survival of the Jewish State is crucial to prophecy (Isaiah 40:1 to 66:24, Zechariah 14:3-4, 8-9, Acts 1:6-7, Romans 10-11, Galatians 6:16, Rev. 7:4). To teach these lessons one of the visitors that Samuel and Dr. Priddy welcomed to the College was the Bible teacher Lance Lambert. Speaking at the College he said, "Has God broken the Covenant He made with the Jewish people? I am not speaking of the Covenant with Moses!" (The Covenant of Moses had terms and conditions; but the Covenant with Abraham is everlasting). "There are no ifs and buts in the Abrahamic Covenant; it is all of grace and promise. There are no judgements mentioned here, and there are no threats made if the conditions are not met; for there are no conditions," he said.

God chose to make an eternal and unconditional Covenant with Abram and his descendants (Genesis 12, 15). God all-knowing, had already foreseen the failings of the Jews, for they would break the conditions of the forthcoming Covenant of Moses (Hebrews 8:8). Therefore this first Covenant with Abraham and the Jews was free of all stipulations. "Then think of the duration," stated Lance. "I will give this land to you and your seed forever" (Genesis 13:15). "It is an everlasting Covenant. This Covenant only ceases when there is no physical seed of Abraham on the face of the earth. It is throughout all their generations. It is an everlasting possession. I'm not talking about politics. This is what the Word of God says."

Even the millennial and eternal prophecies of Christ's reign are coupled to the promises to the Jews. "He shall sit upon the throne of David forever," said Lance. "He was promised by Isaiah in these immortal words: Of His Throne and government there shall be no end" (Isaiah 9:7). "Jesus was born King of the Jews" (Luke 1:33); and when Christ was crucified the title above His head was: 'The King of the Jews.' When Jesus comes back He "will return to Jerusalem" (Zechariah 14:4, Acts 1:10-12); but "before He returns something will happen to the Jewish heart that will lead them to recognise Jesus. Instead of rejecting Him, they will welcome Him!" (Zechariah 12:10, Romans 11:24-26). What deep truths!

Meanwhile, by the beginning of 1967, Jerusalem was still under the direct control of Jordan. How could Jesus return to Jerusalem if the children of Israel were not in possession of all of that Holy City?

Then on 5 June 1967, events suddenly erupted in the Middle East. In a plan intended to annihilate the young nation, Israel was in grave danger as invasion forces were made ready to attack and threats to eradicate Israel were announced. Pressures were mounting and Samuel, deeply exercised in prayer, followed every move very closely as it was released in the media. This conflict was prompted when the Soviet Union sent a falsified report to President Nasser of Egypt stating that Israel was massing troops on the Syrian border. The demonic powers that were working behind Communism were trying to manipulate the nations to annihilate Israel and derail God's end time purposes as stated in Scripture.

President Nasser, knowing that he had Soviet support, expelled the UN Emergency Forces from the Sinai Peninsula and then on 11 May 1967, the Syrian Defence Minister, Hafez-Al-Assad, issued this inflammatory statement, "I, as a military man, believe that the time has come to enter into a battle of annihilation." Similarly President Nasser declared, "The problem before the Arab countries is...how to totally exterminate the State of Israel for all time." Tiny Israel was threatened by Syria in the north and Egypt in the south, with added support from Iraq, Saudi Arabia, Kuwait, Algeria and the USSR.

One expert military observer, Samuel Katiz wrote: 'Never in human history can an aggressor have made his purpose known in advance so clearly and so widely. Certain of victory, both the Arab leaders and their people threw off all restraint. People throughout the world watched and waited in growing anxiety, or in some cases in hopeful expectation, for the overwhelming forces of at least Egypt, Syria, Jordan and Iraq to bear down from three sides to crush tiny Israel and slaughter her people.' Israel needed God to intervene!

The Jewish State was only nineteen years old and the Holocaust was a living memory for most people. Now a second attempt of genocide was broadcast to the Arab world. Egypt's 'Voice of the Arabs' radio presenter Ahmed Said, one of the most famous voices in the Arab world stated on air, "We have nothing for Israel except war. Comprehensive war...destroying and putting an end to the whole Zionist existence. Every one of the 100 million Arabs has been living for the past nineteen years on one hope, to live to die on the day that Israel is liquidated." Having struggled for survival from their very first day as a State, Israel was heavily outmatched. Israel's enemies had fifty-seven percent more troops deployed; they had 657 more combat aircrafts and 1,704 additional tanks. Military analysts predicted the complete defeat of Israel by her enemies.

In the seclusion of his room in Derwen Fawr House, Samuel felt the burden and asked staff members to take the meetings until he found the mind of the Lord. One thing was clear. God was being challenged and He would certainly take up the fight!

For Samuel and senior colleagues at the College they immediately relived those days during World War II, when the Holy Spirit led Rees Howells into the intercession of his life for the preservation of the Jews during the Holocaust and for the establishment of the State of Israel in 1948. For Samuel, this took place less than two decades previously. In the longest closing section of his prophecy, Isaiah deals in detail with the redemption and restoration of Israel (Isaiah 40:1 to 66:24). Such accurate prophecies of Cyrus and the return of the Jews from Babylon, cement into place the fortunes of Israel for the last times, waiting for someone to believe them (Isaiah 44:28 to 45:13). It wasn't human eloquence and ideas which coped with the satanic forces which gripped Europe during WWII, but the Holy Spirit applying the prophetic words of truth to inspire faith, as was originally intended; and this faith was needed again.

Now, in 1967, Samuel put everything to one side once more and called for extra prayer meetings to be guided by the Holy Spirit. After 1,900 years, God had returned the Jews to their land, having preserved them through the most violent of persecutions, and they were not to be annihilated. The prayer was intense, but Samuel found relief through returning to the book of Esther, a record of Satan's attempt to destroy the Jewish people in the fifth century BC. As in the days of Esther, when Haman devised an evil plan to annihilate the Jewish nation, so Samuel could see a modern day parallel. Mordecai had resorted to intercessory prayer and Esther was at first prevented from defending the Jews by very powerful, dark spiritual forces at work in the unseen realm. Meanwhile, Mordecai's intercession prevailed and Esther found complete liberty of spirit and the Jewish nation was preserved (Esther 7-9).

The power of intercessory prayer to break the spiritual forces of evil in the heavenly realms is very potent and will prove again the only means by which the final phases of God's plan for this age will be determined. There had to be an Esther, willing to forfeit her life, to seek audience with the king, but Mordecai told her that another would be found if she demurred. Mordecai was the intercessor.

Back in 1967, the Israeli response to the threat was pre-emptive, sending up all but twelve of their whole available aircraft at 7:14am on 5 June to destroy three hundred Egyptian planes on the ground as their crews had breakfast. Then a similar strike in the north crippled Syrian and Jordanian air capabilities. Israeli tanks rolled into the Sinai Peninsula and engaged Egyptian tank regiments in bitter tank battles in the scorching desert, finally pushing their way to the Egyptian border. On the Syrian front, costly fighting eventually secured the Golan Heights for Israel, and within six days the Shofar was once again sounded in Jerusalem (Luke 21:24).

Despite efforts by the Israelis to prevent any fighting against Jordan, an agreement was broken when Israeli planes were fired upon. Israeli soldiers then stormed the West Bank gaining full control of Jerusalem, including the Old City and the Wailing Wall. Prophecies were being fulfilled before the eyes of the world and Samuel could see the hand of God at work in response to intercessory prayer. On 10 June, Israel and the Arab countries accepted UN Security Council ceasefire demands. History has continued to produce many developments in the Middle East, since it remains the focal point for the future, but through them all the Holy Spirit is ever seeking for a channel through whom He can intercede for the completion of the Divine plan.

There were many miracles during this period; within just three hours of the war, the Israeli Air Force destroyed Egypt's air force and Jordan's air defences were crippled by strikes against their bases. Several Jordanian and Iraqi aircraft were shot down and on the second day of the war, King Hussein and Nasser felt so overwhelmed that they publicly declared that American and British aircraft must have taken part. The humiliating defeat of the Arab Frontline States, compromising the failure of the armed forces of Egypt, Jordan and Syria shocked the world. Before this war, Israel was considered a weak nation in the Middle East, but their swift and decisive victory radically transformed the power balance in the region. The principalities and powers of Egypt, that had harassed the Jews from ancient times were also routed and dethroned. Israel took control of the Golan Heights from Syria, taking back the spiritual and physical 'high' ground from the enemy. Jordan's occupation of east Jerusalem ended and for the first time in 1,900 years, the undivided capital was restored to Jewish control, including the symbolic Wailing Wall (Acts 1:6).

Samuel rejoiced as prophetic events unfolded. "Jerusalem has now reverted into the hands of the Jews!" exclaimed Samuel. Quoting from the words of Jesus, Samuel said, "Jerusalem shall be trampled down until the times of the Gentiles are fulfilled" (Luke 21:24). Think of the signs that are being fulfilled!" The dark spiritual realities working through the Soviet Union, which had provoked the war had planned to annihilate Israel, but by the end of the conflict Israel had gained territory, including complete control of Jerusalem!

Meanwhile at the College visitors would often arrive, romancing the legacy of Rees Howells, expecting Samuel to be an outgoing heroic, intercessory figure. Instead, they saw a shy man who often walked as a public failure, to prove in private the resurrection life! True intercessors are rarely recognised (1 Cor. 9:1-3, Gal. 4:12-20).

Chapter Thirty-Two

The Vietnam War and Mozambique

The growing momentum of the Communist threat around the world had stimulated much deep prayer at the Bible College, which was heightened by events in Vietnam as the Viet Cong threatened to swamp this beautiful country in South East Asia. The College had been deeply challenged through visits from Gordon Smith, working in alliance with the Worldwide Evangelisation Crusade (WEC), whose slides of life among the Rhe people in the interior mountains had shocked everyone. There were still many unreached tribes needing the Gospel and the Viet Cong threatened to bring all Christian witness and outreach to an end. The enemy had to be challenged and only intercessory prayer could penetrate.

In order to contain the Communist threat in Asia, the U.S. went to war. In 1965, 200,000 U.S. troops were in Vietnam, by 1967 this had risen to 500,000. There were many very fierce battles, but conventional warfare did not succeed against an enemy who lived in underground hideouts and fought with great tenacity. At the College, a Vietnamese student poured out his heart to God in prayer for his nation in the many long prayer sessions which Samuel convened. He later returned to serve the Lord in a dangerous area of Vietnam.

There were many battles and intercessions taking place during the Vietnam War and the College was not given personal responsibility to pray for the physical victory of this war; instead their burden was that the Christian witness would not fail and Samuel was exercised about the pastors and missionaries in Vietnam. "You might believe there are no believers in North Vietnam," said Samuel in 1967. "There are believers there and how we praise God for people who are reaching them. Think of the missionaries and the sacrifices they are making! There was a pastor and his brother executed last year. They were on their knees. When they were being executed, they were praising God for embracing martyrdom for His name!"

In the midst of the carnage, God was at work and He found His channels in Vietnam. Samuel took note of one Vietnamese Pastor, Doan Van Mieng and he was giving much time to praying for him. Here was another facet in the Holy Spirit's strategy in leading an individual to intercede for a nation. He will single out one individual, a representative of that nation, so that prayer can be focused.

Following a concerted military offensive, peace talks were agreed by President Nixon resulting in a total U.S. withdrawal from the country in 1975. Thousands of the Vietnamese refugees escaped, some crammed into small or larger craft and others by helicopter, fearing cruel reprisals from their new overlords.

A missionary went to Saigon just before it fell with the sole purpose of rescuing Doan Van Mieng, explained Samuel. "There was a helicopter there ready to take him out, but he said he was an integral part of the Church of Christ in Vietnam. It would be out of the question for him to leave Vietnam." Then Samuel pointed out the spiritual calibre of this man. "An intercessor wasn't he? He wasn't a hireling (John 10:12-13). He remained there and he knew that he would probably be tortured and put to death."

When the war was over, Vietnam appeared to be a disaster, for the Communist forces had won the physical war. Many outside of the College had prayed for military victory, but there was no success. The outward failure of a prayer or faith prediction can often conceal the inscrutable spiritual resurrection that the Lord is preparing. We find this in the Lord's life. When Lazarus was sick Jesus said, "This sickness is not unto death, but for the glory of God" (John 11:4). Jesus knew he had died and waited two days before going. When He met Mary and Martha they were overwhelmed with confusion because Lazarus had died four days earlier! What must the disciples have thought when Jesus wept and the people questioned, "Could not this Man have kept this man from dying?" Outwardly, it was all a disaster. But Jesus turned outward defeat into a greater victory by raising him from the dead! When Jesus said, "This sickness is not unto death," it was a spiritual statement. Lazarus' life was not over, though physically he did die. This can be the case with intercession. Rees and Samuel Howells witnessed spiritual loss in other intercessions, in order that a greater resurrection for the glory of God would prevail. Rees said, "There is a death in every grade, but as really as you die, there will be fruit to a hundredfold" (Matthew 19:27-30, Mark 10:28-31, Luke 8:8).

The responsibility taken by Vietnamese believers in prayer, and the outward death thereof, ensured the future blessing of Vietnam, irrespective of what the immediate picture then might have suggested. Despite continuing persecution, the Church in Vietnam grows and those believing prayers of the 1960s are bearing fruit. Present day reports from very reliable sources state that over 2,300 Vietnamese Church leaders are involved in a biblical training programme and there are over one million Christians in the nation.

Amongst the mountain tribes, which Samuel felt burdened for, there has been a nine-fold increase in the numbers of Christians since the war. There is still persecution, but on 11 December 2009, 40,000 people came to Ho Chi Minh City (Saigon) to worship and 8,000 accepted Christ. The Lord had turned defeat into victory!

Meanwhile, a fresh burden came upon the College when dramatic changes took place in East Africa from 1969-1975, as Mozambique emerged into a Communist dictatorship. The whole country was turned into a bloodbath; hundreds of thousands were exterminated and the brutal secret police hunted down Christians. Rees Howells had wanted to spend his days there as a missionary (then known as Portuguese East Africa), and the Spirit in Samuel responded immediately to the holocaust. Graphic details were shared in meetings from exiled former students and Samuel assured them of his prayers and stated that they would return.

Michael Howard, founder of Kalibu Ministries, is a man with a burning heart for the African continent. He has witnessed the power of intercessory prayer in Africa and Samuel had deep fellowship with this young firebrand. Notable of his fifteen books is *Tales of An African Intercessor* (1998). In *Love Constrained* (1997), Michael Howard describes the intensity of the spiritual conflict that he and his fellowship were plunged into, and Samuel Rees Howells stood alongside them. 'We took up the challenge of the Holy Spirit and locked into battle. It wasn't that we had a few prayer meetings. We carried the burden of the travail on a daily basis for over six long years, agonising, weeping and praying. At every meeting and conversation it would be a major theme. People did not realise the vast networking of demonic control over the whole subcontinent. We were going for the very jugular as it were, and it was a tough one! Most Christians today have no idea what it really means to take on the principalities of darkness. It must be done only at the direction of the Holy Spirit, for to step on to the devil's territory without Divine direction and protection is foolishness and asking for trouble (Jude 8-13). Most Christians think that it is a mere matter of shouting at the devil or a few nice little prayer meetings. The intercessor gives his whole life to the cause for which he is fighting. Can the prayer warrior fight any less hard than those on the physical battle front? Intercession is not dealing with a few little minion demons with a shout, but is taking on the deeply entrenched princes who rule entire territories. Without such, victory shall never be gained; which will bring lasting change.'

God answered the prayer for the nation's liberty; the missionaries returned and Bible believing Christians increased six-fold! "Think of the way Mozambique is opening!" said Samuel. "Think of the ones that have suffered and been imprisoned. What are they longing for now? For the Spirit to descend upon them, so that they can complete the work, not in their strength, but in the Divine strength."

Chapter Thirty-Three

Angola, Lebanon and Cambodia

Samuel loved to walk on the veranda of Derwen Fawr House and from this vantage point he would often catch a passer-by and arrange a visit to his room, or folk would just hear him pacing up and down for long periods, locked in prayer. Samuel was seen there many times in the early hours of the morning 'watching on the walls,' praying 'in the high places' with his view of Swansea Bay, and the bungalows below. Nonetheless, Samuel did not want to be distracted in his intercessions, so the front lawn was sacrosanct in those days, out of bounds to anyone, staff and students, without the nod of approval being given. It was reserved for the Director, Samuel, bowed in prayer, but in later years, this rule was abolished.

On one occasion when he was preaching, Samuel referred to the 'ball of fire' rising slowly over the Bay, early one morning. It had struck him quite forcibly that the One who had created that magnificent sunrise was the One who had died for him and for all mankind, on the cross. How could he not but worship such a wonderful Person and live for Him alone? Samuel was always very quiet and extremely sensitive, particularly in spiritual matters. Before he preached, many hours would be spent in the Lord's presence. Once in the pulpit, with exceptional discernment, he would know exactly where many members of the congregation stood in their relationship with the Lord, and would sometimes speak about these issues to staff members responsible for students. It was this sensitivity and close walk with the Lord which also enabled him to discern what he termed the 'prayers of the Kingdom.' These were special burdens that the Holy Spirit gave him for national and international situations, particularly where satanic forces were seeking to disrupt God's purposes for the advance of the Gospel.

The sixties had been a time of intense spiritual battles for Samuel, and he ended the decade with a greater determination to pour out his life in the ministry God had given for a lost world. On 7 April 1968, he responded to a call for a Day of Prayer for Britain and another on Sunday 20 October. Samuel wanted the College to respond in a similar way and called everyone to special sessions of corporate prayer following the reading of appropriate passages of Scripture around 2 Chronicles 7:14, 2 Chronicles 20:13-14 and Acts 4:23-33. In 1969, the U.S. won the space race and whilst Neil Armstrong was making his first tentative steps on the moon, Samuel was traversing the heavenly realms on his path of intercession.

As the College welcomed in 1970, they held another solemn

meeting and Samuel returned to the Vision to reach every creature with the Gospel. These messages were never routine, but were a part of Samuel's desire to prepare the College for another year of intercession. The prayers of the 1970s were many and the greater details of them cannot be dealt with in one book, therefore the following are selective quotes that speak volumes.

"We feel sometimes that we could put everything to one side and concentrate on intercession," said Samuel in the 1970s. "We feel now that prayer is not sufficient. Ordinary prayer will not touch this at all. There is a need for the ministry of intercession and intercession will succeed each time. We've proved that haven't we, in our experience. The emphasis is on intercession."

In the past, Samuel had believed for many prayers to be answered and often knew when he had gained a position of intercession and was able to apply this position to other burdens, as the Holy Spirit led him. "We know that we have gained the position of intercession," said Samuel. "One has been spending whole nights with God in prayer and you know the moment you touch the Throne. The moment! That's not ordinary is it? Are we prepared to pay the price? We've been keeping intercession to the fore haven't we? Whatever else has been neglected (referring to the maintenance of the properties) we have not neglected that aspect!"

A deep impression was left on the College staff one Sunday morning in the 9:45 prayer meeting in the Conference Hall, when they heard Samuel pouring out his heart to the Lord for the dear people of Angola, who had gained independence from Portugal in 1975. This had not produced stability, but had plunged the country into a long civil war between the government forces and the Unita rebels. The work of the Gospel was disrupted and Samuel, ever sensitive to suffering and every move of the enemy of souls, was alert in the Spirit. "For the first years of the Lord's life, He was brought up in exile in Egypt," he said. "Many are fugitives today. Last week we sent some relief to a society working among the Angolan refugees. Think of the intense suffering of these people, who have been torn away from their country for no fault of their own. It's difficult for you and me to enter into the feelings of those people, because we are not fugitives. But let me tell you, the One that is on the Throne tonight He can intercede for them. He was a fugitive."

There was a similar response to the upsurge of violence in Lebanon, when civil war broke out in 1975, particularly as former students worked in a Christian school in Beirut, which Samuel had visited on several occasions. "One has been thinking of those Lebanese pastors again," said Samuel. "With all of their towns and cities that have been razed to the ground. Don't you think they're crying and weeping these days? Isn't it our duty to pray for them as we have been during the past weeks?"

Samuel was also concerned about the rise of Islamic terrorism in the Middle East, decades before most in the West had even noticed it. "Dr. Priddy was just telling one earlier this evening of the arms that the Israelis have found in Lebanon," said Samuel. "Enough to supply large armies. They were there for a purpose, but it seems the evil designs of Satan have been stalled once again and God is triumphant. Isn't it necessary to press the battle to the gates that God's will shall be fulfilled in Israel and in Lebanon?"

The Bible expresses that God loves all peoples and wants all men to be saved (John 3:16, 1 Timothy 2:4). "We are praying for the people in Lebanon, that the Lord will meet them," said Samuel. "We know that the Jewish people are to be blessed. These blessings are not only for the Jews, but for the Gentiles as well. That is the prayer we go back to. We want the inhabitants of Beirut to be relieved. What is our desire in this time? That these dear people in Lebanon, in Iraq, in Iran, in Israel will meet the Lord in a true and living way. That they will partake of this great salvation!"

Samuel's prayers were drawn towards Asia in 1975. "When you think of those terrible things that have been happening in Cambodia," said Samuel. "There are believers there who are rejoicing in Christ, they have survived. Some people said there wasn't a single believer left. We couldn't accept those things and now these letters have arrived which substantiate our beliefs. The gates of Hell will never prevail against the Church of Christ." Samuel finished one meeting with an open prayer, "We think again of those dear believers in Cambodia, the Spirit is resting upon them, despite all they have endured...continue to be with them and lead them on."

Often criticised for his, at times, frugal lifestyle, Samuel was a man whose companions in the Spirit were the fifty-two members of the U.S. Embassy held in Iran as hostages for 444 days from 4 November 1979, and the missionaries and Christians suffering under strict Islamic rule. "We may be tested, but let me tell you there are some dear children under the sentence of death," he said. "I am referring to Iran. There are missionaries and national believers being imprisoned. If the normal course of events will take place, they will face the firing squad. An urgent plea has come to pray for them. There's no mercy for people in Iran today. Isn't God able to deliver these people, as He delivered Elijah? That's why the Word comes to help us. How could we pray for them in a general sense? But when we base our prayers on the Word of God as Daniel and the others did, then we have something substantial to rest and rely on." 'For the Word of God is living and powerful, sharper than any two-edged sword' (Hebrews 4:12, Psalm 149:6-9).

Then Samuel's prayers turned towards the hungry Africans experiencing the terrible drought of the Sahel, leading to many deaths in the nations of Ethiopia, Sudan, Chad, Nigeria and beyond. "Millions of people in the world are suffering from malnutrition," said Samuel. "Millions are dying every year of starvation. Does anyone care for them?" Samuel was searching for intercessors in the College. "Does anyone care for them? Yes, the One who is on the Throne. You can't suffer for them," he said. "You can pray for them, but you can't intercede for them. Why? Because you are having four good meals everyday." Samuel was explaining the principle of the first sufferer. Before anyone can intercede for another, they have to first live like them and become the first sufferer. "You can't intercede for those people," said Samuel. "If you interceded for those people you would have to live like them – that's the point. There's no intercession otherwise. But the One on the Throne is an Intercessor. I hope we won't spend all of our lives in the shallows. Let's enter into the depths of this life in the Holy Spirit" (Ezekiel 4:11,16).

Throughout the 1970s, Samuel persisted in carrying the burden for the evangelisation of the world, which had been with him since he promised in 1935 to dedicate his life to reaching every creature with the Gospel, and he remained true to his vow. "There are millions in the world yet who haven't heard once about the redeeming grace of the Master and that is our prayer. That is our burden in these days. Prophecies have been made that blessings are to occur in these last days. They're not ideas of our own; no these are beliefs and convictions based on the infallible Word of God."

Samuel was carrying abstruse intercessory burdens, but the practicalities of running an organisation in a living community, led to some criticisms and infighting (2 Corinthians 12:20). When this was the case he would withdraw and intercede on his own (Exodus 33). But at times he confronted the criticism head-on. "It would be wonderful if the Lord revealed the significance of these things to us again. You could be living, oblivious of it all! Just thinking that hardly anything is going on…when everything is going on!" His message was direct – if we try to 'see' with carnal senses, we will never enter into the realm of God. We need to use the gift of discernment and faith to realise that these intercessions are shaping the world!

Samuel always concluded his time of ministry and prayer by declaring a word of faith and confidence, no matter how dark and desperate the situation in question would seem to be. He was believing for blessing in every nation of the world and would round off his prayer with a quote from Isaiah 53:11. 'He shall see of the travail of His soul and shall be satisfied.'

Chapter Thirty-Four

The Yom Kippur War

In October 1973, on the holiest day of the Jewish calendar, Yom Kippur, the Day of Atonement (as the nation was in solemn contemplation), there was a surprise attack on Israel from her neighbours, who were heavily armed with military technology from the Soviet Union. Samuel called the College back to prayer as the Holy Spirit led through another spiritual conflict characterised by many great miracles. After the great victories of this intense spiritual struggle, Samuel aged sixty-one celebrated the triumph of their intercession, as he read reports of the battle to the College. "In the Yom Kippur War, with Egypt's greater numbers they should have been in Beersheba within twenty-four hours. The Arabs had more weapons and better weapons. In the early stages of the war, three out of every five Israeli jets were shot down. Israel suffered terrible casualties. Then Egypt crossed into Sinai and the Syrians took much of the Golan Heights. Egypt and Syria should have beaten Israel." Then Samuel praised the Lord for answered prayer. "If God hadn't intervened in the Sinai Desert and if He hadn't intervened in the Golan Heights everything would have been over. With the arms at the Syrians disposal they should have been in Tiberias at the end of the first day. Who saved that nation? It was the Lord!"

The Lord had stepped in again and saved the unprepared Israel miraculously, yet there was another great victory that most people have forgotten. Near the end of the conflict, the Soviet Union came close to entering the war against Israel. Another Holocaust of God's people was possible. "When the Syrians and Egyptians suffered those setbacks, the Russians became very infuriated," said Samuel. The head of Russia sent Nixon a message stating that if Russian demands were not met they would 'consider taking appropriate steps unilaterally.' Russia was preparing to solve the Arab's conflict with the Jews in the Middle East by fighting with Israel's enemies. "America took this very seriously," said Samuel, as he read from the report. "American reconnaissance flights had already spotted that a large Soviet warship, previously seen headed for Egypt, had now stopped dead. On the deck of this warship were ballistic missiles with nuclear warheads." The Russians believed Nixon had such great domestic problems that he would delay a response.

Seven Soviet airborne divisions were placed on alert and planes were made ready to invade Israel. An airborne command post was set up in the Soviet Union to prepare for war and planes were moved towards the Middle East. Amphibious warfare craft with

40,000 Soviet naval infantry were also moved to the Mediterranean.

In the College, this was recognised as a second Cuban Missile Crisis. The Soviet Union armed with nuclear weapons, aimed its sights on Israel, with the expectation that the U.S. would not be able to support the Jewish nation because of internal problems. A day before the crisis reached its peak, the Lord called the College to urgent intercession. He also called others to pray and Samuel read of these prayers. "I cannot forget the burden of prayer that fell upon some of us on the preceding day, urgent and anointed prayers that were made to God concerning the unmasking of the Soviet Union's plans." Samuel then spoke of the intercession at the College. "The burden came upon us and on other people. We then prayed and prevailed in God's presence and God answered; but not without cost." Satan's plans had failed. "The enemy is so deceitful and we must be aware of his devices. We must be ready at all times. But the Holy Spirit is victorious and the evil one has been bound."

Samuel was then reminded that many Christians were out of touch with the Holy Spirit and had little or no understanding of this spiritual battle, as they continued to 'play Church.' "We were close to World War Three! We were living in a fool's paradise, teetering on the brink of a nuclear war. Christians continued their meetings unaware of the grave issues at stake and the tremendous movements in the unseen world; but think of the extent to which Satan went!"

The demonic hosts that urged the USSR to go to war with Israel were bound through intercession and the Soviets retreated. The Soviet leadership was famous for acting illogically, but in an example of how intercession casts 'down arguments and every high thing that exalts itself against the knowledge of God,' the Soviets responded in a conciliatory manner (2 Corinthians 10:5). The Soviet Premier, Alexei Kosygin stated, "It is not reasonable to become engaged in a war with the United States because of Egypt and Syria," and Yuri Andropov, chief of the KGB said, "We shall not unleash the Third World War!" This overlooked threat was identified and addressed through intercession, as led by the Holy Spirit.

Once again, Israel had been saved by prayer. "Do you see how close things came?" noted Samuel. "The Lord allows them to come close. Is it possible for the Holy Spirit to make us alive to these things? There is a tremendous conflict going on in the heavenlies. Remember the special prayers that we had when this was going on? Everybody else thought it was just covering up for the possible impeachment of the President" (due to the Watergate Scandal).

A few times in Samuel's life, Satan tried to use the USSR to evoke a global war to hinder the Gospel (such as the Cuban Missile Crisis and this conflict), but each time he was bound. Would he try again?

Chapter Thirty-Five

Cyprus and Turkey

There were times at the College when Samuel Howells presented an open word concerning the future, indicating exactly what would happen in a world event, but generally he often preferred to become accountable in his prophetic revelations to a very small number of trusted intercessors. Samuel learnt from bitter experience during the days of Rees Howells that if he shared too much publicly, it could open the ministry of intercession to 'friendly-fire,' where misguided believers, ignorant of the real power of confession and declaration, gossip cynically, negatively influencing the war in the heavenly realm (Proverbs 18:21, Isaiah 46:10, Philippians 2:11, James 3). There are strict warnings in Scripture concerning this: 'If anyone among you thinks he is religious and does not bridle his tongue but deceives his own heart; this one's religion is useless' (James 1:26), and 'these speak evil of what they do not understand' (Jude 10).

Samuel was equally cautious of misinformed believers 'praying' against the revelation, due to lack of understanding because of their spiritual immaturity. He too felt the sadness of the apostle Paul: 'And I brethren could not speak to you as to spiritual people, but as to carnal, as to babes in Christ. I fed you with milk and not with solid food; for until now you were not able to receive it and even now you are still not able. For you are still carnal. For where there is envy, strife, divisions among you, are you not carnal and behaving like mere men?' (1 Corinthians 3:1-3). This is why Samuel was ultra cautious in discussing the intercessions. In addition, if everyone knew the true conflict, it could endanger them and the intercession itself (Daniel 8:26, 9:24, Revelation 10:4). Paul warned that Satan disguises himself as an angel of light (2 Corinthians 11:14). Jesus warned of tares in Matthew 13:24-25, and Satan, the tare was present in Jesus' ministry working in and through Judas, the son of perdition (Luke 22:3, John 17:12).

Samuel may have been cautious concerning making public predictions because he accepted the wisdom of the apostle Paul who stated, 'for we know in part and we prophesy in part' (2 Corinthians 1:9). With this warning in mind, Samuel determined that we must be careful not to overstep the revelation God gives us, or put our own interpretation on a word from Heaven. The prophetic words intercessors receive are usually known 'in part' and therefore they 'prophesy in part.' It is often with hindsight that they begin to learn what God was achieving in the spiritual realm. Samuel's strength was not in knowing the exact details of the outcome, but in the Holy Spirit's ability to lead and provide during the battle. "The Lord doesn't always show us the future," he said, "but we know that there is grace for every test and there's provision for every need."

In 1974, war clouds were gathering in Cyprus and Samuel was not immediately certain of the will of the Lord. Turkey was threatening to invade the island and a wider conflict could ensue. Turkey was an ally of the U.S. and held a strategic position as a buffer zone against the Soviet Union, and Samuel was concerned that any incident in the region could spark a non-nuclear Third World War.

The Cold War was a dark game of military chess, with the Soviet Union, the U.S. and allies fighting each other in distant lands, using proxies to struggle with their enemy to undermine the other superpower's presence in regions such as Afghanistan or Vietnam. The Cold War never led to a direct confrontation of the superpowers on the battlefield, and an invasion force was not taken to the front door of each other because nuclear annihilation would ensue.

As the pressure mounted between Turkey and Cyprus, Samuel gave a chilling assessment to the College. "According to the radio, the situation is as strained as it could be. The President of Turkey has stated that unless the bloodshed ceases tonight they will intervene. Everybody that has been to Turkey knows the military might of the country. Toby (Bergin) and I travelled as far as Istanbul; practically the whole territory was a military zone. Greece is reacting and stated that if Turkey intervenes they will act most decisively. The prospect is war between Greece and Turkey. There are tens of thousands of soldiers ready there."

The North Atlantic Treaty Organisation (NATO) was created in 1949, for the purposes of collective security for all its members. But as Turkey and Greece were both members, Samuel sensed that Satan could manipulate the internal division of NATO; by using the Soviet Union to exploit the situation for its own military advantage to intervene as 'peace keepers.' The general public in the West was largely ignorant of this scenario, which would then escalate into a wider war, but the American President was not. In addition to the threat of another large war, if Turkey invaded Cyprus and the Soviet Union intervened to occupy Turkey, they would have real access to the Middle East and Israel. "We don't know what will happen," said Samuel, "Cyprus may be invaded but the Lord is still on the Throne."

In July, the Turkish military invasion of Cyprus began, deposing the president and expelling large numbers of Greek Cypriots from the now occupied northern part of the island (which then constituted eighty percent of the population). Samuel gave his assessment, "If the war spreads all our future plans (Bible distribution) will be disrupted. What can stop it from spreading? These are members of

NATO, and Russia will take advantage (of the problems at NATO because of the internal dispute of Turkey and Greece)." President Johnson, ten years previously had foreseen this scenario leading to a wider war and in response on 5 June 1964, stated that the U.S. would not come to the aid of Turkey if an invasion of Cyprus led to conflict with the Soviet Union. But that was a decade ago and seemed like another age. The U.S. had a secure treaty with Turkey and could not afford further Soviet expansion. Could intercession stop the Soviets from intervening and leading to another great war?

The Soviet leadership, living under a system ruled by fear and paralysed by the dread of being labelled a plausible defector, were carefully watched by the KGB and often played a highly volatile game of political Russian Roulette to prove their commitment to the system. Leaders were replaced on a whim, and to indicate patriotism many chose violent rhetoric against their enemies as they submitted dangerously unstable policies. This system of intimidation drove many to psychosis and Satan was always willing to manipulate a dangerously lost soul. With this fatal flaw in their evil system of government and military defence, the plausibility of large Soviet aggression during the crisis was always a real possibility. We must also recall that the Soviet leadership had little respect for human life, because millions died under their godless system at home. If Soviet citizens were under threat, what about the world!

If the struggle spread to other nations, a World War was a potential consequence and Samuel warned about the seriousness of such an escalation, "There will be conscription (drafts) again and all the young people will be called up. That's what took place in 1914, and it was repeated in 1939. Every Bible College in Britain was closed at that time and all the young people had to go and fight for their country." His warnings may seem superlative now, but that is only because we are on the other side of the conflict. History warns that small skirmishes can drag entire regions into war. Samuel had witnessed this first-hand in the past and took nothing for granted.

In Cyprus, Samuel's point of intercession was Levon Yergatian, whom he supported in the work of the Christian Literature Crusade, in its drive to distribute evangelical literature throughout the island. However, the Turkish invasion threatened to engulf the whole island, so special prayer was again made in Swansea. With military strength on their side, Turkey flooded northern Cyprus and Samuel's heart went out to the innocent people as he recalled his personal experience of the terror of war, when the bombs fell so close to the College shaking its buildings during WWII. "We are all converted in this room here tonight," he said, "and if a bomb was dropped on us, our lives here would be finished and we would enter into eternal life because we know the Saviour. But if a bomb was dropped on those other people, they would find themselves in a lost eternity. That's the point isn't it! If those people were born of God, they'd have nothing to fear for eternity," (Romans 10:9).

A ceasefire was agreed on 22 July, but talks broke down and the fighting resumed. "Don't think this is a College prayer," stated Samuel. "This has nothing to do with the Bible College of Wales. When we are praying this, we are praying it for the world. This is a world prayer and praise God that we know something about prayer, and can resolve to pray in times like this." In August talks for peace stalled again, as Turkey occupied forty percent of the island.

Some at the College had hoped that Turkey would never invade Cyprus, but Samuel reminded them that even Judah was invaded by the Assyrians, whilst Hezekiah and Isaiah were trusting in God. "That was very real wasn't it?" he said, "but there was one man in Jerusalem that believed God and he had seen that test coming for many, many years. It was no surprise to Isaiah. There was only one person in perfect peace in Jerusalem when it was surrounded by the Assyrians and that was Isaiah. Hezekiah was a good man; but all his confidence and faith went when the Assyrians were outside of Jerusalem! He wanted to pay tribute. Jerusalem was surrounded and there was no hope at all. Are we believing God like Isaiah?"

Samuel's prayers were often directed towards restoring peace and defusing conflicts. The Prince of Peace was his Master, and as he discovered in 1939, war greatly hinders missionary endeavours. Therefore someone must pay the price in intercessory prayer for peace to be restored. "This state of affairs must come to an end," said Samuel. "Who is causing all this strife? It's the enemy isn't it? The enemy doesn't want peace to be restored in Cyprus, because he wants to drag these people down to a lost eternity."

As the dust settled internationally, the Soviet Union's chances of escalating the conflict as two NATO nations were pitted against each other slipped away. The cracks and divisions in NATO were put to one side as Greece removed its forces from the organisation in 1974 for a few years, and the possibilities of an escalation into a larger war diminished. On the island, Turkey held the occupied territory and roughly 60,000 Turkish Cypriots fled from the south to the north. The island was now partitioned, with the northern third inhabited by Turkish Cypriots and the southern two-thirds by Greek Cypriots. The tolerance between the two communities was setback decades, but the war had been contained and international peace was maintained. Samuel's confidence in God's sovereignty, like Isaiah's had been rewarded (Isaiah 37:6-7, 35-37).

Chapter Thirty-Six

Christ Our Lord

The ministry of the Holy Spirit in the Church was central to the teaching of Samuel Howells, but he always reminded the College that the Holy Spirit has been sent to glorify Christ. The relationship of the Trinity working in union is central to the teaching of the Lord (John 8:28, 12:49, 14:10), and He explained to the disciples that He would send the Holy Spirit to continue His work on earth (John 16:7). "When He the Spirit of Truth has come He will guide you into all truth, for He will not speak on His own authority, but whatever He hears He will speak and He will tell you things to come. He will glorify Me, for He will take of what is Mine and declare it to you" (John 16:13-14). Samuel once said, "Let us ask the Holy Spirit to help us understand these deep things so that we do not read them superficially." These were foundational truths in Samuel's life.

The fruit of all of Samuel's intercessions were always grounded in Christ's complete victory over the enemy at Calvary. Christ's death and resurrection enables the intercessor to exercise authority over the enemy, because Christ, *the Intercessor* defeated the devil and made a public spectacle of him, and He released this authority to be exercised by His obedient vessels. As Matthew records, the unity of the Trinity is key to Christian discipleship and victory. "All authority has been given to Me in Heaven and on earth. Go therefore and make disciples of all the nations, baptising them in the name of the Father and of the Son and of the Holy Spirit, teaching them to observe all things that I have commanded you; and lo I am with you always, even to the end of the age" (Matthew 28:18-20).

In one evening meeting, Samuel considered the passages in John 6 where Jesus proclaimed Himself to be the Bread of Life. "A young Man was standing before them and saying, 'I am the Bread of Life!' They could not take that without a revelation. The whole world was to be satisfied with His Body. He was Life. Have we come to the position where we never hunger or thirst? Do we day-by-day feed on Him? Has He satisfied us? Ever since last Saturday afternoon, that company on Mount Zion who have followed Him all the way have been in my mind. Those who do not want any relationship but Himself. It is not anything ordinary. It fills our minds, our affections, which have been absorbed in His Person. He becomes all in all."

Samuel Howells hoped that all students would understand the true meaning of Calvary and continued in the custom passed on to the College family through Rees Howells, where both Easter and Pentecost (Whitsun, as it is also known in Britain) remained very special times. Although no religious fasting period was declared for Lent (the six week period preceding the Easter weekend), Samuel prepared himself prayerfully and his pulpit ministry usually took the form of an intense study of the final weeks of Jesus' public ministry. Such was the power of Samuel's ministry when under the anointing of the Holy Spirit that a wave of conviction would touch the hearts of all present, for reasons known only to themselves.

The Saviour's inner conflict in Gethsemane, the betrayal, the trial, scourging and crucifixion scenes, all were graphically portrayed as the Holy Spirit revealed afresh the agony of those fateful hours in the Saviour's life. On the night Jesus was betrayed, "He went out from the light of Heaven, to the darkness of Hell and did so deliberately," said Samuel "the intercessory walk to Golgotha."

Throughout these times, Samuel's command of English, his second language, was masterly, "His life and ministry had exposed their hypocrisy. Have you paused to consider what the impeccable Son of God has done for you? Have you? The physical suffering was terrible, but it was the dereliction He could not face. Yet He was willing to accept it for you and me. That bitter cry of desolation as Christ plumbed the depths and was accursed by God the heart of our redemption. Aren't you profoundly affected today? Then spend time low at His feet" (James 4:6, 10).

Samuel treated Isaiah's graphic descriptions of the suffering Servant in Isaiah 53 with great reverence and respect as a holy hush descended on the prayer room. It was obvious that each verse touched his tender spirit, drawing from him such phrases as, "We shall never know what it meant for Him to become incarnate. These words haunt one (referring to himself); we don't know what to do, it is all beyond our comprehension. We are not heavy or sleepy today, are we? There is something radically wrong with you if you are. We shall never be able to discharge our debt; all other things pale into insignificance. The prophet was completely taken out of himself and saw the suffering Christ." From the Bible, many know the story of the cross from a historical perspective, but few have 'seen' the full implications of Calvary. Samuel said, "There is no satisfaction nor conviction in anything unless it has been given by a revelation, otherwise it is only mental assent," and "teaching will never change your position, words and phrases do not convey anything." Then he said sternly, "Only one glimpse of the cross is sufficient to change us completely; undoubtedly!" (Romans 16:25-26, Gal. 1:11-16).

Dr. Priddy also had a deep revelation of the cross when he sat under the ministry of Rees Howells, and under Samuel's leadership he shared from the pulpit how hard the process of full surrender had been; but a vision from God transformed him. "In His mercy, the

Spirit drew the veil aside again and gave me a glorious view of the invisible and I saw Calvary!" Taking a deep breath and lowering his tone, Dr. Priddy reiterated, "I saw Calvary." Silence touched the room. "I believed that Jesus died on the cross for me and for the sins of the world. I believed it all, but I had never seen it before! But that day, Calvary was before me." Straining and holding back his emotions, Dr. Priddy continued, "The One on it was the Son of God." With a pause he continued, "The One concerning whom I had been such a humbug and a hypocrite, with all my preaching and talking and yet I remained in the unsurrendered state that I was. In the light of that revelation of Calvary I said, 'Yes' (to God in full surrender) "and He came in and I was living in a different realm after that. It was eternal things that mattered; it was eternal things that were real! It was eternal things that motivated me."

On another day, Samuel examined in-depth the seven sayings of Jesus uttered from the cross, including the assurance given to the penitent thief enduring the same fate as Himself. "Today shalt thou be with Me in paradise" (Luke 23:43). "What a powerful Gospel this is!" he said, "No waiting period necessary even for the worst of sinners who truly repents and believes." Again, in another service Samuel revealed just how much every verse of Scripture was being considered prayerfully in God's presence. 'Behold, the veil of the temple was rent in twain from the top to the bottom; and the earth did quake...and the graves were opened' (Matthew 27:51-52). "I have been dwelling on that verse – all barriers between us and God have been broken; death can hold us no longer!"

During the sacred Good Friday sessions, time seemed to stand still. For some moments Samuel's voice was reduced to barely a whisper. These were not sermons that Samuel was preaching, but everyone knew that it was his life that was being poured into each session, and the physical exhaustion would be very real. At others, his pitch was raised as the Holy Spirit empowered him. So often, passages from the book of Hebrews filled his thoughts, particularly the priestly office of the Saviour, High Priest after the order of Melchizedek. This remarkable figure who blessed Abram (Genesis 14:18-20) was the facsimile of the One to come, Jesus Christ the reality. "Now we can boldly enter the Inner Sanctuary of God's presence, previously only permitted once a year following the most stringent preparations, to the Throne of Grace…We have had many totally impossible prayers recently, almost absurd to pray, but the Holy Spirit has enabled us to present them before that Throne and the Father has answered them all. That's God!" Samuel exclaimed. "We must thank Him as we have never done before and believe Him in ways we have found difficult before" (Hebrews 11:6).

The ministry on Easter Sunday followed closely from Samuel's Good Friday meditations and showed clearly just how much time he must have spent in God's presence beforehand. Every section of the resurrection narrative received his typically thorough attention, interspersed with impassioned declarations, "Despite all the efforts of the Saviour not one of the disciples could understand the resurrection. Neither will we. These truths must be revealed to us – that is the need of the hour...The danger is that we consider these lovely meetings but we are not changed. I have been praying through the night that the Lord will meet us as He did these early believers...How important is Divine revelation. We cannot deal with these matters with our own understanding! I do trust that a large portion of the night was spent at the open sepulchre. You haven't spent all night in sleep, have you?"

Ascension Day never went unnoticed by Samuel, who pondered deeply on its truths and its promises of the King's return to the mountain top of Olives to establish His millennial reign on earth (Zechariah 14:4, Acts 1:10-12). No doubt, these will be troublesome days, particularly in the Middle East, but ones of hope and deliverance for God's people as they anticipate His return.

Then came Pentecost, (also known as Whitsun in the U.K.). The outpouring of the Holy Spirit on the early believers on the Day of Pentecost in Jerusalem had birthed the Church, and only He is totally responsible and able to oversee these end times. The promise of the outpouring of the Holy Spirit on all flesh in Acts 2:17-21, would be a worldwide demonstration of the power of the atonement, completely orchestrated by the Third Person of the Godhead Himself. Samuel's ministry on the Whit-Sunday was, as usual, very powerful once he found liberty. Often he would take time to trace the activities of the Holy Spirit in the Old Testament, as He took possession of individuals for specific ministries. Now, however, the promise is to all men, for all whom the Lord calls to Himself. 'For the promise is unto you, and to your children, and to all that are afar off, even as many as the Lord our God shall call' (Acts 2:39). Sometimes he would read letters and articles illustrating just how powerfully the Holy Spirit was at work throughout the world, particularly in China and Eastern Europe.

Pentecost was always a time of great rejoicing at the coming of the Holy Spirit, and also an opportunity for personal challenge to go further with God. The life of Jesus Christ, *the Intercessor* provided Samuel with a perfect example of intercessory victory. Jesus was misunderstood, misquoted and ridiculed. In His last days He was openly mocked but public failure is often the price intercessors pay for private victory.

Chapter Thirty-Seven

The Falklands War

An unexpected spiritual conflict arose on 2 April 1982, when the lightly defended Falkland Islands, the British territory in the South Atlantic Ocean were invaded and occupied by Argentinian forces under the command of General Leopoldo Galtieri, the Argentine military dictator. Just sixty-nine Royal Marines were present on the vast territory and were quickly overwhelmed as thirteen thousand Argentinian troops flooded the islands. Despite the Falklands having no vital interest for Britain, the 2,500 islanders wanted to remain British and Prime Minister Margaret Thatcher led the country to retake the islands by amphibious assault.

On 5 April a Task Force of ninety-three British ships, including two aircraft carriers, HMS *Hercules* and HMS *Hermes*, carrying fifteen thousand men, set sail from Portsmouth, the largest force since the Suez Crisis. On 19 April 1982, the cover of *Newsweek* magazine featured an aerial photo of the enormous British aircraft carrier HMS *Hermes* sailing to liberate the islands, with the caption 'The Empire Strikes Back.' The prestige of this image gave the impression that a British victory was inevitable, but this was far from the case.

Military strategists knew that those who controlled the airspace over the islands would win the war. Air power counted now and Britain was outgunned in the air by a ratio of almost five to one. Every British pilot knew that the Argentinians were flying first-rate French built jet fighters with the latest technology and for every aircraft they shot down, another four could be on their tail. Britain's closest ally, the United States, asked their Navy to produce a secret intelligence report on Britain's capabilities. The strategic review unequivocally stated that a successful counter-invasion by the British was 'a military impossibility.' Without air supremacy, Britain's Armada would be sunk and America's closest friend in the world would be humiliated. With this in mind, the U.S. tried to mediate an end to the conflict, but the Argentine dictator refused to negotiate. With major economic troubles at home, General Galtieri invaded the disputed islands, to pacify unrest at his tyrannical rule.

At the College, Samuel, who would turn seventy that year, reminded the staff that only God knows what needed to be prayed. "There comes a moment when we tell the Lord in prayer, 'We can't do anything at all about it!' Then He is obliged to come in and help. That is the rule each time in personal prayers and in these prayers that we pray on a worldwide scale." After meditating on God's Word, Samuel sensed that it was God's will for Britain to win the war. If

Britain won, the dictator would fall, liberty would spread, democracy would be restored and Christian revival would follow! But if General Galtieri won, the dictatorship and brutal repression of the people in the Dirty War would continue (over 15,000 people had disappeared in state organised terror), and there would also be a great war in South America. General Galtieri told his generals that after Britain's defeat, they would invade the Chilean islands in the Beagle Channel, starting a significant war between Argentina and Chile. Once again this was not a question of God favouring one nation over another, but God using the aggression of a dictator to bring about His purposes. Samuel was not the only intercessor who could see in the Spirit what God was doing. One of Samuel's friends and a fellow intercessor Michael Howard wrote: 'I came to realise after a while that it was not so much that the Lord wanted Britain to win that war, but He wanted Argentina to lose.' The Holy Spirit had told Michael Howard, "I want the defeat of Argentina because when she is defeated the military Junta will be overthrown ending dictatorship forever in that land, and with the overthrow of the Junta, the power of Rome will also be forever broken. No force will be able to prevent Me from freely presenting the Gospel in Argentina again."

In recession hit Britain, the nation was beginning massive defence cuts, limiting its ability to respond abroad and eight thousand miles away from home, it could only send thirty-four Harrier aircraft confined to win the airspace from the decks of two aircraft carriers!

The physical crisis was just the tip of the iceberg and Samuel could see, in the Spirit, where the real conflict lay. For some years the Holy Spirit had been preparing for a wave of blessing to sweep Argentina and now evil spiritual authorities in the heavenly realms were threatening to hinder the work. Once more, everything was laid to one side to seek the Lord's leading. Three specific petitions were given to pray. First, that there would be a minimum of bloodshed in the conflict. Second, that General Leopoldo Galtieri, the Argentine military dictator, would be removed from office. Thirdly, that there would be, as a result, a spiritual awakening in Argentina.

Once more, passages from the Scriptures, read carefully under the Spirit's anointing with occasional comments, brought inspiration to the prayer. It was always a question of whether the Holy Spirit was able to deal effectively with the situation. A group of Christians could unanimously declare that they believed without a shadow of a doubt that He could, but if challenged as to whether they were willing to be responsible to see that it happened through them that would be another story. Most would baulk at believing even for something much less – £100 ($160) by the end of the week if they had empty bank balances and purses! Real faith must become substance.

Samuel never treated these prayers lightly. Often he found great strength in considering the story of Gideon in Judges 6 and 7, whom the Holy Spirit came upon to liberate Israel. Judges 6:34, literally reads: 'The Holy Spirit clothed Himself with Gideon.' From then on, Gideon remained invincible and there was a resounding victory.

A section of the Italian Gardens at Derwen Fawr

The greatest threat in this war for the British was the substantial Argentinian Navy and Air Force. If Argentina could sink the fleet before it arrived, the war would be lost before it began! On the journey, the fleet had been overshadowed by Argentine surveillance aircraft, so there was no way to hide their position. They were a slow moving target and when they got near the islands the Argentinian plan of attack was launched. The Navy Cruiser *Belgrano* was sent on one side of the Falkland Islands, with an aircraft carrier on the other to catch the British Task Force in a pincer movement. The captain of the *Belgrano*, Héctor Bonzo said, "The navy tried to attack on the first day in the afternoon. They tried a pincer. The planes were ready on deck, ready to begin attack." But prayer was answered as the One who controls the weather took charge. Admiral Carlos Busser said, "Unfortunately something happened, it doesn't happen very often. The wind died down and it wasn't possible for the planes to take off from the carrier." God had intervened and the Task Force sailed through the trap!

The British fleet arrived in safely, but the naval threat was still serious. General Martín Balza said, "I had a conversation with the general and he told me that the Navy Cruiser *Belgrano* was going to put into port in Stanley Harbour." The *Belgrano* was a substantial threat, for its canons could fire shells over the island up to twelve miles away. It was also believed that it carried missiles which could sink the two British aircraft carriers, which would lead to a quick Argentinian victory. Therefore, on 2 May, London gave orders for the submarine HMS *Conqueror* to sink the *Belgrano*. This was the first and only time in history that a nuclear-powered submarine engaged an enemy in direct action during a state of war. The two escort ships failed to come to the immediate aid of the crew and tragically three hundred and twenty men died. The sinking remains controversial, but it transformed the naval war, as the Argentine fleet were neutralised and fled home.

Now the greatest threat was from the air and Britain was in deep trouble. The Argentinians had recently bought French built anti-ship Exocets missiles. These half-ton missiles were designed to seek out and destroy a ship from thirty miles away. On 4 May, the British destroyer, HMS *Sheffield* was hit in surprise attacks by Argentine pilots flying in French-built Super Etendard aircraft. Launching their deadly AM39 Exocet air-to-surface missiles; of the 281 men aboard, twenty were killed and twenty-six were wounded. These deadly attacks were launched six feet above sea level, below radar contact.

The success of the British liberation plan relied on having complete air superiority to provide cover for ground troops, but this was now impossible and the troops were sent in under fire. On 21 May, 3,000 British troops landed, as wave after wave of Argentinian planes flew over, and in four days, eight British ships were damaged and two sunk. On 25 May, the crisis peaked when the *Atlantic Conveyor* was hit and all nine helicopters onboard were destroyed. The troops on the ground had enough rations for just two days and were relying on the helicopters to take them into battle. Now with the South Atlantic winter biting and freezing temperatures at night, they had a four day march, under enemy fire from above and on the ground, with 120 lbs (54.43 kg) of kit on their backs through very uneven ground, with rain lashing down; but worst news was still to come.

Sir Galahad and *Sir Tristram* were packed with five hundred reinforcements to take Stanley, but forty-nine men were killed and a further one hundred and fifteen injured when they were hit. It was a very serious situation for the Expeditionary Force. All the secret predictions of an overwhelming British defeat were now coming true. The British Commander overseeing the liberation of the islands, Rear Admiral S. Woodward said later, "I was seriously considering ringing up home and saying, 'We're losing this.'"

In a meeting at the College, Samuel said, "There's need to believe now isn't there? The dictator (Galtieri) has had great victories. But we want it to be completed with a minimal loss of life. Will God do this? Will He give us liberty again to pray these matters?"

After days of gruelling marching, British troops who had hardly slept fought their way to the mountain fortress of jagged rocks that surrounds Stanley. Exhausted by days of freezing conditions, the battle ahead earned its reputation as a miracle of deliverance. For seven hours they fought up a bewildering maze of narrow gully rocks, as Argentinian grenades rolled down towards them, and snipers in hidden positions picked them off. Only eight weeks before, many of these men had been on duty in London, guarding Buckingham Palace and marching for tourists – now they were fighting for their lives, outnumbered by almost two to one.

At the College, where every news report was followed closely, Samuel led evening intercessory prayer sessions well into the night. Against all the odds these soldiers drove the Argentinians off the high-ground and the demoralised defenders poured into Stanley. By the 14 June, the Argentinians were surrounded, leading to a speedy surrender and saving many lives. Three days later, Galtieri was forced from power and the rule of terror in Argentina ended.

Samuel Rees Howells in 1989, age 77

In 1989, relations between Britain and Argentina returned to normal and with propaganda relegated to history, top British and Argentine Commanders reviewed the war and found several key battles, which if slightly altered, would have led to a British defeat. There were many miraculous events during the conflict, including many bombs that were unable to detonate when they landed on British ships! It is documented in photographic evidence and by eyewitness testimony, on at least fourteen occasions pilots dropped bombs which pierced the ships, bounced off, and at least one cut through one side and flew out of the other! Admiral S. Woodward said, "If they had all gone off, we'd have been defeated."

The Argentinians had occupied Stanley for seventy-four days and due to the conflict, three islanders, 255 British servicemen, and 649 Argentinians died. Had the conflict took longer thousands more would have suffered and the grief for those left behind intensified.

Now that the physical battle had been won, it was the College's responsibility to push home the true spiritual victory to transform Argentina. "The need is dire," warned Samuel in June 1982. "Think of Argentina. The Lord is answering prayer. The process has now been set in motion. Surely the outcome will be a democratic form of government and then there will be freedom for these dear ones. But the Holy Spirit must descend on these."

Samuel was also concerned for the Argentinian soldiers who had been used as pawns by their dictator. He prayed much, sent relief, and received reports back. "It's wonderful what the Lord has done in the Falklands and the blessing among the soldiers. We want to go over and above to help those dear people. I had a letter from a missionary and sent him some help. He wrote back stating every penny was spent on purchasing Bibles for the Argentinian troops."

The true purpose for British victory in the war was to prepare Argentinian hearts for revival, and this prayer of Samuel's was accomplished as his intercession for revival in Argentina bore fruit. The Argentine revivalist Claudio Freidzon explained how defeat prepared the nation's heart for a Christian outpouring. "It was the sorrow and suffering of our nation that prepared hearts for the Gospel. The Malvinas (Falklands) War left a tremendous wound in people's hearts. We lived through days of tension and deep sadness as a consequence of the death of many innocent boys in that frigid place. Our pride was shattered by defeat. In the spiritual arena, this situation led to the willingness of many people to open up to the Lord." General Galtieri was removed from office, and democracy was restored in 1983. The threatened war between Argentina and Chile was avoided; many lives were saved, and all three prayers regarding the Falklands crisis were answered. In 1980, Bible believing Christians numbered only one million in the nation, but after the war, a real wave of spiritual blessing swept across the land; by 2010 there were four million true Christians!

Chapter Thirty-Eight

Rees Howells' Biography

Samuel never toured the world preaching, but he still helped touch the lives of millions of people by working with Norman Grubb to release a book about the intercessory life lessons of his father. To appreciate this legacy, we must now pause and look back to the 1950s and consider how Rees' intercessory burdens were recorded.

Norman Grubb was a true friend of the Howells family and he later became a trustee of the College. "God has given me wondrous blessing through two men," said Norman at the College. "I learnt by the Spirit through them realities which grabbed my life. One was C.T. Studd, the other was Rees Howells. While I lived with C.T. Studd, I learnt total abandonment. I learnt to live with nothing else in life, except Jesus and souls. From my beloved friend Rees Howells, I learnt a principle of the Spirit without which, humanly speaking, the Worldwide Evangelisation Crusade (WEC) of today and the Christian Literature Crusade (CLC) wouldn't be in existence; if I hadn't learnt from him the principle of operating faith. The ways of the Spirit operating by faith became real to me. The principle of faith operating on the basis of intercession – the faith of Hebrews 11."

Norman Grubb then explained how Rees Howells had helped WEC survive some of its worst storms. "When C.T. Studd died in 1931 we were in a helpless condition. That month we had thirty-five missionaries and we had £1 ($1.60) a week for that month. That was all we had! People said to us, 'You'd better give up. Your Founder is dead, the mission is so weak, give up.' But we learnt, mainly through Rees Howells to change our whole attitude and the Lord told us not to give up. The Lord talked to us about going to the world and we laughed. Here we were two missionaries at home, thirty-five starving missionaries on the field and the Lord is speaking to us about going to the world! How does anything get done? By faith of course! Faith is the ability, inspired by the Spirit, to believe something offered to you. It isn't I doing it, it is Him doing it." To help the WEC survive these terrible days, Rees sent great financial aid to them and under Norman's leadership it grew into a large missionary outreach, today with almost 2,000 missionaries, serving among one hundred unreached people groups and CLC works worldwide!

In a letter to Rees Howells on 18 September 1936, Norman Grubb wrote: 'I have often for years wished that someone could take up and write of your experiences and your life, and almost offered to do it myself.' After the death of Rees, Samuel was praying about getting his father's biography produced when Norman Grubb wrote offering his services: 'I do most keenly hope that God will guide you about putting Rees Howells' life story in print. I have felt so strongly that these marvellous stories of God's dealings with him through the years are just full of the teaching which the Church needs. The Church of Christ needs it all! I shall never be able to thank God sufficiently for all the light He poured into me as I drank in the inner teaching in all those experiences...It is so much on my heart, and that the glorious opportunity of giving the world some of the 'deep and sacred things' He taught Mr Howells may not be missed. I am at the service of the Lord and you in this thing.' Samuel replied: 'Only a few days before your letter arrived, some of us were discussing the matter together, and we were all of the opinion that you were the person most fitted for that great task. I can only repeat Nathan's words to David, "Thou art the man!" ' (2 Samuel 12:7).

In these important decisions Samuel had learnt 'always to get counsel from God before you act.' The people of the Spirit in the Scriptures had discernment and would pray only the prayers that the Holy Spirit gave. Each decision that Samuel would make in College affairs was only made after much waiting upon God.

Samuel's motive in publishing the book was to bless the Church with the principles of intercession that Rees had learnt and lived. In a further letter to Norman he wrote: 'While you were down with us in the summer, we agreed that we wished the book to be entirely in accordance with the will and mind of the Spirit.' Samuel also refused any royalties from the biography because he wanted the College to continue to be sustained by faith alone (Genesis 14:22-23).

There was more than adequate material to draw from and Samuel was able to produce the manuscript which Rees had already written as a testimony of God's dealings. In addition, several staff had written copious notes of meetings and provisional accounts of Rees' life lessons made by staff were also available. *Rees Howells Intercessor* was published in 1952 and circulation of the book worldwide, has challenged many to full surrender through the deep experiences of the Holy Spirit recorded with such clarity in the life of Rees. A more recent DVD is now also in circulation.

Samuel and Norman Grubb were deeply encouraged as letters flooded to them, explaining how people were being taught the principles of intercession by Rees' example and how they were now applying them in their lives. Some of these new young intercessors became friends with Samuel. Norman speaking at the College said, "It's also amazing, the way the Holy Spirit is using the life of Rees Howells all over the States today. Wherever I go, I seem to find people whom the Holy Spirit grips through reading about that life. Of course it is something that cannot be imitated, but experienced."

Chapter Thirty-Nine

Rees Howells' Teaching Legacy

When Rees Howells died, many believed that his greatest visible legacy would be the founding of the Bible College. However, Samuel's decision to work with Norman Grubb to release a book concerning his life lessons in intercession transformed this legacy. Countless numbers have been inspired and letters flooded into the College asking for more. In 1980, Samuel responded to one letter: 'You will be glad to know that we are still continuing with the intercessory ministry as it is described in the book. We believe that intercession is more necessary now than at any time.'

Doris Ruscoe, the first head teacher of the Bible College School, was now bubbling over to share her reminiscences of Rees Howells, with whom she had spent many hours of discussion during her early days in the College. Her book, *The Intercession of Rees Howells* was released in 1983. Samuel had received many reports of its progress and was pleased to have the first signed copy, having previously been asked to write a suitable preface.

With the hush of God's presence pervading the College prayer room, Samuel recalled the legacy of his father, "The Founder of the College had to spend days and days in prayer when he was 'climbing' in faith. Surely if he had to go back to God all the time, so must we. But it is worth living to raise a testimony. Shall we believe God? Have we seen Him in all His majesty tonight, in His power and His authority? In the light of that can we believe Him? Let us tell Him tonight that we believe Him for all our needs, spiritual, natural and physical. We believe Him."

Samuel's daily walk with God was always his priority and he fully understood that his entrance into the Divine Presence of the Inner Sanctuary of Hebrews 10:19-20 was conditional on passing through the Veil; that is to say, His flesh. At that point, he would say, the enemy watches you and seeks to spoil the 'abiding.' Quoting from several of his own expositions it can be seen how vital it was for Samuel to be living in the Lord's presence every day, John 4:46-54. "We were thinking of the Life which is still in the Son of God. John had a revelation of Him and to him there was no doubt that Jesus was God. The people of Jerusalem had to accept Him as such or nothing at all. In Him was Life but it seems there had to be a contact, there had to be faith on the part of the individuals. There was a release of Life when contact was made. The Lord perceived that this man had the faith. That was the only requirement, to have faith in the ability of this Divine Person. Again the Life was released and entered into that child and the child was healed. That Life is not dependent on time or space. This is the power and it is just the same today. We may live in Him today – this relationship is essential. We must make contact with Him. We are not going to partake of this Life if we are not walking uprightly. Satan would have us believe that this abiding is unnatural. Let's put it this way – it is the flesh that is the hindrance to us. We need to touch Him whatever is confronting us now" (Galatians 5:17).

When Samuel preached, it was not uncommon for him to read the Scriptures consecutively throughout a whole two-hour session, commenting here and there and pausing occasionally for a hymn. For some, Samuel's ministry did not 'tickle their ears' as they would have liked; usually those who were not used to trusting God even for their day-to-day needs, let alone in greater issues. Sadly, a life of prayer and faith holds little or no attraction for those who are at ease in Zion (Amos 6:1). In addition, in Samuel's international prayers, students needed to exercise personal faith to believe that God was intervening in world events. The father of lies always tries to fill people's minds with doubt (John 8:44), and in these big prayers, he would suggest that the answers to prayers they received were all just a big coincidence. Samuel's reply was to indicate that the success in their small prayers proved that God was working in the bigger prayers too; and over the decades what Satan called 'coincidences' became too numerous to be called anything else but miracles! God had worked, not once, but day-by-day for decades!

Raw faith will always be needed and Samuel once said, "If you lived at the time of the Saviour you would have to judge Him from what you could see and not from the historical standpoint of today."

Engulfed in challenges of faith from day one as the Honorary Director in 1950, Samuel knew first-hand what stress and burdens were all about, but the Holy Spirit would not tolerate those 'tendencies' – as Samuel called them. "No," he would say, "we must live in victory; according to the light the Spirit sheds on the Divine Person of the Son of God." An ounce of experience is worth more than a ton of theory, was Samuel's axiom to live by, a saying he picked up from his father. For those who had the privilege of knowing Samuel at closer quarters than most, here was a genuine, transparent individual, fully committed to God and willing to pay any price to see millions blessed.

After decades of leading the College into these truths, Samuel also welcomed to the College, some children whose parents had attended the School or College. What a wonderful experience to see young people discovering the same principles of faith in their own lives that their parents had once learnt (Ps. 22:30, Mal. 2:15).

Chapter Forty

Ethiopian Dreams

The College had forged deep links in the Spirit with Ethiopia since 1936, when the Holy Spirit had led Rees Howells to pray for the preservation of this ancient people who were threatened by invading Fascist forces under Mussolini's command. These bonds had been strengthened when the beleaguered exiled Emperor, Haile Selassie, visited the Bible College in 1939 and 1940, and marvelled at the Penllergaer Estate that had been purchased by Rees in his desire to help Jewish refugees. The Emperor had also sent several refined young men in his family to study as pupils in the School. Samuel was a member of the College staff by then, and always keen to welcome visitors, had taken a personal interest in their welfare.

The Lord had assured Rees of future blessing in Ethiopia through the promise of Psalm 68:31: 'Ethiopia will quickly stretch out her hands to God.' After prevailing in intercession, that victory was assured and the Emperor returned to his people in 1941.

Capable of experiencing intense feelings of compassion toward those who suffered for the name of Jesus, Samuel knew he had met a man with a true spirit of intercession for Ethiopia when he welcomed Gerald Gotzen as a visiting speaker to the College during the 1970s. Gerald's involvement in Ethiopia was deep and when Communism swept the nation, he did his utmost to encourage the persecuted Christians and earned the reputation of 'Mr Ethiopia.'

Ethiopia was devastated by many long hard years of famine in the 1980s, and Samuel prayed much for them. Finally Communism crumbled, giving way to liberty and democracy – allowing steady growth in the churches. Samuel would again give himself to pray for Gerald, who took full advantage of the country's new found freedom to arrange for consignments of Bibles, New Testaments, Christian booklets and books etc., to be printed and distributed in the land.

When Gerald testified at the College on one occasion, Samuel was animated. Afterwards, Samuel could hardly wait to declare with such excitement, "What my father prophesied I have seen and witnessed today." This was one of the fulfilments of Psalm 68:31. Ethiopia was stretching out her hands to God! Praise the Lord!

In a letter written to a friend in October 2010, Gerald writes: 'The first occasion when I visited the Bible College was in the autumn of 1973. I praise the Lord for this wonderful association over many years with Mr Samuel, Dr. Priddy, yourself and so many other beloved Christians. It was also the connection with Ethiopia and the regular support for the ministry, especially the Bibles that I received from the Bible College. I am firmly of the conviction that the Bible College under Rees Howells, and then continued by Mr Samuel and the staff in the ministry of intercession for Ethiopia, is definitely one of the main factors of the tremendous movement of revival and renewal. The seed of intercessory prayer was sown in tears of time over seventy years ago, and now we are witnessing this wonderful harvest and the Kingdom being established in Ethiopia today.'

During troubled times in Ethiopia, Samuel was alerted to the plight of the Beta Israel Community, known as Falasha Jews (invaders) by their enemies. Living in thatched huts around Lake Tana in Gonda, this unusual group of people with distinct Jewish origins were under attack. Samuel prayed much for them and the answer came when the Israeli Defence Force began operating a special plan to escort members of the fleeing Beta Israel community by covert means, into Israel. It was a slow process and eighteen hundred reached their destination safely in 1983. It was then that a carefully devised initiative named Operation Moses (Mivtza Moses), using Hercules Transport aircraft fitted to carry two hundred refugees at a time, snatched eight thousand emaciated, destitute Beta Israel citizens and flew them safely home to Israel. Flights continued from 21 November 1984 until 5 January 1985, when the operation was brought to a sudden end as a result of leaked news. Arab nations objected to this mass exodus, and over one thousand refugees were left behind. For many who had never seen an aircraft before, Exodus 19:4 took on a new meaning. "You yourselves have seen what I did to the Egyptians and how I bore you on eagles' wings and brought you to Myself." The small remaining remnant was later retrieved in operations Joshua and Solomon. For Samuel, this was yet another wonderful answer to prayer, for this ambitious deliverance could never have proved such a success without the assistance of the God of Heaven, who kept the enemy at bay and it had been a further opportunity to believe God for the impossible.

The College also had a friendship with another ministry which helped Jews return to Israel to fulfil their end time destiny. 'Let the redeemed of the Lord say so, whom He has redeemed from the hand of the enemy and gathered out of the lands, from the east and from the west, from the north and from the south' (Psalm 107:2-3). Gustav Scheller, a friend of Dr. Priddy, often visited the College during the foundation period of Operation Exodus, a ministry of assisting Jews to make Aliyah (to return to their Homeland from countries around the world) by ship. Gustav became the Founder Director and was much encouraged through Samuel and Dr. Priddy, who had both received the revelation of the Jews' destiny under Rees Howells' ministry during World War II.

Chapter Forty-One

What is Intercession?

Intercession, as Rees Howells showed Samuel, is the burden to become responsible for a prayer given by the Holy Spirit. Prayer opens the door for God to work in the world and for this reason the Lord taught His disciples to pray stating, "When you pray" (Mark 11:24). If the Church does not pray, the door for the Lord to work cannot be opened. However, Samuel also learnt that an intercessor cannot pray 'stray prayers.' These prayers are 'good ideas' which find their genesis in human reasoning. An intercessor can only pray as he or she is led by the Holy Spirit. This is the golden law of all intercession (1 John 5:14-15).

Intercession can never begin until the believer has surrendered all to the Lord. If there is one area which a Christian refuses to yield to the Lord, the enemy will have a foothold and will manipulate it ruthlessly to undo the work of intercession. The intercessor is never humanly perfect, but must be fully surrendered and always be 'willing to be made willing' to lay down whatever the Holy Spirit asks. The intercessor has to fully embrace the cost of discipleship. "But why do you call Me, 'Lord, Lord' and not do the things which I say?" (Luke 6:46). A surrendered life is the cornerstone of all intercession.

Rees Howells always taught Samuel and the College the principles of intercession through his life experiences. He learnt the Bible as the Holy Spirit made him live it. Before he began his life of faith, the Holy Spirit asked him, "Can two persons with different wills live in the same body?" Rees responded, "No, it is impossible." The Holy Spirit said, "I need a body I can speak through, intercede through and show the Saviour through!" Rees realised, "If He was to come in (and live Christ's life through me), I was to give way. It was a sentence of death!" (2 Corinthians 1:5, 9). But the reward of a life of full surrender is an intimate life in Christ. "The Holy Spirit will be your Teacher, Guide and Intercessor," said Rees Howells. "You will have to believe Him and you will be tested in your obedience. The Holy Spirit is a Personal Guide, but He will never guide where self is."

Rees taught Samuel that no-one can begin to intercede until he or she has received the Holy Spirit as a Person. If the Holy Spirit is going to live the life of Christ through a person, there must first be in the words of Rees, "A full and complete surrender of the will." The Holy Spirit is the Intercessor on earth; we are only His vessels. If we are full of self or the world, we cannot be full of the Holy Spirit.

After the believer has been suitably prepared, intercession begins when the Holy Spirit shares the burden with the surrendered vessel and then he or she must become entirely responsible to believe that prayer into being. The intercessor must learn that prayer means answer and cannot pray whatever he or she likes or feels. The intercessor can only pray as the Spirit leads them, and must learn to 'pray through' – to carry the prayer into everyday life.

Intercession is not only to set aside a regular time to pray each day, but a daily abiding in the concern. There is no escape from the intercession, day or night. When the Holy Spirit places the prayer into the intercessor's spirit, he or she must then be committed to it, whatever it costs and however long it takes. The Holy Spirit's role as the Intercessor on earth, praying through Christians cannot be minimised; He must have supremacy in the believer's life and in the intercession. It is He interceding, just as Christ is interceding on the Throne in Heaven (Romans 8:26-27, 34, Ephesians 1:20-23).

To make the prayer 'real,' the Holy Spirit leads the intercessor into a process of identification with the prayer, through encountering similar situations or by identifying with the subject. This process is costly and leads to the crucifixion of the flesh life. As the crucifixion of self proceeds, intercession begins to gain ground. In this context, intercession will always cost. The style or form of the identification with the situation or subject of an intercession can vary, but as we learn in the Scriptures, the Holy Spirit can take the intercessor to extremes. Isaiah, Ezekiel, Daniel and Hosea were all led into a costly path of identification as they prevailed in their generation.

The process of identification with the intercession leads to agony. As the prayer warrior becomes one with the intercession, the enormity of the prayer comes upon them. In the Garden of Gethsemane, the Lord's sweat was like drops of blood (Luke 22:44) as His identification with mankind was reaching its peak; the agony of bearing the judgement for their sins was coming upon Him with ferocity. For those who follow the Lord into intercession, the agony with the subject of the intercession may be placed upon the intercessor in stages, making them share the pain and suffering of those they are praying for. The process of identification and agony in intercession are not theoretical, but become as real and as heavy as the crises that are the subject of the prayer.

To maintain his or her place of intercession, the prayer warrior must abide in the Lord. The position of abiding is often a practical demonstration of the ongoing nature of the intercession. Abiding is the physical side of a hidden prayer. The intercessor may need to fast, give, or change his or her lifestyle or attitude, in order to prove to the Lord his or her willingness to abide in the prayer. As long as the intercessor abides in this practical obedience, the prayer continues to go through. The intercessor must always rely on the

Holy Spirit to teach him or her how to abide in God's will. It is the Holy Spirit who will lead an intercessor to 'pray through' and abide until the prayer is fully answered.

After identification and agony goes through, the intercessor enters into a prevailing place of prayer in God. He or she then receives the authority to prophesy God's remedy for the situation or subject that the intercessor is praying for and through. Once this authority has been gained in one position of intercession, the prayer warrior enters into the 'grace of faith' and is able to walk in the gained position of intercession; but only as the Holy Spirit directs for it to be used in other cases. The measureless realms of God's grace are open for the intercessor to prevail through and believe upon!

Intercession is completely voluntary and the prayer warrior is never forced into a burden; but if we choose to sing, "I surrender all," the Holy Spirit will take us at our word, or we shall be found to be lying, in what we call 'worship!' Once a prayer has been accepted, quitting is never an option. Therefore, the believer needs to be willing to enter into the next phase of intercession and the individual's readiness to pay the price is anchored in the love of Christ.

Intercession is costly and the intercessor will discover wave upon wave of evil as he or she prevails upon God, to bind the strong man and witness demonic spiritual systems broken. As the individual confronts the powers of darkness, he or she learns that there is death involved in intercession. There may be setbacks, confusion and defeats, but the focus is never just death, but upon the promise of resurrection. The Spirit of God is gaining ground all the time.

The principle of 'death and resurrection' is a reoccurring theme in intercession. A prayer may outwardly fail and be buried in death, but when the human mind is at a loss and reputations have been called into doubt, the resurrection life of Christ can explode with far weightier fruit than was anticipated. Sometimes after completion of an intercession, the Holy Spirit reveals the greater significance of the burden, as the full implications of the victory are unveiled. But before that happens, the outward 'death of an intercession' may lead to sharp criticism of the intercessor's prayers, prophecies or beliefs. In these circumstances, only the inner few can appreciate Jesus' teaching: 'Woe to you when all men speak well of you, for so did their fathers to the false prophets' (Luke 6:26). The intercessor will find that a great public failure gives him or her authority to make a claim on a substantial private victory! The Holy Spirit is always able to turn defeat into victory. When Samuel was at university, a friend wrote to him stating: 'The Director taught by experience 'the path of intercession...death, life, death, life. Except a corn of wheat fall in the ground and die!' We leave the meetings not knowing where to stand after being stirred inside and turned upside down by messages which simply come from the Throne. The blessing in the College continues to flow wider and deeper every day.'

Intercession in many ways is hidden. The world does not see the prayer until it is fully completed. Jesus Christ, *the* Intercessor, was misunderstood in His intercession. Not until after the resurrection did the disciples begin to understand why He came. Even then it was not until after His ascension that they began to understand His work as the great High Priest, who embraced death to destroy it.

On an international level, the final word on intercession is found in the Lord's Prayer, "Your Kingdom come, Your will be done, on earth as it is in Heaven" (Luke 11:2). Three of the great chapters on intercession in the New Testament are found in John 15, Romans 8 and Ephesians 6. The first chronicles the Lord's teaching to the disciples concerning the principles of the intercessory life of abiding, and Paul teaches the Romans of the Holy Spirit's supremacy in intercession in the Church. It is He, the Holy Spirit, interceding through the human vessel with groans that cannot be expressed. To the Ephesians, Paul explained that our spiritual struggle is never against human beings, governments or physical systems of power, but against principalities, powers, rulers of darkness and spiritual wickedness in the heavenly place. Only the Holy Spirit knows how to lead the intercessor to prevail in this spiritual realm and the intercessor cannot walk away from the prayer or find freedom until the Lord's perfect will has been applied (Luke 9:62).

Intercession is not an intensified version of prayer, but to lay a foundation for intercession, every believer must first know and apply all the conditions as revealed in Scripture for answered prayer. Christians and their leaders sometimes take the Lord's promises on prayer out of context and plead for answers with many loud cries, when the conditions have been ignored! Before we pray, we must first humble ourselves and make sure that our lives are right before God. We must repent of all sin. Trying to pray without repentance is totally ineffective (2 Chronicles 7:14, Proverbs 28:13, Rev. 8:4).

Some of the basic principles to answered prayer are:

1. We must pray according to God's will (Matt. 6:10, 1 Jn. 5:14-15).
2. We should pray with unselfish and right motives (James 4:3).
3. We must confess / forsake sin, in order to pray with clean hands and a pure heart (Psalm 24:4, 66:17-19, Prov. 28:13, 1 Jn. 3:21-22).
4. We should pray in Jesus' victory for God's glory (John 14:13-14).
5. We must have good relationships (Matthew 5:23-24, 1 Peter 3:7).
6. There needs to be unity based on the Holy Spirit's anointing but not compromise (Psalm 133, John chapters 13, 15).
7. Be persistent in your prayers (Luke 11:5-10, Luke 18:1-8).

Chapter Forty-Two

Spiritual Warfare for Eastern Europe

In the 1930s, Rees Howells said of Stalin, "The devil has used and may yet use this man to be the greatest foe to the Church that the world has ever known." After WWII, Stalin swallowed up Eastern Europe, forcing the people to live under a system of dictatorship within the Soviet Union (USSR) or the Soviet Satellite States. It was for the spiritual freedom of these enslaved peoples that Samuel Rees Howells prayed.

There are some prayers that find childlike release and there are other prayers that stay with the intercessor for life. In the 1950s, Samuel spoke on 1 Samuel 7:2 and reminded the College that for twenty years the prophet interceded for Israel. "Why didn't Samuel the prophet succeed in his mission in one year, in two years, five years or ten years? He didn't. There are times when we make that cry to the Lord when we are alone and it penetrates." Samuel explained that true intercession can last decades and along the way, there may be many setbacks before victory. "We shall have to be identified with the Saviour in His death and walk with Him, before we are identified with Him in His resurrection." Samuel taught that in the Bible, there are many intercessors like Jeremiah who were called to intercede for decades concerning God's will to be fulfilled. Little did Samuel realise that decades of intercession were before him for one cause – the demise of Communism worldwide.

Over the years Samuel had prayed for many peoples, nations and conflicts within the Communist world, but it was in 1962 that the full weight of the burden of intercession for the demise of Communism worldwide began to come upon him. All the other burdens in past conflicts in Communist nations led as an introduction to this intercession, as he gained greater positions of grace in each case.

The Holy Spirit introduced this burden to Samuel after his second missionary journey in 1962, when he went behind enemy lines and witnessed first-hand the horror of Communism. This journey and the people he met represented 'points of intercession.' Those whom he met with, prayed with, supported and interceded for were his 'points of contact' to become identified with. By standing with these believers, he was gaining ground in practical identification, as if he was standing with every person living under Communism. He accepted this intercession after he was looking at a photo of five Russian pastors who were imprisoned for their faith, and during the same period he was pondering Rees Howells' intercession for Russia during WWII. "It was on the basis of that intercession that

God spoke to us years later with regards to the USSR," said Samuel. The first recorded prayer of Samuel for the demise of Communism worldwide is dated to 3 July 1962: 'Prayed for the 900,000,000 under Communism.' This note announces the beginning of the titanic spiritual struggle that Samuel embraced for the next twenty-five years of his life! In this same year, Samuel welcomed to the Bible College, God's smuggler, a famous missionary who smuggled Bibles into Eastern Europe and beyond. In his diary, he wrote: 30 November 1962: 'Brother Andrew gave a wonderful account of the activities of God's servants behind the Iron Curtain.'

Samuel Rees Howells (inside doorway, right) at the Bible House, Istanbul, Turkey, with other men of God, 1962

As Samuel surveyed the Communist world, he saw that Satan had placed a stranglehold of impenetrable darkness over the millions in Eastern Europe, Russia and the Soviet Satellite States. In every corner of the world, the demonic hosts were working through the USSR to prop-up failed regimes, dictators and amoral atheistic rulers. In these nations, Christians were being terrorised by the state, churches were closed and the Bible was often outlawed. If these suffering people were to be reached with the Gospel, intercession would need to penetrate beyond the walls of the Kremlin and strike into the heart of darkness.

Samuel was in prayer for many peoples, nations and conflicts as they arose, but he always kept the spiritual liberty of Eastern Europe as a central theme in his life of abiding. "The Holy Spirit is working all over the world today," Samuel added, referring to several recent letters written to thank him for timely financial gifts sent to agencies distributing Scriptures to China, Russia and various countries of Africa and Indonesia. "Being one with Him is the secret."

Throughout this period, the intercession for the emancipation from spiritual slavery of the Eastern European peoples had continued. The burden for liberty was heavy and as the years went by, Samuel began to enter into a fuller realisation that he was interceding not only for those nations, but for the dark influence of Communism to fall all over the world – for true Gospel liberty!

Intercessors may find that the Lord speaks to His servants in a way that is mysterious and puzzling (Numbers 12:6, 2 Corinthians 1:9). Very rarely does the Lord give His intercessors the full picture of the burden that they are carrying. It can be normal to get one piece of the puzzle of intercession, to carry the prayer through, until a larger revelation is needed. This experience is a practical demonstration of the operation of the branch and Vine (John 15). Guidance and life are gently filtered down to His intercessors, giving them time to stop, meditate and pray on God's purposes. Intercessors do need time to stand back and look at a situation in its fullness. This path keeps them abiding and completely dependent on Him. In 1978 Samuel said, "Now there are these prayers. We want to continue the prayers for Eastern Europe. We want to continue these prayers for these countries. How can we do so? Only as we draw near. It is necessary for God to reveal these realities to us."

Samuel discovered in his burdens that the enemy would contest his intercessions and he found encouragement in the Scriptures, by others who had overcome satanic attack (Romans 15:4). The work of building the Second Temple was suspended for fourteen years because the enemy resisted the work and Samuel found his prayer for Eastern Europe was also withstood in the spiritual realm. These setbacks were often perplexing, just as Job was confused when his faithfulness to God caused him to be attacked by the enemy (Job 1:22, Job 2:10). "We have been perplexed often," said Samuel. "In great perplexity and in great bewilderment...until the Holy Spirit comes and He's the only One who can come to enlighten our minds when we are facing the impossible. We've had to wait on the Lord haven't we? Some of our prayers have been of the impossible nature, but God proved Himself to be the God of the impossible."

When the College experienced terrible grief in their identification with the believers in Eastern Europe (and as Samuel felt the pressure of the life-and-death decisions that the Soviets were forcing on Christians), he referred to Luke 22:31-32, "Simon, Simon, behold, Satan has demanded permission to sift you like wheat; but I have prayed for you, that your faith may not fail; and when once you have turned again, strengthen your brethren."

As God had saved and delivered His people in the past, Samuel had faith to believe that God would do it again in the modern world. He recalled God's miraculous deliverances from the hands of Pharaoh in Egypt and then, much later, through Isaiah's own ministry from the Assyrian monarchs. Samuel would remind his listeners that God Himself had raised up those pagan overlords in order to demonstrate for all the world to see, that by simply stretching forth His hand, they were utterly destroyed (Exodus 9:16). It is exactly the same today with respect to all the current world powers and religious systems and will be in the future, even when the antichrist is manifest. However, in each case, God must have a pure channel, as with Moses and Isaiah, through whom the Holy Spirit can exercise the commensurate Divine faith.

Samuel Rees Howells preparing lunch, Yugoslavia, 1962

Meanwhile, Samuel's abiding for Eastern Europe continued day in, day out, as the unspectacular aspects of life and ministry continued. Bills needed paying, problems had to be solved, paper work needed completion, and the students had their issues to be worked through. To outsiders, the story of these intercessions may seem romantic, but these burdens were a titanic up-hill struggle against the forces of darkness, in the setting of routine community life.

Chapter Forty-Three

Intercession Only

The path of intercession is a lonely one. Isaiah and Ezekiel were never free to forget their identification with God's people, and Daniel, who could have enjoyed great riches, was led by the Spirit to withdraw into fasting and prayer. Let's imagine the life of Jeremiah; do we really believe that it was easy for this weeping prophet to joke around and talk about casual things? Neither could Samuel.

For Samuel, dark clouds were gathering at home and he resorted to prayer. God was taking him along the pathway that all true intercessors have trodden through the centuries; that of loneliness, misunderstanding and unpopularity and for him, identification with those believers whose suffering he was sharing. In the past, Samuel could enjoy the strength he found in those who were leaders in the days of Rees Howells, but the loss of Dr. Symonds in September 1970 and his own dear mother, on 9 August 1972, increased his grief. Not all could understand the cost of intercession and there were hardly any he could fellowship with at these deep levels. Very few had walked this path (2 Corinthians 6:4-10). Meanwhile, Samuel did become a spiritual father to younger intercessors, like Michael Howard, and Dr. Sam Matthews, of Family of Faith, USA.

Samuel was experiencing for himself what it means for any real intercessor, as opposed to a praying Christian, to contend with the powers of darkness in order to see God's covenant purposes established in the world. He knew that the 'gates of Hell' (Matthew 16:18) could not prevail against the Holy Spirit's intercession. However, in correspondence he did share with a close friend that the pathway was proving a deep and costly one. It was a matter of looking to God for strength, not only for each day, but each hour.

Every night was spent in agonising prayer and intercession, but the Holy Spirit was giving him strength to continue. Samuel realised that it was an essential part of the intercession. Despite the awful cost it was unquestionably a privilege to be identified with the Master in His death and to become a partaker of the Divine Nature (2 Peter 1:3-4). When Samuel's leadership abilities were doubted, as far as he was personally concerned, he did not wish to continue in the leadership of the work a day longer than it was the Lord's will for him to do so. How many critics realised that or had ever walked that way themselves? On one trip in Wales, Samuel pointed towards a lonely farmstead and remarked with a broad grin, "What do you think; shall we buy a farm and come and live out here?" Being free of the burdens of leadership, especially for praying in the thousands needed to continue the work each week, was a temptation Samuel never succumbed to. He thought it must be lovely to live a simple life; but a life of intercession is never simple!

By this time, intercession had burned its way into Samuel's life and it soon became obvious to his congregation, whenever he touched on the subject in ministry, that he was 'on the inside of it' and knew from experience what he was talking about. Once he spoke out quoting from an article he had read, "The highest form of Christian service is intercessory prayer. The high water mark of spiritual experience is an intercessory life. I care not how emphatically you may boast of your spiritual experience and of the special gifts you have received, your ministry is void of power in the sight of God if you know not how to intercede on behalf of others. The Throne life is what counts." To emphasise his thoughts Samuel banged the pulpit and continued, "Apart from intercession you couldn't carry this place on (referring to the College). That is what His servant (Rees Howells) used to say and the work was far less complicated than it is today. I remember those last years of his life when he said that he used to get up in the morning feeling so physically weak and exhausted. He said that a man couldn't carry this place on for a day. Well, could a man carry it on today?" reasoned Samuel. "It is the Holy Spirit who is carrying the place, but He is seeking for bodies. That is the price you have to pay. Think of the people whom we have helped. One (referring to himself) is going back to the Throne. You may think it good if you lose yourself in enthusiasm in prayer (and most of us are guilty of that, we must confess!). Are you sure you are touching the Throne? If you intercede you are touching the Throne each time. That is the need, and we heard it every day and every hour with the Founder. That was the revelation. I believe, you know, that the importance, the significance of intercession was revealed to him by the Holy Spirit just as salvation was revealed to the apostle Paul in the deserts of Arabia (Galatians 1:15-17). That became His servant's ministry and it was on intercession that the Lord worked; and it is important to see that intercessions of the Holy Spirit are always made within the orbit – do you follow me – of the atoning work of our Lord, not outside of it, and it is by way of intercession that the Holy Spirit proves the fullness and completion of the atonement." (Isaiah 53, Romans 5:6-11).

These deep truths which the older staff members had learnt, through bitter experience during the war, needed to be revealed to the younger generation of Christians entering the final phases of the spiritual battles of the ages. There is no substitute. Samuel knew that he needed to guard these deep truths, without any distraction, no matter how legitimate any other causes seemed to be.

Chapter Forty-Four

The Fall of the Soviet Union

Throughout the years, Samuel learnt that he was called to a living intercession. His places of abiding and identification were designed by the Holy Spirit to make him share the pain, grief and struggle of those that he was interceding for. Now he had been interceding for the demise of Communism for two decades, and during this period, many events at the College would make the intercession real for him. In a practical sense, the Lord caused him to share the reality of the burden of those he identified with, by allowing circumstances at the College to make the intercession and identification real. When three classrooms at Glynderwen burned down on 4 April 1981, he felt the burden of believers who lost their churches and homes. When staff in the College died, he felt the loss of believers whose friends were martyred in Christ (Isaiah 57:1-2). The costly prayer for the Communist world had drawn a cry from Samuel as he had been identified with countless thousands of suffering saints, all of whose cries had not gone unnoticed by the Covenant keeping God.

Amidst his trials, Samuel declared in one Friday meeting in April 1979, "It is all right in fair weather to say that Jesus is King and that He is on the Throne, but things were very rough when the apostles wrote their letters." For many years, Friday was set aside in the College to pray for Eastern Europe, and Samuel read out many reports from friends who had risked border crossings to encourage the believers there. The news emerging was of such a phenomenal growth of Christianity in areas where it was hardly known a century before. The emptiness of life without God was a stark reality and proved the failure of Communism. Samuel solicited urgent prayer, especially for the dissemination of the Scriptures, because without the Scriptures and without a preacher, how could the people in the Communist world be saved? (Romans 10:14-15).

As God wove His tapestry through the lives of Samuel and the College fellowship, the silver thread of intercession became more evident. Reports from Russia told of underground printing presses where young Christians were committing themselves to work for life in the secret hideouts, never again to see the light of day, if necessary. The Scriptures meant everything to the Russian believers. Additional lunchtime prayer sessions were introduced at the College and Fridays remained as voluntary fast days when staff and students could meet for prayer for Eastern Europe and the Communist world. For Samuel, carrying the full weight of the intercession, there was a bitter price to pay as one by one fifteen key workers in the College died either through illness or old age. Samuel was identifying with believers in the Communist world, whose own leadership were being decimated by firing squads, deprivation and inhumane treatment in brutal prison camps. To make things worse, news came that the young underground printers had been discovered and arrested, and Samuel was deeply touched for them and their families (Hebrews 13:3).

Samuel was never able to walk away from the burden he carried for the demise of Communism worldwide, for those who suffered under it could not escape. Weighing heavily upon Samuel, were the letters he received concerning Christians in Communist prison camps. "Think of the corns of wheat that have fallen to the ground in Siberia," said Samuel in 1982. "I think it would be good if we prayed for these people. How can we pray effectively for these people in Siberia? We can only do so in the Spirit. We don't want to multiply words, they are vain. It's praying in the Holy Ghost that will touch these people" (Isaiah 61:1, Matthew 6:7, Jude 20).

In the College there was a 'real grip' in the prayer for the demise of Communism and each victory on the way served to strengthen the main prayer. Intercession was now breaking through and change was taking place. In 1986, Mikhail Gorbachev called for Glasnost (Openness) and Perestroika (Restructuring), a dramatic change!

Samuel's ministry through the book of the prophet Isaiah became very relevant as it had been during Rees Howells' ministry. With the threat of invasion from the Northern Kingdom and Syria hanging over the nation, God gave Ahaz, the new King of Judah, opportunity of His help which he refused. In chapter 8 the consequences of Ahaz's foolish stubbornness are spelt out as the Assyrians would sweep across Judah like a razor. Like flood waters, they would overflow the land and reach right up to the neck (v8) and then God would intervene. Samuel would relate Assyria to the Communist domination of Russia throttling the life of Eastern Europe. God had given Samuel three distinct prayers to pray:

1. That God would grant religious liberty in these lands.
2. That God would make it possible for the Christians in Communist countries to teach their children about God.
3. That God would make it possible for Scriptures to be printed and distributed in these countries so that everyone could have a copy of the Bible of their own.

It was not a political prayer; but it would change politics, because liberty would only come with the end of Communism in Eastern Europe, the Soviet Union and in the Soviet Satellite States!

In Isaiah's case, another forty years elapsed as the Assyrian threat increased, but his great intercession continued. Hezekiah brought sweeping religious reforms into the land – almost a revival in modern terms – as detailed in 2 Chronicles 29 to 32, but when the full force of the Assyrian flood reached the gates of Jerusalem, he found the situation more than he could cope with. He appealed to God in prayer and solicited Isaiah's help. Isaiah remained unmoved in these years of intercession till the end, because he knew without any shadow of doubt that 'the flood would only reach the neck.'

The word from God pronounced a conclusive end to the plans of Sennacherib, King of Assyria, "Because you rage against Me and because your insolence has reached My ears, I will put My hook in your nose and My bit in your mouth, and I will make you return by the way you came. He will not enter this city or shoot an arrow here. He will not come before it with shield or build a siege ramp against it. By the way that he came he will return; he will not enter this city," declares the Lord (Isaiah 37:29, 33-34). Samuel could see clearly before him, in the spirit realm, the picture of God putting a hook in their nose and a bridle in their mouth to turn them back by the way which they had come. Communism was doomed and he knew it – it was a matter of waiting to see the Communist Empire crumbling. Samuel was able to declare with confidence that the impregnable 'Wall' would crumble too. After seventy years of oppression, God's time had come. Samuel had entered the grace of faith.

In 1987, Samuel now aged seventy-five declared, "The Lord has said I may stop interceding for Eastern Europe and the Soviet Union. The Berlin Wall is coming down and they will all be free!" In the same year, he received a visit from his friend Michael Howard, who recalled these events in a letter: 'Each time I arrived at the Bible College of Wales it was always with the greatest excitement and anticipation of seeing Mr Samuel and finding out what the Lord had been saying. There was one most memorable occasion in 1987 that I shall never forget. I was taking tea in the drawing room (of Derwen Fawr House)...Mr Samuel walked in with his ever warm and most generous Welsh greeting, "Ah bach!" (a Welsh term of affection). His face was really shining like that of an angel. "Mr Samuel," I asked, "what has the Lord been saying to you?" With his hand raised in a familiar gesture of love, joy and victory he responded, "It is too wonderful – too wonderful indeed!" I was all attentive for I knew what an enormous burden Mr Samuel had been carrying for many decades for Eastern Europe and the Soviet Union. It was an agony that had consumed him, as does any burden that an intercessor carries from the heart of the Father. "The Berlin Wall is coming down!" he declared most precisely and significantly. "The Lord has heard our intercession. Eastern Europe and the Soviet Union are free." Samuel's declaration of faith is remarkable.

In 1987, Eastern Europe and the Soviet Union were not at liberty, yet in the heavenlies intercession had prevailed and the captives had been set free. This news had already been proclaimed in Heaven, now events on earth had to catch up! 'Forever, O Lord, Your Word is settled in Heaven' (Psalm 119:89). It was with this confidence that Samuel spoke in the present tense stating: "Eastern Europe and the Soviet Union ARE free." Samuel had now gained the position of intercession and was walking in the grace of faith. His confidence was found in one of his sayings, "The Holy Spirit is THE authority on telling the future. He is God and He has foretold everything accurately till the end of time" (John 16:33). In 1989, nine months before the fall of the Berlin Wall, Samuel wrote to an intercessor in the U.S. stating: 'The day of fulfilment is dawning and the whole world is going to feel the impact.' One month later Samuel said, "We must be obedient. We must be in that state of abiding and then we can ask what we will. Not for ourselves, but for others."

Three months later in June, the first major crack in the Iron Curtain opened, as Poland was allowed to vote and by September they were free. In October, liberty spread to Hungary. "We as a little company here," said Samuel, "in our weakness and in our extremity, we've had a burden for Eastern Europe. But we knew that we couldn't do anything at all. There was only One person that could break Communism. It was the Holy Ghost. The work in Eastern Europe is the work of God, nothing of the work of man. God is changing history and He's giving us opportunities we've never had before, and we believe that God has put His mighty hand on the Eastern European countries. I've just had this letter from one country stating that religious outreach is no longer a crime against the State. One of the most antireligious and atheistic countries made this announcement last night, granting the right for passports for foreign travel. God is truly at work. We must continue in earnest prayer until there is complete religious freedom in Eastern Europe. God is changing the whole situation for His own glory and for the uplifting of His Son. God the Holy Ghost is going to work powerfully undoubtedly in these lands."

Dr. Sam Matthews was staying at the College when the Berlin Wall finally and officially fell in November 1989. The evening before, as he was ministering, there was such a release of the Holy Spirit in the meeting that everyone knew for certain that a significant event had happened in the spirit. Samuel was seen later in ecstasy on the landing of Derwen Fawr House waving his handkerchief and declaring, "The Wall is down, the Wall is down!" The Wall certainly had come tumbling down – physically and spiritually. Samuel believed without doubt that many more walls would fall around the world as intercession is made through the prepared, consecrated lives of believers, and the Vision for the complete fulfilment of Joel's prophecy for the outpouring of God's Spirit on all flesh takes place.

Speaking in November 1989 Samuel said, "This is the ministry of the Holy Spirit Himself. When you think of what is happening in the countries of Eastern Europe. Who'd of dreamed that these events would occur in Eastern Germany. Just a few months ago, no-one (in the world) would have dreamt such a thing. The people of Eastern Europe are on the march towards freedom and true democracy. This is God's work, this is God's day!"

Two thousand years ago, Peter received the revelation that Jesus Christ 'has gone into Heaven and is at the right hand of God, angels and authorities and powers having been made subject to Him' (1 Peter 3:22). Now Samuel Howells was witnessing once again, that the intercessor can be grafted into Christ's victory, by abiding and following the leading of the Holy Spirit (John 15). Over the decades of intercession for the demise of Communism worldwide, there had been many setbacks, but victory was always assured. There may be postponements in intercession, but no lasting failure.

On New Year's Day 1989, Samuel said, "Every day incredible changes are taking place in Eastern Europe. The Bible has been taken off the forbidden list. That has been an intensive prayer of ours and a host of others for years and years. It seemed to be an impossible prayer, and how often the evil one taunted us and said that we were praying in vain. No prayer is in vain if it's offered in the name of the Lord Jesus Christ. Bibles and New Testaments are being conveyed over the frontiers in large supplies and Scriptures are being sent by post to the Soviet Union. Who has brought these changes? God Himself! God is working! God is magnifying His name and God is answering prayer. What an answer! These are the results of costly and prevailing prayer down the years."

With joy, Samuel spoke of the Christian prisoners whose plight he had followed for decades. "We praise Him for the prisoners that have been released. Think of those little families that have been divided for years, with their fathers and brothers in prison." Then in an emotionally strained voice he continued. "Most of them have returned home to join their families. Isn't that the work of God? Do you thank God from the bottom of your hearts for these dear ones? They are members of the body of Christ!" The tone of Samuel's voice and the tears that he was holding back showed how deeply he had been identified with the prisoners of Christ (Hebrews 13:3).

As the principalities and powers in the heavenly realm were routed, they withdrew in lightning speed, as liberty swept across Eastern Europe and the USSR. Beginning in 1989, Poland, Hungary,

Bulgaria, Czechoslovakia and Romania were at liberty. In 1990, East Germany was reunified with West Germany. When the Soviet Union was dissolved at the end of 1991, freedom shook Armenia, Azerbaijan, Belarus, Estonia, Georgia, Kazakhstan, Kyrgyzstan, Latvia, Lithuania, Moldova, Tajikistan, Turkmenistan, Ukraine, Uzbekistan, and the Russian Federation emerged. Communism also fell in Albania, Yugoslavia and even in Cambodia, Ethiopia and Mongolia! All over the world governments who received support from the USSR spun into crisis and sought inspiration from Western liberty. The ideology behind the system received a severe deathblow and Communist political organisations worldwide receded in membership or collapsed altogether. In fifty nations, there was a direct traceable response as the dark cloud of Communism withdrew. The U.S. then emerged as the world's sole superpower, strengthening Israel's existence in the Middle East.

The experts in the West were taken by surprise by these events, as Soviet leaders lost all control and credibility. Even the warmly regarded Soviet President Mikhail Gorbachev was shocked by the changes sweeping over his world, and his personal vision for a reformed Soviet Union capsized. Only the true intercessors and Christian prayer warriors worldwide knew what was happening. 'Surely the Lord God does nothing unless He reveals His secret to His servants the prophets' (Amos 3:7). By August 1991, the Cold War was history and those once obsessed with Communism were now free, and asked themselves, "What were we thinking?" The Scriptures were fulfilled: 'Casting down arguments and every high thing that exalts itself against the knowledge of God, bringing every thought into captivity to the obedience of Christ' (2 Cor. 10:5).

In 1992, as Samuel prepared to enter into his eightieth year, he received a wonderful gift, purchased through years of intercession, the return of peace. In early 1992, Russian President Boris Yeltsin visited Britain and said, "We don't want to consider the U.K. a potential enemy ever again." Then he signed an agreement to turn thousands of nuclear missiles away from British cities. This act freed Britain from any nation-on-nation threat for the first time since the end of Pax Britannia, the one hundred years of relative peace and prosperity from 1815-1914, when Great Britain was the world's superpower. Similar treaties were signed with the U.S. and other Western powers, ensuring a lasting settlement.

'This is the victory of the intercessor,' wrote Michael Howard in a letter. 'He knows that he can claim no glory for his travail, for all glory belongs to the Lord. But the intercessor has the deep satisfaction of the tremendous breakthrough and the task accomplished for the King.' In 1987 'there was not a shred of doubt in Mr Samuel's mind, and neither in mine, that this spiritual giant had heard from God and gained the place of intercession after some twenty-five years of battle. It was not simply about Eastern Europe and the Soviet Union being free politically, socially and economically, but of the glorious Gospel having free access into these lands which for so long had been bound by satanic Communism. This was the great victory of light, order and freedom over darkness, confusion and bondage. Yet again, true intercession had prevailed. Many may ask, "But what a price!" Yes, but the fruit of that price can never be measured in earthly terms. What a price Jesus paid for my redemption. Ah, but what fruit for such a price for the Lord.' 'He shall see of the travail of His soul, and shall be satisfied' (Isaiah 53:11). Samuel's twenty-five years of intercession for Eastern Europe were complete.

Samuel was quick to remind the College that there was no glory for them in the answer to these prayers, and they were not the only ones praying. "We saw the prayer answered, not only in response to our intercession," said Samuel, "but the intercession of these other dear people who have suffered so greatly in the meantime." Samuel rejoiced as their faith bore fruit and he continued to pray for the beloved Russian people. Speaking in December 1992, on the anniversary of the day the College received the Every Creature Commission, fifty-seven years previously, he said, "Hasn't He dealt with atheistic Communism? Who had dealt with it? God Almighty!"

The joy and glory that flooded Samuel's spirit were beyond measure, as he witnessed the dramatic changes in the world being registered in every Communist country. Once more it was proved that, for the intercessor, apparent failure in the past twenty-five years had not been the end, but the beginning (Romans 6:5).

Now that this intercession was complete, he wanted to press home the prayer for global Christian revival. "I know that the Holy Spirit is interceding for that vast country and for the Russian people so that they might have an opportunity of hearing and accepting the Gospel," said Samuel in 1992. "Are they not having an opportunity of hearing today! Their country is in a state of upheaval and confusion, but there is freedom for the Gospel! There is a tremendous response to the Gospel. Many are accepting the Lord as their Redeemer and Saviour. Do you remember what we prayed? We had the privilege of praying for about twenty-five years for Eastern Europe to be open! It was a stubborn prayer, but God answered it. It was nothing in us, it was all God. Shouldn't it be all God today! There was believing; believing of the Holy Spirit. Are we maintaining that believing? Isn't it for this that we are living?"

Chapter Forty-Five

The Charismatic Renewal

The last true Heaven-sent revival in Britain, when people fell to the ground on the roads weeping under conviction, took place in the Hebrides in 1949-1952, with Duncan Campbell. Since those days, many Christians had been crying out to God to endue them with power, to revive the Church and to reach out to non-believers. The statistics revealed that the Church in Britain was in decline. Much of this was due to watered-down beliefs and compromise. In response to prayer, God began to pour out the Holy Spirit in the 1960 / 70s, restoring the gifts to the Church and baptising His people afresh.

The Charismatic Renewal, which broke in 1960, proved to be a divisive, yet biblical issue, which emerged and passed through various phases. At the College, staff and students had varying church backgrounds and all visiting speakers were welcome in the pulpit. Occasionally in services a message would be given in tongues with interpretation and there were healings. Samuel himself at times pronounced a prophetic word, often concerning national issues. When very unwell he would call the 'elders' up to his room for prayer for healing, and the Lord would touch him (James 5:14). Several of the former students such as Bryn and Keri Jones and Alan Scotland were associated with emerging leadership in these circles in the U.K. Samuel prayed for each one, recognising the blessings and pitfalls that they faced.

Samuel pondered these developments in the Christian Church and sought to know how to pray for those involved. The charismatic experience of 1 Corinthians 12, widely referred to as the Baptism of the Holy Spirit, accompanied by speaking in tongues, was brought to the fore at the Azusa Street Revival in Los Angeles, U.S., in April 1906. Similar manifestations attended meetings in Britain at Sunderland in 1907, with Alexander Boddy, from which the first British Pentecostal movement began. These outpourings led to new denominations being founded, and Christians blessed by God often felt constrained to leave their old churches to be with others who had received a similar experience. The Charismatic Renewal led to an acceptance of the Holy Spirit's gifts that touched churches and denominations that had traditionally shunned or rejected them, and a new oneness was found in the body of Christ. BCW soon received students who came from churches that welcomed the gifts of the Spirit. After their two or three years of study, some students became staff members whilst BCW remained non-denominational.

Without doubt, there were many casualties in the developing

House Church Movement, as giftings were sometimes being expressed through unchanged natures. In some instances, the movement was bringing great disservice to the Christian testimony. So, without placing any restriction on the private exercising of the gifts of the Holy Spirit, which he had no authority to do, Samuel did express his wish, publicly and privately to some staff members who had been blessed through charismatic experiences, that the main College services should be focused around the intercessory ministry which was continuing. Repeating truths he had heard from Rees Howells, Samuel stated that to step into the realm of intercession was as different as an unbeliever stepping from darkness into the Kingdom via the gateway of the new birth. As with everything spiritual, it comes by way of revelation.

In sharing his heart privately, he referred to his views in this way. Paul mentions in 1 Corinthians 12:31: 'Eagerly desire the greater gifts and now I will show you the most excellent way.' "Sermons are very good," Samuel would say, "but they do not touch the nature."

As the gifts in the wider Church were often operating through people who had not surrendered *all* to the Holy Spirit, a cross-current was witnessed in some cases. Samuel always wanted to emphasise full surrender and he welcomed the Holy Spirit, not to bless, but to possess. "Have you overcome the temptations of the world? Is the Saviour in you greater than them?" he asked. "Will He live anything in you differently from the Sermon on the Mount? Would the Saviour in you live with sin after He has conquered and destroyed it?" Samuel reminded all that the Holy Spirit is God, and 'without holiness no man can see the Lord' (Hebrews 12:14); for God will not share His temple (our bodies) with corruption. 'Do you not know that you are the temple of God and that the Spirit of God dwells in you? If anyone defiles the temple of God, God will destroy him. For the temple of God is holy, which temple you are. Let no one deceive himself...' (1 Corinthians 3:16-18a). Our bodies and our spirits belong to God Himself! (1 Corinthians 6:19-20). Samuel was not indicating perfection, but a sentence of death before a holy God. "The Holy Spirit will never come out of the Kingdom to live with a corrupt nature," he said. "When the Holy Spirit comes in, man must go out. Two persons can never live in the same body. He will put the old nature to death and it will be a complete and total death."

Then, quoting 1 Corinthians 4:15-16 he said, "Even though you have ten thousand guardians in Christ, you do not have many fathers, for in Christ Jesus I became your father through the Gospel. Therefore I urge you to imitate me." Samuel would add, "It is fathers the Church needs." His aim was to reach upward and to believe for the "greater works" of John 14:12. That is exactly what was happening through his ministry around the world, although very few recognised the depth of ministry that was operating through him.

In Samuel's lifetime, there were many Bible Colleges around the world where students could learn to exercise the gifts of the Spirit, but there were very few who had learnt and understood the ministry of intercession, such as Rees Howells had experienced. "This is a privileged place here," said Norman Grubb at the College in 1979. "I don't know another Bible School that believes in the Holy Ghost. I don't mean the terms baptism, power and tongues. I love the men of Pentecost because they are alive; people who haven't had Pentecost are usually half dead! I love to be with people who have the Holy Ghost in the fruits and gifts, but what I say is this, don't stop half way! The gifts are not the Person. We need to go back to the Person. When you've got Him, you've got the lot. Someone asked me, "Mr Grubb have you been baptised in the Holy Spirit?" I said, "Yes I have praise the Lord. I've been more than baptised, I'm drunk on Him. I'm a Holy Ghost alcoholic!" We admire the gifts, but we admire the Giver!" (Mark 16:17-18, Luke 11:13).

Then Norman pointed to his head and said, "I'm not too keen on all the training up here. C. T. Studd said in the old days, 'Give me people who've got the Holy Ghost, any old turnip will do for a head.' Your turnip may be valuable, but don't make too much of it."

Samuel taught the College that the Holy Spirit wants to 'abide' in the life of every believer. There may be times of special blessing and outpourings, but the Holy Spirit Himself wants to live His life in and through surrendered vessels. It is this life, a life in Him, which Christians are called to. The gifts may come and go in meetings as the Holy Spirit enables them, but He, the Person is to remain in all His fullness. "Has the Holy Spirit been revealed to you?" asked Samuel. "Have you seen Him? If He has not, then why not?" Full surrender will always be the price of full possession; this was Samuel's message to the Church (Luke 14:26-33).

The variations, but unity in the Body of Christ was taught by Paul. 'There are diversities of gifts, but the same Spirit. There are differences of ministries, but it is the same God who works all in all. The Body is not one member, but many' (1 Corinthians 13:4-5, 14). The mistakes of the early days of the Charismatic Movement have been recognised and as the Movement matured, many witnessed fathers of the faith emerging, such as Alan Scotland, an apostolic leader of a global network of churches and the successor of Samuel Howells as Director of the Bible College. It was men such as Alan that showed the Church that the fruit of the Spirit is just as important as the gifts. Therefore, we must receive the Giver, in all His fullness, as well as His gifts (1 Corinthians 12, Galatians 5:22-25).

Chapter Forty-Six

Hope in South Africa

In South Africa, the system of apartheid, where Africans were treated appallingly by their Caucasian overlords, was an offence to God. Many Christians in South Africa were campaigning for and praying for change, and these suffering people were akin to the ancient Hebrews who prayed for deliverance from Pharaoh. Then in the modern world God's prophets cried out, "Let My people go!"

In 1986, Samuel Rees Howells, aged seventy-four, responded to an invitation to speak at a conference in Pretoria, South Africa. The conference was hosted by a Christian organisation with a multiracial evangelistic fellowship looking to God alone to supply all their needs, which also placed great emphasis on weeks of prayer before embarking on any of their campaigns. Their teams worked in the dangerous, troubled areas of the townships.

Samuel was deeply moved when he was introduced to Spirit-filled black African Christian women who had suffered much for their faith in that cauldron of unrest. Oblivious of all inner pain, their faces shone as they magnified the Lord Jesus through their triumphant broad smiles, so much so that the visitor from Wales declared that it was worth travelling all the way to Africa just to meet them. He genuinely felt the great privilege that was his. They bore the true hallmarks of Spirit-filled servants of the Living God and he knew that they were all one in Christ (1 Corinthians 12:13).

In one meeting, Samuel was reading and expounding from the first five chapters of Daniel with deep fluency and passion. The Holy Spirit had truly taken hold of him as he portrayed the vital part that Daniel's intercessory ministry played in laying the foundation for the Jews return to their land, following seventy years of captivity in Babylon. Samuel had the witness that the leaders present in the congregation, and many others, had received the Word and would be giving themselves wholeheartedly to see a turnaround in the destiny of South Africa. They would not be disappointed; the sinister system of apartheid was broken (elections were held in 1994), and against all odds (and many predictions), a bloodbath was averted. True intercession prevails every time, but remains a costly process.

Commenting on the proceedings later, Samuel affirmed that he had never before experienced the Presence of God in such a manifest way in ministry as he had that that night.

During his mission trip in Africa, Samuel was also driven to Rusitu, Zimbabwe, to the old mission station where revival first broke out in 1915, under Rees Howells' ministry. There he met Moses, an old

African Christian with a glowing countenance, who was able to lead Samuel to a certain spot and say, “Here the Spirit fell.” He was referring to the moment when, like thunder and lightning, the power of God had fallen on the congregation. Heaven had opened and there was no room to contain the blessing.

Samuel returned to the College from his trip to Southern Africa renewed in every way, inspired by the deep response to the challenges of intercession by so many who were prepared to pay any price to see the evils of apartheid destroyed. Speaking at the College he reminded them of Rees' ministry in Africa, “When I was standing in that little Church outside the compound, the pastor of the mission station said, ‘It was here that the Holy Spirit descended. He descended like a bomb, and they were all on their faces before God and that extended throughout central Africa and South Africa. Tens of thousands of people were brought into the Kingdom!’ ” Samuel loved this account of revival and mentioned the outstanding manifestations of the Spirit that were evidenced during that spiritual outpouring. Always wary of the counterfeit, Samuel would recognise this as the genuine article, which he was praying for worldwide.

He then reflected on some of the salutary lessons on the ministry received through the life and example of Rees Howells who had made it abundantly clear that in the spiritual conflict between God and Satan, both have channels and the warfare is fought through those channels. The Holy Spirit must find individuals who are totally committed to God's will, and they are bound to the will of God in every detail of their lives until the battle is won, or the intercession is through. The ministry cannot be undertaken without the Holy Spirit, who is the only living witness to Christ's atoning work on the cross, His resurrection and ascension. Only the Holy Spirit knows when the total victory is gained in each given situation. Unless the channel allows the Holy Spirit to deal with every facet of his or her life, the enemy will take hold and prevent victory. It is a very close walk with God leading to a complete destruction of Satan's power, a wonderful victory releasing much joy as the deliverance is witnessed on earth (Ephesians 1:17-23). The intercessor never comes out the same person; each intercession brings about a further radical change as the Divine Nature takes over. ‘He has given us His very great and precious promises, so that through them you may participate in the Divine Nature’ (2 Peter 1:4).

Through Rees Howells' ministry, Samuel had been deeply taught that these God / Satan conflicts will only ever be won through the ministry of intercession. The offer is open to every believer, and the Holy Spirit will take us as far as we are prepared to go. Samuel was certainly resolved to go as far as possible (Philippians 3:13).

Chapter Forty-Seven

War in Iraq

The final decade of the century had hardly adjusted to the many changes that were taking place across the world, when ominous events clouded the Middle East once more. On 17 July 1990, President Saddam Hussein of Iraq (who had sided with the Soviet Union during the Cold War), accused Kuwait of oil overproduction and theft of oil from the Rumaila oil field, and despite United Nations pleas, invaded the region on 2 August, seizing them. Ten days later Saddam denounced Israel on the radio and stated that if any action was taken against Iraq, he would bomb them.

Samuel followed the progress of this rapidly escalating situation prayerfully, as the UN Security Council issued an ultimatum for Saddam Hussein to withdraw by 15 January 1991 or face military action. On the surface it seemed to suggest a face-to-face conflict only, but the Lord's hand came powerfully upon Samuel and steered his attention in a different direction. Having enlarged his borders into Kuwait, Saddam was turning his anger towards Israel. Lethal Scud missile launchers, hidden in skilfully disguised bunkers, were poised to release their deadly weapons on Israel. Saddam, manipulated by Satan, hoped that by attacking Israel, he would provoke a war against them, forcing Arab nations to change their alliances with the West and possibly join him in a war of annihilation (Esther 3:8-11).

At the College, about to enter its new term in 1991, special prayer sessions were convened to consider this crisis as the United Nations deadline approached. "We find ourselves these days in our extremity," said Samuel "and we wouldn't take a step without the help and assistance of God." In a late night session on 15 January, Samuel commenced his reading from Ezra 1. The Lord moved Cyrus King of Persia to restore the Jewish people to their land which was the fulfilment of the Word spoken by Jeremiah. God's revealed will became reality through the intercessions of Ezekiel and Daniel, who, like Isaiah and Jeremiah, knew the mind of God for their generation. "They were pure instruments, there was no hindrance in the flow," continued Samuel. As he developed his ministry, those present in this late meeting sensed again that God was speaking through him, and guiding him in focussed prayer as General H. Norman Schwarzkopf, the Commander-in-Chief of U.S. Central Command for Operation Desert Storm, signalled the launch of a military offensive to liberate Kuwait from the Iraqi aggressor.

When the Holy Spirit came on Samuel in this distinct way, each phrase rang out from the depths of his being and gave no quarter for unbelief. He had seen the hand of God stretched out in the Communist world, following his twenty-five years of deep intense intercession, when satanic forces had resisted stubbornly. Now there were other spiritual forces to be broken in the Middle East countries, to enable tens of millions of people to receive salvation through Christ in the future. It was to be a work of God. "I believe we have the mind of the Lord in these matters," said Samuel. "As Paul mentions in 1 Corinthians 2:16, we have the mind of Christ. We cannot place our weight on anything else, only on the Divine Word."

In a late prayer meeting again on 17 January, Samuel developed the theme he had touched on previously. As soon as the returned Jewish exiles from Babylon commenced the rebuilding of the Temple in Jerusalem, Satan came in with all his force to prevent the progress (Ezra 4). He does that vigorously, for every phase in the development of God's plan, even today.

Profession / Profession: THEOLOGICAL TUTOR.
Place and date of birth / Lieu et date de naissance: BRYNAMMAN 31st AUG. 1912
Residence / Résidence: SWANSEA.
Height / Taille: 5 ft. 10 in.
Colour of eyes / Couleur des yeux: BLUE.
Colour of hair / Couleur des cheveux: DARK BROWN
PHOTOGRAPH OF BEARER
FOREIGN OFFICE
7 JUN 1948

Samuel Rees Howells' passport, issued in June 1948

Aerial bombardments began on 17 January and Samuel's concern grew. "In face of what is happening, we feel that Israel is in mortal danger. What does the enemy desire to do? To destroy Israel, and in the event of destroying Israel, the Word of God will not be fulfilled." Then Samuel recalled the events of 1948, when the College had prayed and Rees Howells' intercession bore fruit in the establishment of the State of Israel. "We have seen in recent meetings that it was God's will to restore Israel. We remember the prayers that we offered to that effect during the war years and in those succeeding years. The faith that God gave at that time to see them, for the most part, back in the land." Then Samuel focused on Israel's role in the end times as revealed in the Bible. "But Zechariah has told us what will happen in the land when God visits them, when the people are to see their Redeemer. It will be a wonderful day when the arm of the Lord will be revealed (Zechariah 12:10). The iniquity of that land will be removed in a single day. A Divine act and they will repent and will be born anew as a nation (Isaiah 40:1-66:24, Zechariah 9:16, Hebrews 8:8-10, Revelation 21:12). These are the ultimate purposes of the Almighty. The enemy at this time is challenging. Don't take it for granted because I tell you that prayers, even ordinary domestic prayers, sometimes baffle us. I wouldn't be honest if I told you otherwise. How many times during these past weeks we've been baffled, we've been at the end of ourselves – that is our experience. We only speak experimentally, not theoretically; we've proved it. We've gone back to God in our extremity and we have seen, not the hand of man but the hand of God, as it was manifested in the days of Haggai and Zechariah. Now there is an enemy," Samuel continued, and he was speaking very clearly about Saddam Hussein. "He is satanic and once he will see that the day is turning against him, what is the danger? He will unleash everything that he has in his armoury." Samuel's concerns were beginning to be realised on 18 January when eight missiles were launched at Israel. 'Pray for the peace of Jerusalem. May they prosper who love you' (Psalm 122:6).

Samuel was covering new ground in his intercession and was totally dependent upon the Holy Spirit to inspire and lead him through; "We are treading a path that we've never trodden before and we do not know exactly how much faith we require to believe these things." Apart from the men in the Scriptures, there were very few to whom Samuel could go back for inspiration in similar circumstances. Speaking on God's deliverance of Jerusalem from the Assyrian army, Samuel said, "We know that God has not changed. All He is looking for these days is people of the calibre of the prophet, who are prepared to believe Him in the impossible. Not to look to man and the threats of man, but to look to God alone. We've got a lot to learn. It's all right to take these things in theory, but are we conducting our lives as Isaiah did? Isn't it time for us to change?" 'Be doers of the Word…' (James 1:22).

Samuel was not making vague declarations, but was taking personal responsibility for the intercession. In the same way that he was obligated to pray through for the money needed to continue the College, he was carrying a burden to believe that Israel would be protected from the demonic spirits working through Saddam. Once again his 'small' prayers indicated the credibility of the 'big' prayers.

As tiny Israel was being pounded by Iraqi missiles, the U.S. urged them not to respond to defend themselves, because the Muslim nations of the coalition would effectively be fighting with their hated enemy Israel, against Iraq. Instead, on 24 January, forty percent of the coalition air sorties were diverted away from bombing key Iraqi targets to search for Iraqi Scud launchers. British Special Forces (SAS) were also sent to destroy them on the ground. However, the Scud attacks continued heavily to rain down on Israel, and General Schwarzkopf stated that seeking out the Iraqi Scud launchers was like "searching for a needle in a haystack."

In the prayer meetings, Samuel recalled those critical days during the war years when his father, Rees Howells, had led the College in prayer in the battle for an Allied victory. Samuel spoke of those wartime battles in private talks with his closest staff friends and they had made an indelible mark upon his spirit. They helped him find strength to press the spiritual battle to its end in this challenge, although every step forward required Divine inspiration. Those in the meetings were asked to consider placing their lives in the prayer, to allow the Holy Spirit to deal with any part of their lives. Samuel was deeply concerned too for the ordinary people who would be caught up on the ground, and for the many young men flying dangerous missions in over 110,000 sorties, and who could be facing death. Then there were the innocent civilians invariably caught up in these carnages of war. He solicited earnest prayer for them all, with the same sincerity and passion as we would like people to plead for us if we were facing similar conditions.

He reminded all, how during the twenty-five year intercession for the demise of Communism in Eastern Europe and Russia, it had meant a day in, day out involvement. The evil spiritual forces behind the scenes had to be bound, and only the Holy Spirit could do that, but the blessing that ensued across Siberia and the northern regions was beyond imagination. Taking encouragement from the past, in a powerful prophetic utterance from within, Samuel spoke again. "We firmly believe that through the agency of the Holy Spirit that power is to be manifested again in the Middle East. We are not praying in a fog; the Word of God will never fail." It was certainly a Kingdom battle and many participated in it during the following weeks and months. God's will had to prevail!

When these opportunities are given by the Holy Spirit to enter into Kingdom intercessions, personal response is very important and it is relatively easy to discern those who are 'in' and those who are not, even in a Christian community. How essential it is for the believer to be walking daily in fellowship with the risen and glorified Lord Jesus Christ through the ministry of the Holy Spirit. There were those in the Founder's day, Samuel recalled, who had been asked to leave the College for not showing interest or response in these vital spiritual exercises of intercession (Joshua 24:15).

The prayer deepened in the lives of those who were responding, and Samuel set some very pressing domestic prayers aside as he reached out to God for the faith required to see His purposes fulfilled. Samuel exhorted the students to follow the prayer diligently and as always, he urged them not to pray 'stray prayers' – that is, their own ideas – but what God was giving through the ministry. Stray prayers weaken a prayer meeting and should be discouraged, but you must be persistent, importunate, explicit and direct.

Samuel Rees Howells (left), age 29 with Tommy Howells (no relation) August 1941. Tommy Howells had been a miner with Rees Howells and was known as a man of prayer. Pupils of Emmanuel School affectionately knew him as Uncle Tommy.

Samuel reminded the College that doubt undermines prayer. He recalled how unbelief completely ruined the wonderful opportunity Israel were given to enter the Promised Land at Kadesh Barnea. It was theirs and God promised He would defeat every enemy who opposed them. Sadly only two, Joshua and Caleb, believed God. "There are great prayers that we are engaged in at the moment," said Samuel on 7 February 1991. "We are praying for the protection of Israel and we do not know what this evil man (Saddam Hussein) will do next. He may resort to extreme measures. Israel is as dear to God, as the apple of His eye and He means to make them a praise in all the earth" (Zephaniah 3:20). "If the enemy can cause that Word to fall by destroying Israel, He will do so. But we must confess that we cannot pursue a prayer of this magnitude in our own stride. We will not do so unless the Holy Spirit has anointed us and possesses us as He did with Elisha. We're just temples of His, but they must be clean and pure temples." Samuel was standing in the gap for Israel (Ezekiel 22:30). There was a physical war and a spiritual war, and he had to intercede to bind the strong man (Mark 3:27), from enlarging the war towards Israel.

On a strategic level, Saddam knew that Vietnam was a deeply painful experience for the U.S., and he calculated that he could win this war by inflicting punishing casualties on coalition troops. Just two years earlier, in March 1988, the Iraqi army had released chemical weapons on a Kurdish village in Iraq, killing 5,000 civilians. If he used these weapons on his own people, what would restrain him from using them on enemy troops from foreign nations? In response, coalition soldiers were trained with gasmasks and many suffered heat exhaustion, as they prepared for a chemical attack.

To avoid coalition casualties, there continued a prolonged series of air strikes for many weeks, but Saddam finally forced ground action as he created a massive catastrophe by igniting six hundred oil wells in Kuwait. The combined military force began an assault on 24 February to liberate Kuwait. Samuel prayed much for the American troops consisting of 543,000 personnel and Britain committed the second largest contingent with 43,000 personnel, 2,500 armoured vehicles and various Royal Navy vessels being mobilised. Under the cover of the aerial bombardment, General Schwarzkopf had secretly shifted the bulk of his army three hundred miles to the west, to invade not only Kuwait, but Iraq, in a left hook thrust to trap the enemy troops in Kuwait. But would this be another Vietnam War?

Iraq had one million troops, the fourth largest army in the world, supported by oil wealth. In the first major ground engagement in the war, called the Battle of Khafji, forty-three coalition servicemen died and fifty-two were wounded, just in liberating a small city. If the same casualties mounted in the rest of the war, tens of thousands of troops would be killed or injured; and secret U.S. documents now released indicate that coalition commanders expected one in three of the U.S. marines to be killed or injured! With one million troops, Saddam had the means to turn the war into a prolonged nightmare.

Samuel sensed how serious the war was and stressed throughout "this great crisis," as he called it, the need for strength to believe God. Prolonged prayer was directed by Samuel and his team to restrain the enemy from within, by binding the strong man in the heavenlies. Saddam had to be stopped from using the same chemical weapons which he used on his own people, and the one million Iraqi troops needed to lose the will to fight. If each one fought with all their might, coalition casualties would be very high.

When the main thrust into Iraq began, coalition commanders prepared for the worst; but instead of finding entrenched Iraqi positions and soldiers fighting with zeal for their homeland, a miracle happened as Iraqi troops surrendered en masse. The enemy melted away and General Schwarzkopf was concerned that the advance would come too quickly to fully encircle the fleeing enemy!

Prayer was constantly offered for the protection of Israel and the Scriptures already foretold what would happen to those who supported and those who attacked Israel. 'I will bless those who bless you, and will curse him who curses you' (Genesis 12:3). Saddam's eventual end would be coupled to this promise.

In a further declaration of faith on 11 March 1991, clutching the pulpit firmly Samuel spoke these prophetic words, "We are convinced that the time has come for the Lord Jesus Christ, who has died for mankind, to be uplifted not in some parts of the world, but in all parts. 'He shall see the travail of His soul and shall be satisfied' (Isaiah 53:11). There will be no rivals to the peerless Son of God...Abraham's covenant is still valid and also the Covenant that God has made with His Son. In the validity of that Covenant we are believing tonight and basing our full and entire confidence in it." Samuel was now moving beyond the immediate prayer for military victory and was believing for the impenetrable fog, which had taken captive over a billion souls, to be cut open by the illuminating power of intercession. He prophesied that one day, something will break in the spirit realm, releasing millions of lost souls in the Middle East and beyond to believe on Jesus Christ and be saved.

In the immediate crisis, Western military strength was now crushing Iraq's army, the fourth largest in the world. But the threat to Israel was still severe and Saddam still intended to deflect pressure from Iraq by dragging the Muslim world into war against Israel. "These prayers have not been completed as yet," said Samuel. "We have to continue diligently, earnestly, zealously in this matter. But how can we do so in our own strength? Elijah was weak; he didn't want to face Jezebel (1 Kings 19). But when the Spirit of God was resting upon him – could he have been afraid? Not at all. He was the representative of the Almighty. The strength is in God the Holy Ghost, not in the channels. We can only pray as we are moved and directed by the Spirit of God."

There were great financial burdens at the College that needed prayer, but now the Holy Spirit was broadening the challenge and Samuel was not to be deflected by lesser issues. "We have all got a long way to go," he added. "We haven't exercised the faith that Joshua exercised that day, (referring to the miraculous crossing of the River Jordan) no, not one of us. It was the faith of God." With the end of the financial year looming, the domestic pressures were mounting, and Satan was telling Samuel all the time to neglect praying these Kingdom prayers and attend to the financial needs. This was pressure that few of us have experienced, but Samuel reiterated the truth that it is easy to be deflected, but he had persisted. Then, in one late evening meeting he paused, "There have been some wonderful deliverances this week. We have never appealed to anybody, our minds have been engaged in prayers of the Kingdom. The week is not complete; there will be more deliverances on the way." God was fulfilling the promise: 'Seek ye first the Kingdom of God and His righteousness and all these things shall be added unto you' (Matthew 6:33).

As staff and students stood with Samuel, the believing of God would descend in the services, with the assurance that God had everything in hand. Countless miracles took place as the Lord mighty in battle intervened in the war. Prayer restrained the brutal dictator from using chemical and biological weapons against the troops, and the mass casualties that had been planned for by coalition commanders never materialised. It was one of the most one-sided wars of modern history! In total, only one hundred and ninety coalition troops were killed by enemy action, far less than any commander had dared to hope for. Saddam's cynical war had also tragically led to 30,000 Iraqi deaths. Hostilities were formally brought to an end on 28 February 1991 and ceasefire terms negotiated on 1 March, but these were not accepted until 6 April.

Forty-two Scud missiles were fired into Israel during the six week war, each with six hundred pounds of explosives raining down upon innocent civilians. Miraculously, only two Israeli civilians died and there are at least thirty documented testimonies from people who should have died in the attacks, but events turned fantastically to save them. In Jerusalem, the city where God dwells (Ps. 132:13-14, Joel 3:21), not one missile was able to hit and several missiles were blown off course to barren land or over water. One missile struck the only vacant lot in a city and another hit an empty factory. Official reports state that Israel was very 'lucky,' but we know otherwise!

Saddam, inspired by Satan, had intended to drag Israel into the war, causing a division in the coalition and forcing the Arabs to break with their Western allies. His plans failed, for there was no war against Israel. Operation Desert Storm had liberated Kuwait, but a deeper spiritual conflict had resulted in a more significant victory for the Kingdom of God, with the promise of future blessing.

The Gulf War crisis was the last 'visible' intercession at the College whose outcome could be practically measured. After this Samuel's burdens largely remained private and without a way to tangibly 'see' the impact of his intercessions, it became difficult for students to appreciate them. The carnal 'entertainment' factor of answered prayer at the College was now absent in international events and some critiqued Samuel's spiritual life as nil. As with Moses after the parting of the Red Sea, God's people easily forgot the miracles of yesterday. 'So Moses brought Israel from the Red Sea...and the people complained' (Exodus 15:22-24).

Occasionally Samuel spoke out against the doubts and criticisms with a familiar striking phrase. "Think of the prayers that have been answered! And sometimes we think that nothing is taking place." Then with passion he stated, "Everything is taking place!" It was unusual for Samuel to speak like this, for he had accepted many years before, to be used by God he had to renounce all confidence in his flesh and be prepared for his reputation to be nailed to the cross. He was following in the Lord's footsteps as He 'made Himself of no reputation' (Philippians 2:7).

Meanwhile, in the subsequent years, Samuel's deep commitment to intercession compounded and his veiled messages to students reminded them how deep he was secretly going. "How could we go on in the impossible, to deal with the things we are obliged to deal with day-by-day if we were not refreshed by the Word of God? Things can be so difficult. The expense is so great, but when the Holy Spirit makes Jesus real, everything becomes practical. That's not in theory, that's in daily living. There's no good talking about a lot of theory, unless we're proving it. That is our case day-by-day."

Dwelling on the costly path of intercession that Samuel was privately walking, he considered all these sacrifices in the light of the Lord's unmatched identification with all of mankind. "It's worth carrying these burdens," said Samuel. "However heavy they may be and they are very unpleasant. But it's worth carrying them. We shall never carry the burden that our Lord carried, particularly in the Garden of Gethsemane. We wouldn't be able to carry a burden of that intensity. There are burdens reserved for the children of God and if we refuse to carry them, if we refuse the impossible, what will the Lord tell us on the day of judgement? We are going to meet Him one day, our Redeemer and Saviour."

Perhaps some who consider Samuel's ministry may think that he was a 'super' Christian. But there are no such people; there are only empty vessels and God used him in measure to his surrender.

Chapter Forty-Eight

Faith to Open the Treasury

Samuel Howells learnt that God could open the treasury of Heaven to those who believe in His ability to provide, but God's abundance of supply will only be given to those who refuse to use this provision to indulge the flesh. The earthly symbols of success are loved by the carnal nature but the Bible reminds us to 'set your minds on things above' (Colossians 3:2). In fact, the Scriptures stress that the evidence of Christ's resurrection power working in us, is the change in our attitudes towards the symbols of worldly success. 'If then you were raised with Christ, seek those things which are above…not on things on the earth' (Colossians 3:1-2). The words of Jesus were real to Samuel: "Beware of covetousness, for one's life does not consist in the abundance of the things he possesses" and "no servant can serve two masters…you cannot serve God and money" (Luke 12:15, 16:13, 19-31, 1 Timothy 6:17-19, James 5:1).

On 9 December 1954, Samuel said, "We all have prayers. Can we go back simply and get the answers? The needs this week are very great, between £600 ($960) and £700 ($1,120). I was at it all yesterday and most of the night…these are realities. I want to help those people abroad this week and I am going to help them. Pray and continue to pray. Put every activity on one side and spend your time in prayer. If you get this now, it will make men and women of you. Why did our Lord have to spend nights in prayer? Because He is our Intercessor. It is in the secret place we are proved."

Samuel's preaching was practical and spiritual. He showed the students that the disciples never lived a life of self-indulgence; instead they refused the symbols of human prestige. Teaching on the spiritual calibre of John the Baptist, Jesus said, "What did you go out to see? A man clothed in soft garments? Indeed those who are gorgeously apparelled and live in luxury are in kings' courts" (Luke 7:25). John was a prophet and a man of God must be dead to the self-indulgences of the carnal nature. The flesh lusts incessantly after visible signs of achievement, but the Holy Spirit is grieved by pride. "Jesus was born in the lowest place," said Samuel. "He lived a life of a peasant in Nazareth. He wasn't brought up in a palace."

In the ministry of all the prophets, they never sought the accolades and rewards of fame. Daniel proved that gold and silver had no hold on him (Daniel 5:16-17). Elisha was offered wealth but he said, "I will receive nothing." This prophet did not want his ministry to be tainted by greed and when his servant betrayed this stance he asked, "Is it time to receive money...?" (2 Kings 5:16-26).

Samuel's attitude to money was similar. How could Samuel live an opulent life, living off people's tithes and offerings, when millions were unreached with the Gospel and countless believers could not afford a Bible? The people whom Samuel identified with were in the prison camps of Siberia, not in the million pound mansions of London. How could this preacher claim to be dead to the desires of this world, yet still possess the symbols of human prestige? When Samuel passed into glory, there was practically nothing that he could call his own. It was this private stance that gave him authority with God to make a claim on the hundreds of thousands for the Kingdom, which he needed for the College and to support all the overseas outreaches, missionaries and Bible distribution.

In his lifetime, Samuel needed enormous resources for the Kingdom of God. With this in mind he was astute in the handling of money received through Bible College student fees. For those unable to pay immediately for various reasons he was always prepared to subsidise. Students remained at the College helping with practical work, until they prayed through for the term's fees. Often this meant weeks, but staff prayed regularly until the full amount was paid. He had learnt and taught that every penny has to be prayed through. He discovered that God never releases substantial amounts to new ministries etc., in order to teach them to trust the Holy Spirit. Without the Holy Spirit's leading, they will build a work that has nothing to do with the Lord! This daily dependence put such restrictions on Samuel, that he was not free to have a 'great idea,' which was nothing to do with the Lord. Only through fasting, prayer and strict abiding could the work continue and then a fruitful work would be built. For Samuel, this was a daily abiding, as he fulfilled the biblical conditions for claiming answers to prayer. The flesh resists this abiding and screams, "Why can't the Lord just give me the money and I will get on with the work!" But what work will the flesh build (The Tower of Babel), if the person is not in fellowship with the Holy Spirit? 'If I have made gold my hope or said to fine gold, "You are my confidence"...this would be an iniquity deserving of judgement, for I would have denied God' (Job 31:24, 28).

Sometimes Samuel attended rallies or large meetings convened for visiting evangelists or those gifted with the healing ministry. He would often return to the College with a heavy heart. The main purpose of the meeting was overshadowed by emotional appeals for money, even secular style fundraising as distinct from honest appeals (1 Corinthians 16:1, 2 Corinthians 11:7-9). With that familiar twinkle in his eye Samuel would explain to students, "You won't emulate Rees Howells unless you've done it in the small things. You won't learn it by theory. You may know all the theory of the life of faith, but you won't walk it unless you've been tried. Don't try and get weak deliverances. Don't try and influence people, but influence God. The experiences that you will derive from those processes will never cease. The value will stand you in good stead in the future."

This spiritual exercise of 'touching the Throne in prayer' was one Samuel felt strongly was missing in the Church, and it was his desire that all the students passing through the College should learn. First of all it would commence with praying for practical needs, from a tube of toothpaste to fees for the term, but then it would progress to larger issues in the Church or nation, and eventually would lead to participation in world challenges involving God's Kingdom. Beside the hundred and one practical needs in the work, Samuel with his keen spiritual discernment was also deeply sensitive to the needs of the students struggling in their walk with God, often discussing each one with their resident tutor. Samuel sought answers for everyone before he finally switched off his bedside lamp in the early hours of the morning. Summarising the principles of faith, here are five requirements for consideration:

1. We must have surrendered all.
2. We must have been proved faithful with that which has already been given to us.
3. We must be prepared to use our own limited provisions (when led by the Holy Spirit and not by our own ideas).
4. We must be a generous and cheerful giver.
5. We must continue to give tithes and offerings.

Some believers who resist the concept of tithing, state that it is Old Testament teaching. Actually, it is a Kingdom principle highlighted in 1 Samuel 8:10-18. When Israel wanted to be like other nations and have a king, it was pointed out by Samuel the prophet that the principle of biblical kingship requires that the tithe (ten percent) of all possessions were the just claim of the king. As Christians enjoying the privilege of living within God's Kingdom, through Christ who is our King, we should automatically gladly ensure that ten percent belongs to the King. As Samuel had learnt through Rees Howells, there is a step further, a full and complete surrender of ourselves and all that we own to the Holy Spirit. What a wonderful privilege. It could be argued on a biblical basis that if we haven't put anything into the heavenly treasury, we cannot make a claim to take anything out! If you have not made regular deposits how can you make a withdrawal? The Bible states that there is seed time and harvest, and if there is no seed time, there can be no harvest (Genesis 8:22, Psalm 126:5, Malachi 3:8-9, Matthew 6:33, 22:19-22, Luke 9:23, Luke 16:10-12, Galatians 6:7, Romans 13:8, 2 Corinthians 9:6-8, 1 John 2:15-16). If we don't pass these tests from the Lord, we don't fail; we just repeatedly retake the test until we pass or die! Israel spent forty years in a desert preparing for their re-sit. Then, after we have met the biblical conditions, we can stake a claim in Heaven for God's provision!

The final rule of living by faith is to accept all the sacrifices and the provisions which the Lord supplies. Elijah's miraculous supply was sourced when he lived with a starving widow (1 Kings 17:9), and John the Baptist lived in a desert, eating locusts and wild honey (Mark 1:6). Sacrifices are always required to follow God. Jesus said, "The Son of Man has nowhere to lay His head" (Matthew 8:20), and the apostle Paul stated: 'We both hunger and thirst and we are poorly clothed...and homeless' (1 Corinthians 4:11).

Samuel believed that God would only release a claim to the heavenly treasury to those who had proved themselves faithful in the small things of God. His father had spent eighteen months being taught and tested by the Holy Spirit concerning the value of money. He was not allowed to spend money on anything that was not an essential. The test came for Rees when he wanted to buy a New Year's card for a friend and donor, but the Holy Spirit forbade him. After this testing period, Rees was never again asked by the Lord to give an account of his spending habits, for the lesson had been learnt. Samuel, having lived through the Great Depression, knew the value of money and would never waste it. He would convey his feelings strongly to staff members asking them to ensue that electricity, water and heat (especially the coal used for College boilers, later replaced with wood) were never to be wasted. This was relayed to students, many not used to such a strict regime. If a student was ever asked where he was trained he or she could honestly reply, "Knocks College!" (The College of Hard Knocks). Having learnt its value, Samuel knew that God would only release money to him if it was to be used for His glory alone. He learnt from his father Rees that he could not ask God to supply anything that he had not been willing to give to another. With these principles in-hand, Samuel staked a claim to God's promises of provision.

In the 1970s, Samuel spoke of the large financial deliverances that he had been given and said, "We have not been in touch with people. We have not written to people...and still God delivers! 'Seek ye the Kingdom and these things shall be added' – that is our daily experience. We are doing it hour by hour!" Some may believe this life is easy, but Samuel refuted this claim. "In the life of faith, we need the Holy Spirit. Answers to prayer don't come simply. If you need thousands and thousands of pounds and you're not in touch with anybody, I can tell you it's not as simple as that. You try! Try it and you'll find out that it's not simple. You become utterly dependent upon Him and upon the Spirit of God. But in our weakness and extremity He comes and helps and answers. What we need now is faith in Him" (Hebrews 11:6).

In his ministry of faith, Samuel believed not only for himself, but for many other organisations and missionaries around the world. Letters continued to pour in from all corners of the world, from missionaries and national workers with whom Samuel was in touch. The demand for Scriptures and Christian literature was so great. Samuel would read out in the meetings, quotes such as these:

- Thank you for your generous gift for Bibles.
- Thank you for your letter and for the gift.
- This place is full of Tibetan refugees, thank you once again for your timely gift.
- I have received your letter and a sum of money you sent to help the work here recently. Thank you very much.
- The Lord led us to move to a newly rising city (in Japan) where there is only one tiny church for 50,000 inhabitants. Thank you for your gift (2 Corinthians 8:14).

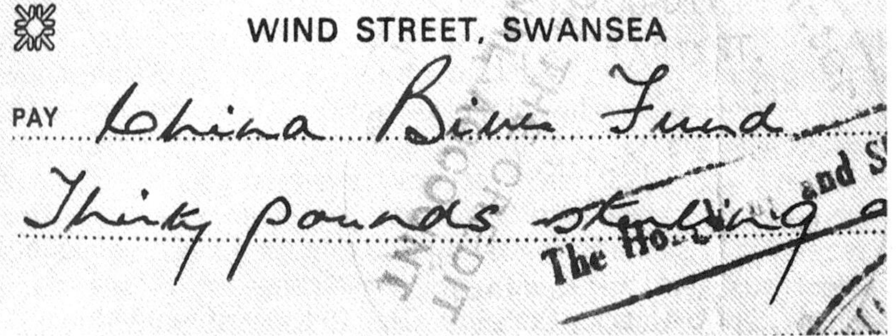

Section of a cheque (check) for Bibles for China, mid-1970s

The life of faith is often portrayed as something romantic, as if money floated down from Heaven. The reality however, is that Samuel's prayers had to reach the Throne. Afterwards Heaven had to find an obedient soul who could be moved to respond and give sacrificially. Delays can be the result of Christian disobediences in financial affairs but Samuel's faith was always in God and not in donors. This is when importunity in prayer and real faith triumphs. Through the decades, Samuel's life of trusting faith was maintained, and as the years passed, many of the early supporters from the 1930s (whom God had used to answer Rees Howells' prayers) were passing into glory. After the 1970s, the College's relationship with the wider Church was weakened and a new generation of Christians in Wales knew nothing of the ministry. In fact, many churches in

Swansea did not even know that the Bible College existed! The strain on Samuel to believe in God alone was very real. For most of his life, he did not know anyone, other than God who could meet the needs. There was no other possible explanation to the College's existence, than raw faith! "You have to find thousands and thousands of pounds every week just to carry on. Isn't this impossible?" said Samuel in 1982. "The expenses would swamp us if they were left to us. When we think how many hours during the nights of this week we have spent in the presence of God! We are going to spend hours tonight constrained by the Spirit."

The burden was heavy, but when prayer was answered, Samuel preferred to send money abroad rather than invest in the properties at home, and he received many letters of thanks for his support. 'May we thank you for your letter,' wrote one missionary in the 1980s. 'Our Scripture fund for India was almost finished. We had been praying for further deliverances and your letter arrived and the answer to our prayers. We have now been able to restock with Scriptures. Our teams are more active than ever. A great number of people have responded to the message of the cross.'

In 1989, Samuel said, "We want to thank Him for all He has done. It's been the most expensive year since the inception of the work. We haven't held one deputation meeting. We haven't written a letter to any person. We can truthfully say that. Not to one person. All has been committed to God alone and if He didn't answer the thing would fold up. More has been given this year for the dissemination of the Word (the Bible) than in any year past. Oh the work of grace! This is what His servant (Rees) wanted to do, but he didn't have the opportunity. Our hearts are full of praise. We love lost souls. Think of the tens of thousands of them that have been saved this year." In 1989, gifts totalling £260,000 ($416,000) were given away by Samuel Rees Howells to a number of ministries across the world (including some former students) ranging in size from £500-£5,000 ($800-$8,000). £260,000 from 1989 is the equivalent of £504,500 ($807,200) in 2012; this was a special year of giving!

In 1991, Samuel said, "I believe the expenses now, including the ministry (of giving to others), average weekly about £12,000" ($19,200, which is £624,000 / $998,400 per year!). "How can we deal with such a situation, (without partners, fundraisers and appeals?), only by the anointing of the Holy Spirit. Let alone all these other big prayers." Samuel had no newsletter, no list of donors he could appeal to, no radio or TV ministry to ask for partners and no wealthy benefactors. In addition, to teach the principle of faith to the students, Samuel subsidised their fees by two-thirds, making BCW the cheapest college in the West! The same principle of faith that Rees Howells had lived by, Samuel followed, but the burden was very real. "We need the Holy Ghost in these matters or we wouldn't be able to cope with them at all," said Samuel. "We confess that. We are seeking His help everyday."

At the end of 1991, Samuel reviewed God's faithfulness to the College. "Forty-one years ago He took His servant (Rees Howells). The testings down the years have been great, sometimes overwhelming. But we have proved throughout the grace and sufficiency of the Lord our God. This is our testimony. Hitherto has the Lord helped us. From a human standpoint, we never make any appeals. We never held a meeting. During the last forty-one years, not a single meeting has been held on behalf of the work here. We appeal to God and God alone and we leave all the other matters in His name. But it's not an easy matter. We have to be renewed everyday. The anointing of yesterday is not sufficient for today."

On 26 December 1992, Samuel looked into the eyes of the elderly intercessors who were sitting before him, who had responded to the Every Creature Vision in 1935 and said, "I was thinking again on this special day, of the day when the Vision was given. We always go back to it and draw comfort from what God did on that great day. We always find something new. He (Rees) was coming to these meetings straight from God's presence, and Mrs Howells who knew the Spirit's ways with him, was conscious that God was preparing him for something." Samuel then reminisced how Rees received the Every Creature Vision and how they all became responsible to intercede for everyone to hear the Gospel. "All who took the vow with him would be bondservants for the rest of their days for this one task to intercede, to go, to serve others who go," said Samuel. These were not words; they were Samuel's life and sitting before him with the students, were the remaining intercessors who had taken the vow. "They were to be responsible for seeing that every creature heard the Gospel," said Samuel. "Finances would be needed in abundance, but the one who gave millions to David for the Temple, would give the same to those who are building a far more precious Temple. Buildings not made with hands, eternal in the heavens."

Samuel was often criticised for neglecting the College buildings, but he reminded them why he had preferred to give to others abroad. "It is only the Holy Spirit Himself that can enable us to withstand the enemy and to go right through. God knows that we are not so much concerned about ourselves and our work here; but rather about the commission of giving the Gospel to every creature. It was that consideration that counted each time" (in every prayer, giving and in intercession. During the intercessions for various wars and conflicts, the College was not praying for itself, but for Gospel freedom). "You cannot bring self into this prayer," warned Samuel, "In any shape or form, you must be dead to everything. Are we dead to everything? Are we dead to public opinion? Are we really? We must be dead to everything and alive to God and to His Kingdom."

After speaking about the heavy financial burdens of the College Samuel said, "Our main burden for this time is always for the Kingdom. The Lord knows that we never prayed so earnestly for these domestic affairs as we have done for the Kingdom. We pursued that prayer for Eastern Europe for about twenty-five years. It was hard at times; the enemy taunted us as he taunted Elijah. But we continued in His grace. We saw the prayer answered. God will open mainland China again, and we firmly believe that it is God's will and God's purpose to open these Islamic countries. We declare that again in His presence. That is what we believe."

"It is important that we believe God," said Samuel in 1997, "despite the circumstances in which we find ourselves. It's easy to make these statements if we are not personally tested. But if we are tested, God expects us to believe Him at all times."

Samuel always praised God for the strong Christian heritage owned by many countries around the world. Christians in these lands had given liberally to support Gospel endeavour. However, since World War II society had changed dramatically and in many cases the interest in supporting world missions had declined. Samuel aware of this, determined to increase his efforts, particularly in a fresh intercession which was gripping him day-by-day. This was to provide Christians around the world with Scriptures of their own. Whilst Christians in the West have ready access to many translations, there are millions of people without their first copy or without a translation in their own language. Despite the great challenges in the College, Samuel determined in his heart that this was the priority need. Having given everything to the Lord, including the right for the Lord to direct his giving, Samuel solemnly declared on one occasion, "Think of the economy, it's most unstable. We don't know when there will be a recession, not only a recession but a depression. Missionary societies will be the first to suffer. All these things will come again. The affluent society today is built on flimsy foundations. This affluence could disappear overnight, with mass unemployment. That will come back again!" Despite the turbulence in the economy over the decades, God always provided. "Has He failed us once?" asked Samuel. "Not once. Everyday He has furnished our table. He will continue with that Divine supply. We don't believe it will ever be exhausted."

Chapter Forty-Nine

Emmanuel School

'Retired' was never a word that Samuel or the College staff had considered in their early days of enthusiasm and expectation. Carried along by the river of faith that the Founder's ministry had created, they could see all the time, with their spiritual eyes, the whole world being reached with the Gospel in their lifetime, to herald back the King. That was the essence of the Vision which took them through the darkest of days, similar to the hope which the apostle Paul presented to the Thessalonians in their day (1 Thessalonians 4:13-18). Jesus had declared emphatically that, "This Gospel of the Kingdom shall be preached in the whole world as a witness to all nations and then the end will come" (Matt. 24:14).

Samuel Rees Howells was brought up in a generation where Christianity had penetrated the culture, convincing people that vows and promises made are sacred. The deepest form of any commitment that a Christian can make is a covenant with and before God. Samuel and his staff had made sacred vows to the Lord in 1935, promising to serve God till the end, without pay, living by faith and now many were elderly. Nonetheless, in practical terms the ageing resident teaching staff were no longer physically able to continue teaching in a very vibrant Emmanuel School. Dr. Priddy had retired as head teacher in 1980, at the age of seventy-two. That generation made remarkable sacrifices and they had been (and were being) replaced by younger employed teachers, more able to cope with the changes in the developing educational system. Costs for running the modern school in a very competitive local environment were escalating. The issues of retirement of resident staff, and in many cases the death of key resident workers (another twenty were called Home during the 1990s), were added burdens for Samuel and he was anxiously monitoring the rapidly rising costs.

The original vision for the School was to provide a home and education for children of missionaries. The School for missionary children opened in September 1933 and was able to protect many missionaries from the heartache of uncertainty, when their children could not go with them. It grew into Emmanuel Grammar and Preparatory School and for sixty years it served, developing into a first-class provider of education to children in Wales and from around the world. Family members of the Emperor of Ethiopia had studied in these classrooms, and thousands of memories were formed. In the 1960s, the School was still expanding with new buildings and it had 450 children, 50 of them being missionary children. However, as overseas educational facilities improved, the number of missionaries wishing their children to be in the U.K. decreased, and by 1993 there was only one.

Some staff members of Emmanuel Grammar School c.1970. 1. Norman Brend, 2. Miss Joan Rush, 3. Miss Ruth Williams, 4. Miss Doris Ruscoe, 5. Miss Valerie Sherwood, 6. Geoffrey Crane, 7. Dr. Kingsley Priddy and 8. Mrs Winifred Jones.

The School was highly regarded in the area, but was running at a considerable annual deficit since the mid-1980s and that could not continue indefinitely. Although financially the right decisions had to be made, the spiritual ministry of the School was an important consideration, as a ministry to young people would end. One trustee involved in the process was deeply troubled through the night and found strength in Isaiah 30:21. 'Thine ears shall hear a word behind thee saying, this is the way, walk ye in it.' Early next morning he was asked to see Samuel. "I hardly slept all night," Samuel told him, "and I believe the Lord was speaking." Before he could continue, the staff member shared his experience and they found an agreement in the Spirit concerning the decision. "If two of you shall agree on earth as touching anything that they shall ask, it shall be done for them of My Father which is in Heaven" (Matthew 18:19).

The closure of the School was announced in July 1992, causing great concern among many who recognised the School's value in the district. An Association ran the School for the academic year 93/94 but they too could not make the school financially viable. In August 1994, in Samuel's eighty-second year, the doors finally closed. It was hard to enter into the personal feelings of Samuel during this dark and difficult period since he shared his thoughts with very few (Mark 6:46). Several years previously, Samuel and the trustees had been led to engage the services of a national legal organisation, which provided round the clock professional advice, and legal services. Every step in the School's closure had been monitored by this group, who represented the College successfully in the legal wrangles that ensued in 1995, following appeals by teachers against unfair dismissal.

A section of Emmanuel Grammar School, Glynderwen House (back left), El-Shaddai (back right), fields, and classrooms (right)

As the latter 1990s proceeded and Samuel continued into his late eighties, he began to withdraw even further away from the public eye. Formal testimonies of his intercessory burdens and answered prayer became less frequent and the controversial closure of the School led to aspects of the College becoming seemingly defensive in nature. Visitors to the College were shocked at the deteriorating buildings and thought the intercessory work must have finished too.

Many years before, Samuel's lectures were handed over to others, even his much loved Church History. Samuel really was a very shy person and over the decades it was becoming increasingly difficult for newcomers to the College to feel that they could really get to know him as a person. It was possible to spend years at the College, yet have only an occasional brief conversation with him in private and many students felt this was wrong. The College seemed to have an unapproachable leader, only occasionally seen at a distance, unless in the pulpit. In addition, Samuel rarely appeared at the meal table, except when there were visiting guests, because of distracting conversations. Usually he remained in his room, at times without taking food at all. His normal diet was always simple.

For many students who had seen lively charismatic preachers, here was a College apparently without a Director; just a solitary, lonely figure who appeared at the pulpit several times a week, then disappeared. Although the older staff, who had spent years with the Founder, fully understood and appreciated that Samuel needed to be alone in this way (and that he was by temperament a retiring person), it did present a problem for the new students. It was difficult for many to understand what was actually going on behind the scenes, as Samuel concentrated on the major challenges which faced the development of the College ministry and intercession.

Samuel Rees Howells at Southbourne Evangelical Church 1966

One very sincere and much loved former student wrote: 'One of the biggest issues for me as a student was to comprehend the ministry of Mr Samuel Howells. I soon realised that under the peaceful atmosphere that pervaded the College was a constantly raging spiritual battle (Ephesians 6:12). I learnt from Mr Howells that prayer was more than words – it was a life poured out. I remember seeing the famous walk of Mr Howells on the veranda outside his room, where he would pace up and down, head bowed, in intercessory prayer. To me, this very misunderstood man of God became one whom I trusted and loved and had the privilege to get to know, and I feel, to understand in a small measure.'

Visiting preachers shared many testimonies with students, but as Samuel stopped sharing his, they were unable to be inspired by his life. Vague theological concepts (from books) rarely motivate people to believe for the impossible, but first-hand testimonies prove that the impossible is possible! Samuel had many of these, but he was protective of the wonderful answers to his prayers (Proverbs 20:5).

Chapter Fifty

A Deep Christian Walk

As the years passed and Samuel became elderly, he preferred to wear a dressing gown in the cold Derwen Fawr House, particularly in his own room, and it became an essential part of his uniform on top of his normal clothes. Throughout his life, Samuel was always turned out well, despite the austerity of the war years and he always wore a very traditional style of clothing, familiar to that generation. However, one local Gentlemen's Outfitters had heard that Samuel was finding difficulty in acquiring the traditional style of clothing, that gentlemen wore in their latter years. The Outfitter arranged to visit Samuel at the College and Samuel asked for a photo of this man's family and he committed himself to pray for them. Those prayers had a profound influence upon them, as all three of his daughters committed their lives to the Lord to serve Him in one way or another; and the Outfitter received 'a prophet's or righteous man's reward,' which is given to those who serve God's servants (Matthew 10:41).

Samuel never married and therefore did not have a family. His personal stand as a single man lay in the truths of Matthew 19:12, where Jesus taught that some people choose singleness to become completely devoted to the Lord. Samuel had faced this position of celibacy many years before and made an unqualified response. Samuel also recognised marriage as a very solemn, life binding union between a man and a woman before God; but he felt that young people would be wiser to seek their own ministry first, and the Lord would then guide them to find a suitable, supportive marriage partner in that ministry. Jesus warned that if we fill our lives with things outside of His will, they will keep us from Him. 'Another said, "I have married a wife and therefore cannot come" ' (Luke 14:20).

It was always very clear to Samuel that for people to become part of the Bride to the Saviour, He must become all in all to them. It is a position gained only through the process of death to the self life. Unless that process is worked out in practical living, they can only claim that position falsely. A deep and solemn silence would pervade meetings whenever Samuel touched on the life of Esau, who sold his birthright so cheaply (Genesis 25:29-34). The Holy Spirit will never fully take His rightful place in a person's life unless that individual has 'died' (Matthew 16:24, Romans 6:11, 12:1-2).

Throughout his ministry, Samuel Howells never lost the sense of responsibility for introducing the students (who studied for two to three years) to the deeper aspects of the Christian walk. He knew how essential was this section of the students' spiritual education, this window into prayer and faith. He himself was involved in bitter spiritual conflicts and he expected their full cooperation and attention in the meetings, in some of which he spoke for almost ninety minutes without a break. Normally such a quiet, gentle individual, in the pulpit he would speak straight, "Be careful how you conduct yourselves in these meetings. Be very serious. We are dealing with very serious matters tonight which require your full-time and attention. Behave yourselves (and pointing), I am speaking to you. There are great needs and it would be better if one spent time alone, but we have an enemy and we have to watch him. We cannot afford to have the spirit of levity when we are dealing with these weighty matters. He can come as a roaring lion, or he may come as an angel of light, so we need the spirit of discernment."

On the other hand, he would give himself to prayer for anyone in the fellowship in need or trouble, and as many will testify, dealt with them in great tenderness. Samuel would also read excerpts from letters received from friends all over the world whom he was supporting. He was touched by their suffering. "Their concerns are our concerns and we must stand with them. We think we are going to live normal lives, don't we? I don't think so. That is a false idea. Take heed to what the prophets said."

Satan constantly buffeted Samuel by asking him how he was going to cope, trying to do what large recognised missions were doing, by supporting so many individuals. His emphatic answer remained the same, "The Holy Spirit will help." Samuel reminded his listeners that Satan would always try to keep them busy all day thinking about themselves, when so many other people in need should have their prayers and support. However, to say words is one thing, but to produce the finances was another. To take hold of the promises of God for finance when you do not have the resources requires faith. In one meeting, Samuel thundered out, "Theories will not help you, I tell you that. You try it! You won't go very far, you have to live it out day-by-day, hour by hour. What I am telling you is very elementary, very rudimentary compared with the intercessions for the nations."

Here was teaching in the Holy Spirit that the young generation of today need to hear. There was a grip in it. Immersed in these intense spiritual conflicts and striving to believe God for complete victory in them was a realm some, even prominent believers, could not appreciate. He was often heavily criticised for being cold, aloof and distant, but he would recall comments once made by his father in similar tests, "When God is speaking to you and man speaks contrary, you don't want to be near them. I always keep those people at arm's length!" (2 John 1:9-11).

Samuel had learnt a hard truth in his life; if he was to find a place of peace in his mind to focus all his strength on intercession, he had to protect his 'thought life' from enemy attacks (Luke 4:1-15).

Misguided believers often think that spiritual warfare only happens at a distance, but the first battleground is always waged in the mind. Satan will bombard our minds with fear, doubt, negative thoughts and criticisms of others. When Christians have learnt to 'cast down arguments and every high thing that exalts itself against the knowledge of God' (2 Corinthians 10:5), the enemy may then send critical people to them in an attempt to fill their heads with thoughts which steal their peace and hinder them from focusing on prayer. Samuel would resist these attacks upon his mind (Colossians 3:15).

Satan even managed to manipulate Peter's flesh to attempt to place the idea of avoiding the cross into Christ's mind (Mark 8:31-33). Satan also planted a tare amongst the twelve disciples; therefore will it be any different in other ministries? To be able to serve God, Samuel knew that like Paul, he would not be able to please men (Galatians 1:10); and over the years Samuel had to lay much on the altar, including friendships and even College staff. He always accepted that trying to maintain popularity and serve the Lord is incompatible. Abram would not have been popular when he left a great city to risk all in the deserts, but he had personal victory.

Victory always begins in a personal way. It's not possible to bind the strong man in an international situation, if we are bound ourselves by unforgiveness or any other sin. We need to find victory for ourselves first, before we seek to gain victory for others. Every Christian should consider what they think about. We should not allow ourselves to dwell on negative thoughts which Satan drops into our minds, nor should we get bogged down in the cynical comments made by others. When this victory was gained by some students, the Holy Spirit revealed to them that the music they listened to and some of the media they consumed was also affecting their spirit. Instead of engaging in prayer, their minds were singing the words of a secular song or dwelling on something they had watched. Samuel knew that wisdom was needed (1 John 2:15).

It is equally true that Samuel and all intercessors need to be able to rest and enjoy the blessings of life in an edifying way. Saturday afternoons were certainly days of relaxation and reflection for Samuel, as he would occasionally slip into a nearby sitting room to watch the news on television, or especially if Wales was involved in an International Rugby match! Watching Welsh rugby (a game similar to American football) gave Samuel the opportunity to give his mind a rest from the issues which kept him up at night in intercession. There is no point being so spiritual that it leads to 'burn out' – physically or mentally (Mark 6:31).

Chapter Fifty-One

Overwhelmed and Exhausted

There are occasions when an intercessor can enter into a period of desperation. Unless carefully managed, the immense burdens of identification, agony, spiritual leadership and the daily demands of ministry can lead to 'burn out.' This was the case with Evan Roberts and has been for many others, including Samuel. His first case of burn out happened at the end of his first decade in ministry, but it was not the last; and this was also the experience of the prophets.

After his great intercession for Israel to be released from the spirit of Jezebel, Elijah had a breakdown. "It is enough! Lord take my life!" he said (1 Kings 19:4). God's remedy was food, rest and a new spiritual revelation of God's sovereignty, power and mercy (1 Kings 19:5-6, 11-18). Amos too found himself under terrible strain when a religious leader told the king, "Amos has conspired against you" (Amos 7:10). This undue pressure from religious leaders, the government and public opinion led him to cry out, "I was no prophet, nor was I the son of a prophet, but I was a sheep breeder" (Amos 7:14). The weeping prophet Jeremiah cried out to God, "You have deceived me," as opposition overwhelmed him. "I am in derision daily, everyone mocks me" (Jeremiah 20:7-9). The Lord Himself, in the final hours of His identification with mankind's sin cried out, "My God, My God, why have You forsaken Me?" (Matthew 27:46).

Rees Howells had also walked through the Valley of the Shadow of death and Samuel had witnessed every step (2 Corinthians 1:5, 9). As a son, he also experienced personally the attacks made on Rees. As all leaders find, everyone has an opinion concerning their decisions, when few understand what it means to have the full weight of responsibility upon them (Exodus 18:17-18).

At the College, many had challenged Samuel's ideas and style of leadership, but it will always be easy to demand new projects to begin when someone else is responsible to fund them! During these great intercessions, Samuel often came under attack from every angle and found himself camped out in the darkest valley of them all (Psalm 23:4). Writing once to his dear friend and confidant Dr. Thomas in 1960, he shared a little of the intensity of those experiences: 'The burden and tension lately have been well nigh insufferable, and if things continue I am afraid one would experience a complete physical breakdown. Sleep seems to have departed, and all one can do at present is to spend most of the nights in prayer and intercession. Incidentally, there are now just ten years since father was called home. That was an awful test, and the pressing needs of the work at that time, together with the great liability, seemed insurmountable. But God gave us the grace and strength to get through...The one desire father had before he passed on was to gather enough means to help needy missionaries who are labouring for God in the different parts of the world. Mother and I have now assumed this responsibility and we hope to give thousands away in the near future, for the help and support of these Christian workers. To be quite frank we have no other aim in life and I believe the Lord will enable us to fulfil this great task.'

Not for the last time would Samuel feel so weak as he pursued this very costly intercessory path. As one observer has noted: 'I remember Samuel as having a global interest in the work of God; his outlook was not parochial so much as international, neither confined to the past but with interest in the future.' Samuel carried the burden for world blessing and coupled with this were the domestic issues, dealt with through prayer, one by one. In the early years, the sale of Penllergaer Estate and the burden to gain suitable charitable status weighed upon him, along with the intercessions.

Knowing the many deep trials that he was experiencing, Samuel once counselled his congregation never to sing lightly the words of John Bunyan's hymn, 'He who would valiant be 'gainst all disaster.' He was referring particularly to the phrase, 'I'll fear not what men say, I'll labour night and day to be a pilgrim.' "How many are really prepared to follow like that?" was his challenge. It is easy to state we are dead to man's opinions, when no-one is saying anything about us, but Samuel had vocal critics on a regular basis. 'But God,' was a familiar vital expression in Paul's writings and Samuel's indomitable spirit enabled him to 'lay hold on God' once more.

When Samuel found time to get away, he did enjoy taking a few breaks in the Welsh mountains and beyond. Perhaps the most frequented trip for Samuel was to the 'bridge,' crossing a stream in the Black Mountains where his father had once held his hand up to the Lord and promised, "I shall not take a thread to a shoe latchet from any person unless the Lord tells me. I do believe You are able to keep me better than the Mining Company." That solemn transaction with God had been a foundation stone in Rees Howells' life and in the beginning of the College, and Samuel drew strength from every visit. It was God who had built and sustained BCW!

Nonetheless, in the economy of God, He will allow the intercessor to enter into situations that bring them to the end of self. These crises expose all hidden self-confidence and trust, nailing them to the cross. These painful crushing and breaking experiences bring intercessors to a place where they lose all confidence in the flesh, so they can enter into the inexhaustible realm of God.

Chapter Fifty-Two

Never Let Go

Samuel never 'forgot' the direction that the Holy Spirit gave him in the past. He did not receive a new 'word' or vision every month, but his whole life was shaped by several direct leadings from God and they lasted a lifetime. In one meeting in 1994, Samuel preached and shared the lifelong intercessions that shaped his call. He read from Ephesians and Colossians; familiar truths took on a new meaning, particularly as he pointed out that, although a prisoner for some five years, Paul was not mentioning the conditions of his imprisonment. He was not confined to the measurements of his cell, but was living above his circumstances – a man in Christ. Samuel continued, "The emphasis is on revelation all the time. The great mystery is that the Gentiles will be fellow heirs with the Jewish people." 'The mystery that has been kept hidden for ages and generations, but is now disclosed to the saints. To them God has chosen to make known among the Gentiles the glorious riches of this mystery, which is Christ in you, the hope of glory' (Colossians 1:26-27).

Then, for those who had ears to hear, Samuel explained many of the intercessions that were still gripping him; which he had never let go. "The burden now is that the dear believers around the world should be able to share these blessings with us" (by having a copy of God's Word). When Rees Howells died in 1950, God spoke to Samuel saying, "The gap is there. Will you fill it?" That was a long time ago, but the voice of God that day was very clear. Since then grace has been commensurate with every test.

"God again spoke to one as clearly as He spoke at the beginning, 'Give ye them to eat.' " Samuel had to take personal responsibility to support missionaries and Bible distribution around the world. "But Mark's Gospel says their heart was hardened (Mark 6:52). Make sure your minds are not closed to these things." Samuel was also responsible to carry the College on by faith. "You take this week, there are very heavy expenses to be dealt with. The electricity bill for three months is £2,400 ($3,840) for these buildings alone. I do trust we use electricity with care. We would be failures every day apart from the Holy Spirit. There is greater truth than you realise in the words that Jesus spoke – 'Without Me ye can do NOTHING' (John 15:5). Nothing is done without Him. There are other bills to be paid tomorrow also. Whatever the domestic needs, however, are we still remembering the ministry which God has given us to the world?" Then Samuel Howells listed many nations where he supported Bible distribution. "Further letters are going to Mozambique, Zimbabwe,

China, Israel, Cambodia, Poland, Mongolia and Russia and so it goes on, week by week. Do not be too active and then miss out on prayer. It is better to drop activities and to make time for more prayer. Spend time, not to pray for our own blessing, but to pray for others of the household of faith." Samuel was always very sensitive on this point, recognising that in some Christian groups the focus is upon what the Lord has done for 'us' alone. He pointed out that there is an element of selfishness and self-centredness generated. In his experience and that of his father, the Holy Spirit had always sought to reach out through them to others for whom Christ died. As they did so, their personal joy and worship increased all the time. "We do not want to forget these objectives," Samuel continued in his ministry. "If we seek first the Kingdom and His righteousness all these things shall be added. It is not what a person says that counts. No, you watch their conduct" (Matthew 6:33, 7:16).

Samuel had become a regular supporter of Christian workers, some of whom were former students, in about forty countries in the world, as well as sending substantial gifts to agencies distributing Scriptures particularly in India, Africa, Eastern Europe and China. In one year, he recorded 103 large gifts totalling £108,677 ($173,883). It was a mammoth task, repeated throughout the 1990s. A summary of gifts given over six years (excluding 1989) ending on 31 March: 1988, £33,913 ($54,260); 1990, £45,061 ($72,097); 1991, £52,717 ($84,347); 1992, £52,320 ($83,712); 1993, £34,719 ($55,550) and 1994, £39,847 ($63,755). These gifts total £258,577 ($413,723) and represent an average gift of £525 ($840), or £881 ($1,410) in 2012 sent to about eighty-two individuals or organisations per year.

There was further work to do for everyone and Samuel was supported by his team. On an editorial note, it is worth recognising that Samuel was only able to find the time to spend hours in intercession, because many of the practical burdens of leadership in the ministry were borne willingly by the staff at BCW. Some bore responsibilities for a range of duties, from arranging the Bible College curriculum, to teaching classes, the headaches of charity law, health and safety, governance concerns and the lengthy work of administration that came with the legal issues of the College. The editors recall that the College Principal, Richard Maton, took a heavy workload from the Director, which enabled Samuel to remain focused on the burdens of intercession. Without Richard Maton's assistance, Samuel's wholehearted dedication to intercession, night and day, would have been impossible. Richard, nearing seventy in Samuel's last few years, would often begin his day before 6am, working until the early hours of the following day. Nonetheless, Samuel was kept up to date on every issue at the College and had the last word on every subject, as he took personal responsibility for his decisions in directing the staff. His work of intercession was hidden, but not to all.

The ministry of intercession was the focus of the College, but there were many other practical realities of life at BCW. To run the three estates of Glynderwen, Derwen Fawr and Sketty Isaf, it needed many full-time staff living on campus. The intercessors in the meetings would also be responsible for various duties from cooking to cleaning, teaching to maintenance, from preaching to painting. Upon graduation it was not uncommon for students to stay on, helping until they had secured their future ministry. In addition, many of the lecturers at the Bible College were local ministers giving freely of their time to teach students. At the weekends, often a visiting speaker would be welcomed to one of the carefully prepared visitor's rooms. There was always activity and work to be done!

From the 1930s onwards and for several decades, hundreds of people lived on campus in a very austere community life – at one stage, nearly one thousand meals were prepared each day! There were over one hundred staff, plus a large number of Bible College students and the School boarders / missionary children living in various buildings. Glynderwen was the home of the School and due to limited space, children had to share small rooms and the attics of some buildings were converted into dormitories. Then in the day, the site would explode with life as the children who lived outside flooded the classrooms ready to learn.

In the latter years, after the School was closed and many of the elderly staff had been promoted to glory, the community reduced to less than seventy but it still felt like a very active, vibrant communal life, as staff and students lived side-by-side, seeing each other all day, everyday. All shared the facilities, from the washing machines to communal meals. The Bible College students were expected to begin their day at 6am, for devotions, with their first prayer meeting beginning at 6:45. In one week, students would be required to attend at least thirty meetings, from lectures to services, plus there was coursework, daily duties and two full mornings of chopping wood or cleaning etc. Every Sunday, pairs of students filled local pulpits of two or three chapels or mission halls of differing denominations in a maximum radius of forty-five miles from Swansea; to Cardiff in the east, Haverfordwest in the west, to Llandeilo and Abergavenny, both north of Swansea. Community life had its ups and downs, and not everyone was able to cope well with losing their freedom, privacy and personal space. To an outsider, it may have felt like another world, but community life developed and over the years Samuel guided this large ship into deeper waters.

Chapter Fifty-Three

10,000 Believers Possessed by God

Samuel often stated that Rees Howells had received "a unique revelation of the Holy Spirit." It was not that the Holy Spirit gave a one-off special revelation of Himself to Rees, but that he had made an unconditional surrender of himself to the Lord, enabling the Holy Spirit to work in and through him in an exemplary deep way. This offer, Samuel explained, was open to everyone who was willing to pay the price of total abandonment and obedience to the Holy Spirit.

Throughout his life, Rees Howells delved into the unplumbed depths of a life of faith, intercession and discipleship. The Holy Spirit revealed to the College that Rees was not going to be unique in his experiences with God; because he told them to believe for 10,000 other Christians, who would be 'willing to be made willing,' to surrender all to the Lord and obey Him unconditionally. When these 10,000 believers put all on the altar, they too would be completely filled with the Spirit, and the Spirit would take possession of every part of their being. 'The Lord possessed me...' (Proverbs 8:22).

The 10,000 was never set aside as a 'special spiritual' number, because the opportunity of full surrender is made to all who may respond, but it did represent a target of faith for the College. To protect a prayer from becoming incomprehensible to ordinary understanding, it is good to have a goal to raise one's faith towards.

Samuel and the young people at the College were the first to respond to become a part of the 10,000 that the Holy Spirit had laid on Rees' heart, and in the ministry of Samuel he too sought to teach each generation of students the lessons of complete surrender. He believed that the Lord would find his 10,000 surrendered vessels from all over the world. "See that the Holy Ghost has taken possession of you," said Samuel to the students. "Use any term you desire. You can use any of these terms the Baptism of the Spirit or the infilling of the Spirit etc. The important feature is that the Holy Spirit as a Person has taken possession" (Ephesians 3:19).

For Samuel, an act of total surrender to the Lord, allowing the Holy Spirit to possess his empty vessel, was the door to the often untouched life of complete fellowship with the Third Person of the Trinity. But as Samuel surveyed the Church, he was troubled that many Christians seemed content to invite Jesus into their lives, in order for Him to make their lives in this temporal world better. They were not going out into the depths of all that is possible in Christ, by inviting the Holy Spirit to live His life through them. This reversal of the Divine intention will ultimately lead to frustration and failure, which is always the experience of the Church devoid of the Holy Spirit's infilling and leading (Jude 1:5, Revelation 2:5, 3:19).

"Please don't misunderstand this," said one preacher. "But I think sometimes we make too much out of church – as a building we go to, thinking that we are putting in our time with God. The fact is this, we are the Church! We should be living this life everyday." The Holy Spirit does not want us for an hour on Sunday; He wants us every hour. He does not want to meet us weekly, but to live through us.

Samuel shared with the College that the Holy Spirit wants to possess every believer, so that Christ can live and love through them. On earth, only the Holy Spirit knows how to win souls, heal the sick and dismantle the demonic strongholds that bind millions. Jesus taught that the Church would need total dependence upon the Holy Spirit, who is His representative to believers, to be our Teacher, Guide and In-Dweller (John 14-15). If Jesus Himself was physically present in the Church, many would love to sit at His feet to listen and learn; but Jesus sent the Holy Spirit in His place and we should become completely dependent on Him (John 16).

To Samuel, allowing the Holy Spirit to live the life of Christ through the surrendered vessel was the broadest expression of the Christian life and the deepest reflection of the mystery that Paul wrote about: 'Christ in you the hope of glory' (Colossians 1:27). Throughout the Old and New Testaments, the revelation of God living His life through empty channels is reiterated; but the Church, so often content to live in the shallows can overlook the fact that Moses, Jeremiah, Isaiah, Peter and Paul all paid the ultimate price to become living martyrs for God. When a martyr lays down his (or her) life for Christ, a one-off offering of his human existence is placed on the altar of sacrifice. Yet the Holy Spirit showed Rees and Samuel Howells that there is a greater privilege and that is to become a living martyr; one who chooses to be dead to his own desires, in order that the resurrected Christ can live His life through him. Paul wrote about this position in Christ, when he told the Corinthian Christians, 'I die daily' (1 Corinthians 15:31).

The expression 'possessed by the Holy Spirit,' used in various translations of the Bible (Amplified, New Living, Darby, Revised Standard, New American etc.), has prompted many debates among scholars. The root word for complete possession as in Judges 6:34, 1 Chronicles 12:18, 2 Chronicles 24:20, means 'the Spirit clothed Himself with the individual,' later repeated in the lives of the apostles at Pentecost (Acts 2:4), and to the Gentiles (Acts 10:44).

The complexity of translating the Bible from the original languages into English has led to great struggles as scholars have tried to convey the original meaning into English vernacular. Some words are arduous to translate and the meaning of various words depends on context. Translation has always been a very difficult process. Imagine how difficult it must be to translate 3,000-year-old Hebrew and 2,000-year-old Greek into English! Finding a modern counterpart to express in English the *fullness of the Holy Spirit's indwelling* has often been hard. What does it mean when the Hebrew states that 'the Spirit clothed Himself' with people in the Old Testament? Scholars have tried their best to find accurate words and phrases but it must be hard to convey an experience, particularly if it is personally unknown. Perhaps the translation may technically be accurate, but the full meaning was not rendered. Scholars will always debate the exact meaning of difficult to translate passages from Scripture, but Paul recognised that only the Holy Spirit can give us true revelation of their original meaning. 'The natural mind does not receive things of the Spirit of God...they are spiritually discerned' (1 Corinthians 2:14).

When Rees Howells read the translations of the Bible that state, 'the Spirit took possession of Amasai' (1 Chronicles 12:18), and 'the Spirit of God possessed Zechariah' (2 Chronicles 24:20), he recognised this. The Spirit had taken 'possession' of Rees Howells, just as he had with these people in the Bible. Rees Howells was not trying to interpret Scripture based on his encounter with God, but his knowledge of the ways of the Holy Spirit with an individual, acted as a confirmation that the expert translators had found a more accurate way of expressing the original meaning from the text.

At home, some students had been taught they had received 'all there is to receive' at conversion; but this was not the testimony of the first Christians! Paul was born again after he was challenged by the Lord and he was convicted – then quickened by the Spirit, (John 16:7-8, Acts 9:3-8). He was 'sealed with the Holy Spirit of promise' (Ephesians 1:13). However, there was more. Three days after his conversion, Paul received the fullness of the Holy Spirit, (Acts 9:6, 9, 17). Many years later Paul wrote: 'Do not be drunk with wine, in which is dissipation; but be filled with the Spirit' (Ephesians 5:18). In Greek 'be filled' means to 'keep on being filled constantly and continually.' He desired that the Ephesians would be filled / possessed by the Holy Spirit, because he prayed that they 'may be filled with all the fullness of God' (Ephesians 3:19).

Samuel taught that the disciples were born again when Jesus breathed on them saying, "Receive the Holy Spirit" (John 20:22). But the Lord also commanded them to wait in Jerusalem, to receive the fullness of the Spirit, (Luke 24:49, Acts 1:5, 8, 2:4). Then, in Acts 4:31, they experienced another infilling! In the Authorised Bible (King James) an excellent contextual rendering of John 3:34

explains how Jesus was completely filled with the Spirit: '...for God giveth not the Spirit by measure unto Him." Matthew Henry's commentary states that Jesus 'had the Spirit, not by measure, as the prophets, but in all fullness.' John Calvin wrote: 'The Spirit was not given to Christ by measure.' Rees Howells explained this as 'being possessed by the Holy Spirit.'

Rees and Samuel Howells both used the expression 'possessed by the Holy Spirit,' but they were not trying to introduce a new doctrine into the Church, but rather to clarify the depths of the workings of the Holy Spirit in surrendered vessels, clearly revealed in Scripture. In recent history, many have been baptised in the Holy Spirit and spoken in tongues, but most did not give the Holy Spirit permission to fill every area of their lives, allowing Him to have all. There is an opportunity for a deep work of grace in our lives, and it penetrates far beyond the blessing of the gifts of the Spirit! Many Christians are chasing after the next experience, or the new wave that is sweeping the Church, but they are not fulfilling the conditions to meet the Holy Spirit in all His fullness. We seek experiences with God, but we have not met Him in a way that changes us forever. We are hungry for Him, but we have allowed ourselves to be satisfied with the passing shadow of His Presence. We have been touched, but not transformed. We have been blessed, but not possessed.

Samuel often used the expression 'possessed by the Spirit' to clarify that the experience in the wider Church of being baptised in the Holy Spirit is not the end. This experience is the beginning of the possibility of a far deeper walk with the Holy Spirit, who wishes to possess every area of the believer. If our lives are still filled with our own ideas, desires and love for the things of the world, there will be no room for God to fill us and live through us. But if we surrender ourselves to Him, He is able to 'take possession' of all we give to Him. In this way, Samuel taught that we can be 'possessed' by the Holy Spirit, because He possesses all of us and through our unconditional obedience, He lives His life and advances Christ's victory through our 'empty vessels.' There is no room for self.

We may state that we are full of the Holy Spirit, but in truth, we have only been introduced to Him. Only when we surrender all and invite Him in to possess, do we begin to learn what being filled with the Holy Spirit means. When we are baptised in water, the water washes over us; but to be filled we would need to drink the pool dry! It's the same with the fullness of the Spirit; many have been washed over, but not filled. We have been blessed, but not possessed. When we surrender all to the Lord and allow Him to live through us, His life and His faith then operates through our bodies. Possession is not the Spirit blessing someone, but the Spirit fully entering them.

The person voluntarily gives the Holy Spirit control, allowing Him to assume control. “Then the Spirit entered me” (Ezekiel 3:24).

Samuel was deeply concerned that some of the modern Church bears the characteristics of the Church of Corinth, which enjoyed His presence with all the gifts, but had little fruit. The carnal nature (or self) is far stronger than many Christians acknowledge. Many disobey the Lord on a daily basis, refusing to forgive and forsake sin because their lives are dominated by their feelings. Instead of obeying the Spirit, we state, “but I want or feel.” ‘In my flesh nothing good dwells’ (Romans 7:18). ‘Then a dispute arose among them as to which of them would be greatest!’ (Luke 9:46). It is a cross that the Lord has called intercessors to, not to a position of privilege (or a title) in the Church, which the flesh lusts for (1 Timothy 3:6).

“Two people can’t live in the same body,” said Samuel. “Either we live there or God lives there. The Holy Spirit is not going to share our lives. If He is coming in, He’s coming in to live His own life. He’s coming to live His own Divine life and we’re not going to bring the Holy Ghost down to our level, but He will raise us to His level.”

When believers invite the Holy Spirit to possess their lives, they do not lose their personalities, but day-by-day the Holy Spirit takes possession of them; spirit, soul and body. They are called to a daily renewing of their mind and actions, as the Holy Spirit leads them (Romans 12:1-2). As all of their own hopes and dreams are put to the cross, the resurrected life of Christ, the fullest life of all, can be expressed through their ‘empty vessels’ (Amos 7:14-16, Heb. 8:10).

Samuel realised that what we feed on will possess us. If we feed our flesh with its desires, the flesh will overcome our spirit and take possession of our soul and we will remain carnal. But if we feed on the will and Word of God, the Holy Spirit will lead us to starve the flesh, leading to its crucifixion, and He will be given access to possess and transform us. Samuel showed the College that the entrance fee to this life of possession by God is a complete surrender of self to the Lord. This decision involved a ‘one-off’ laying down of his life and rights; but the practice of allowing the Holy Spirit to possess every area of his life was ongoing. ‘Whoever of you does not forsake all that he has cannot be My disciple’ (Luke 14:33).

In the context of world evangelisation, Samuel perceived that if the Every Creature Vision was to be fulfilled, ‘normal missionaries’ (despite all their sacrificial work which they have achieved) could never complete the task. If every tribe, tongue, people and nation is to be reached with the Gospel, the demonic strongholds which have held millions captive for millennia would have to be bound and rendered powerless through Holy Spirit led intercession (Ephesians 3:8-11). After binding the enemy, their strongholds could only be plundered by men and women filled and led by the Holy Spirit (Mark 3:27, Matthew 3:11). The challenge ahead was immense and man could never accomplish this task. Therefore Samuel continued to believe that the Holy Spirit would find 10,000 Christians (and more) who would become 'living martyrs' for the Lord. Only the Holy Spirit has the knowledge and power to win the world for Christ, only the Holy Spirit can lead the Church into victory and only the Holy Spirit can win the world for Christ! Therefore if the Every Creature Vision was to be completed, the Holy Spirit would need to find men and women who would become His channels of blessing to the world.

The record in the book of Acts is often called, 'The Acts of the Holy Spirit' in theological circles, because the account always refers to the Holy Spirit. It was He, the Third Person of the Trinity who was leading the apostles and transforming the world. The Holy Spirit's supremacy in the life of the Church is clearly laid out in Jesus' teaching and was obeyed unconditionally by the first disciples. It was the Holy Spirit's outpouring that led to the first 3,000 converts in the Church (Acts 2). It was the Holy Spirit that led Peter to Cornelius' house to open the door of faith to the Gentiles (Acts 10). It was the Holy Spirit who through prophetic revelation told the Church to set apart Paul and Barnabas and send them out on their missions (Acts 13:2); and it was the Holy Spirit that forbade them to go into Asia, leading them to Europe where the Gospel thrived for centuries (Acts 16:6-9). The Holy Spirit was also central in the life of Paul (Acts 13:19), and his understanding of the Gospel which he wrote in his epistles, came from direct revelation by the Holy Spirit (Galatians 1:11-12, Galatians 2:2, Ephesians 3:3). No Holy Spirit, no blessing! Speaking on Acts 1:8, Samuel said, "The doctrine of the Holy Spirit is one of the most neglected aspects of Christian theology. Yet is a truth which is firmly embedded in Scripture and it was cardinal and unmistakable teaching of our Lord."

When the Every Creature Vision was first presented to the College in 1935, they believed that the Lord would find His 10,000 and a new age of the Acts of the Holy Spirit would begin. It was He, now working through empty vessels that would reach the world. These 10,000 believers would not go out and 'build a work' for the Lord, it would be He, the Spirit who would build His Kingdom through their complete obedience to Him. The Holy Spirit would lead and guide them, as He spoke to them in gentle promptings with an inner witness and clear guidance wrapped in love, joy, peace and patience. To save them from being led astray, the gift of discernment would be greatly needed to distinguish the difference between God, the flesh and the demonic counterfeit, (1 Cor. 12:10).

In their youthful enthusiasm, the College had once believed that every creature could be reached within a generation. Rees Howells was not the first to believe in reaching the world in 'this generation,' a phrase that became popular in the late 1880s. Men such as Hudson Taylor (China Inland Mission) and A. B. Simpson (Christian and Missionary Alliance) all preached the possibility of evangelising the world in their generation. In 1910, the first International Missionary Conference was held in Edinburgh, Scotland, its motto was: 'The Evangelisation of the World in this Generation.' It takes great faith to commit oneself to a goal publicly, rather than cynically retreating into unbelief and stating, "It's not possible."

The Vision Rees Howells received added great emphasis on individuals, for their responsibility in world evangelisation which meant a full surrender and consecration (Romans 12:1), coupled with power for service (Acts 1:8). "Go ye into all the world and preach the Gospel to Every Creature" (Mark 16:15), became the motto of the Bible College of Wales. However, for decades they found themselves interceding against principalities and powers that were challenging God's plan to reach every creature through many great wars and conflicts. These intercessions were costly and draining. As the decades drew on, Samuel had to lead the College forward into the future, with the knowledge that the intercession to reach every creature would now stay with them for the rest of their lives. 'For the vision is yet for an appointed time...though it tarries, wait for it, because it will surely come' (Habakkuk 2:3).

Over the decades, their faith and intercessions for the 10,000 were publicly rewarded, as they witnessed many former students go out into the mission field and experience revival. Former students have been involved with revivals and tens of millions have responded to the Gospel message under their ministry. Many of their converts have in turn brought up their children in the ways of the Lord and have been used to lead others to faith in Christ. This compound expression of faith is unstoppable and unsearchable. The blessing on their ministries was not the result of training at the Bible College, for many other students did so and have seen no fruit; but the blessing on their ministries was in proportion to their response to the revelation of the Holy Spirit. Very few of these former students use the phrase 'possessed by the Holy Spirit,' in their preaching, but the principles of possession are expressed as they speak of being filled with, anointed by or led by the Holy Spirit.

The revelation was not that there is one Bible College where all who want to be used by God must be trained, but there is One Person, the Holy Spirit who must be received unconditionally. The work at the grounds of the Bible College of Wales in Swansea would one day end, but the work of the Holy Spirit would never end.

Chapter Fifty-Four

Possessed by the Holy Spirit

In January of the first year of the new millennium, Samuel now aged eighty-seven, shared his concern once again that every student and believer should surrender themselves unconditionally to the Lord and give permission for the Holy Spirit to take full possession of them. "We've been thinking of cases in recent meetings when the Spirit of God took possession of ordinary people," preached Samuel. "We've been thinking particularly of the example of Gideon. In that era, Israel was being oppressed and Gideon regarded himself as the most ordinary person in the land, but when the Holy Spirit came upon him and indwelt him and made a garment of him, he wasn't ordinary. From that point on he knew that he had been appointed the leader of that nation and that victory was inevitable." Samuel was trying to make a clear point: The Holy Spirit had transformed a nation by one young man who surrendered himself to the Spirit. He could do the same with us today if we would pay the same price (Judges 6-8).

When Jesus was baptised by John, the Spirit of God came upon Him. "Why was there need for the Spirit to descend on the Second Person of the Trinity?" asked Samuel. "He was Almighty! He was sufficient for every eventuality! If Jesus needed the Holy Spirit, how much more us! Before we are effective in any way in God's service, it's absolutely necessary for us to be possessed by the Holy Spirit. That is absolutely essential; otherwise nothing will be done of any eternal value. Jesus needed the Spirit, and to think that He was *the* Intercessor! Jesus was then driven into the wilderness, but He returned in the Power of the Spirit...Did you notice that? He returned in the Power of the Spirit. The emphasis throughout is upon the Divine Spirit." Samuel wanted the students to realise that if they too surrendered their lives entirely to God, they might be driven by the Spirit into the wilderness of testing like their Lord (Luke 4:1-14), but when they would come out, they would be walking in the power of the Spirit! There is a big difference between claiming to have the power and exercising that power!

The heroes of the Old Testament needed the Holy Spirit and Jesus was led by the Spirit. What about the apostles? Just think of Peter, the Rock before he was possessed by the Spirit. During the Lord's trial, Peter went to pieces. However, at Pentecost, the Holy Spirit came upon him and he spoke like another man. "Was it the old Peter?" asked Samuel. "No. It was the new and transformed Peter. The Holy Spirit had taken possession of him and it was the voice of the Holy Spirit speaking that day. Not the voice of man."

After the apostles surrendered their lives to the Holy Spirit, He became their Teacher and Guide, just as Jesus said He would (John 14:26). The Holy Spirit then used the apostles as channels to reach the world with the Gospel. "Peter was the one used by the Spirit to open the door of faith unto the Jews on the day of Pentecost," indicated Samuel, "and some years later it was he who was instrumental in opening the door of faith to the Gentiles, as a result of his mission to Cornelius." Peter had to reject his own culture, in order to obey the Holy Spirit unconditionally and go to Cornelius' house (Acts 10). "The Holy Spirit told Peter that he was to accompany those people without any questioning at all, and he did so," said Samuel. The Holy Spirit was the missionary! Peter was the body – an empty vessel of the Holy Spirit. "At this time too, Saul of Tarsus had been converted," Samuel preached. "The Lord had sent Saul to Ananias to receive his sight, and to 'be filled with the Holy Spirit.' Those were the important words," he indicated.

"We know the way the Spirit led Saul. If a committee were in charge of Saul, they would have sent him back to Jerusalem to be instructed and be enlightened by the apostles there, but He didn't do anything of the kind. After spending some time in Damascus, Paul went to the deserts of Arabia. There were no human beings there to help and instruct him in the faith," Samuel observed. "He was there for years. Who was his teacher? The Third Person of the Trinity." Samuel said this sternly and then repeated it solemnly once more, "The Third Person of the Trinity! The next ten plus years were unquestionably a time of intense training by the Spirit. The Gospel that Paul proclaimed in the Gentile world was received by revelation (Galatians 1:12). He hadn't received it from the apostles, but from Christ Himself, through the ministry of the Holy Spirit."

The students sat quietly amazed, with their eyes pinned upon Samuel. Many recognised that a special anointing was resting upon him, as this elderly man shared with atypical exuberant passion.

"Who had trained Paul? Human beings?" asked Samuel. "No! But the Third Person of the Trinity. Is there a wonder that he was so strong in the presentation of the Gospel," remarked Samuel. "If he had received it from a human being, perhaps he would have wavered like some of the others. But he was steadfast. The Holy Spirit had revealed it all to him."

"Let us consider carefully the following words of Paul's testimony in Romans 15:19. 'Through mighty signs and wonders by the power of the Spirit of God, so that from Jerusalem and round about to Illyricum I have fully preached the Gospel of Christ.' " Now drawing upon his experience of travelling Samuel remarked. "That vast area, comprising of some of the most important and populous provinces of the Empire was evangelised just by the apostle Paul and a few companions! Was that the work of man?" Reverently he replied, "It was the work of the Third Person of the Trinity. It could never have been accomplished otherwise. Those vast provinces had been evangelised in a period of about a decade! It was the work of God, the work of the Spirit of God. Is there a wonder that the Holy Spirit kept the man for all those years in His presence, with very little outward activity? He was preparing him for this very great ministry."

"Whenever we read these passages we are under conviction," he said. "We will not follow in the footsteps of the apostles unless we have received the Holy Spirit and have been possessed fully by Him, as was the case with Paul." We have spent two thousand years attempting to accomplish around the world what the apostles did in the Roman Empire in a few decades. They reached the Roman world by surrendering to the Holy Spirit and following His leadings, but do we still trust in the flesh? Do we still have plans, strategies and ideas that originate in the human intellect?

The Holy Spirit is not an influence, but the Third Person of the Trinity. He is God. "The Lord spoke concerning the Holy Spirit as a Person," said Samuel. "Not in any vague sense. He did not say 'it', no...when HE will come." The Holy Spirit has a mind, will and emotions (1 Corinthians 12:11, Ephesians 4:30, 1 Thessalonians 5:19). The Holy Spirit wants to call apostles, evangelists, prophets, teachers, pastors, missionaries and intercessors. He is not only the gift Giver, but the Sender: 'Now the Holy Spirit said, "Separate to Me Barnabas and Saul for the work to which I have called them" ' (Acts 13:2). In the early Church, it was the Holy Spirit who chose people and sent them forth to the mission field! They were fruitful because the Holy Spirit was the evangelist! They were empty vessels.

Christians are always in danger of stepping ahead of God's will, especially those who have been called to serve Him. We may have been called, but if we do not welcome God the Holy Spirit into our lives and abide in Him, we will run ahead of Him and appoint ourselves to our own ministry. If we do this, we will unknowingly be promoting 'our vision' and 'our mission.' Due to God's grace, He may bless our best efforts, but it will still be a work of the flesh, because hidden motives are at work. Paul wrote about this: 'Let nothing be done through selfish ambition or conceit' (Philippians 2:3). One intercessor once explained that the saddest thing she ever witnessed was ministers and missionaries all over the world that had not surrendered all to the Lord. They had given up so much to serve, but they had not given up self. There was much on the altar, but still the most important part of their sacrifice remained unsurrendered. They had a blessing, but not *the* Blesser.

If we do not know the Holy Spirit, we will love doctrine more than devotion to Christ. We will have a denomination, but no dynamism. We will know about God, but not know Him. We love the written Word, but not the Word, Christ Himself. 'You search the Scriptures, for in them you think you have eternal life; and these are they that testify of Me, but you are not willing to come to Me that you may have life' (John 5:39-40). In the same manner that Jesus Christ was rejected by those who claimed that they knew God, so too the Holy Spirit is often rejected in the Church (John 7:16, Revelation 3:9).

The Holy Spirit is frequently regulated to the role of silent observer in the Church, but the eternal, omnipotent and omnipresent One has been sent from the Father to teach us all things and lead us into all truth (Psalm 139:7-10, Luke 1:35, Acts 20:28, Hebrews 9:14, 1 John 2:27). The Holy Spirit is eternal and should have supremacy in the Church to glorify Christ Jesus, for He wants to indwell, intercede through, distribute gifts to, love through and guide believers (Romans 8:26, 1 Corinthians 12:8-11, Ephesians 6:18, Hebrews 9:14). However, the Spirit does not force His way into someone's life, He must be invited and His leadership must be accepted. As Dr. Priddy said, "The Holy Spirit is sensitive and gentle like a dove." The Spirit of God will always glorify Jesus. "About whom did the Holy Spirit speak on Pentecost?" asked Samuel. "About Christ, not about Himself." The Holy Spirit's desire is to glorify *the* Intercessor, the Lord Jesus (John 15:26).

Christ called the Holy Spirit "the Spirit of Truth" and Jesus clarified the role of the Holy Spirit in His teaching (John 16:7-15). The Trinity works in complete unity and it was the Holy Spirit that raised Jesus from the dead (Romans 8:11, Ephesians 1:17-20). We have access to the Father by the Holy Spirit and the sign that we are sons of God is that we are 'led by the Spirit of God' (Romans 8:14). 'For through Him we both have access by one Spirit to the Father' (Ephesians 2:18). Samuel warned the College that if they ever tried to become familiar with the Holy Spirit, it was because they have never truly met Him as God. "One thing you know dear friends, we can never become familiar with Him. These are the modern tendencies, but they are not biblical. Study the Word of God and find it so. He is as holy today and pure, and majestic as in the days of old."

Moses walked with God, and Peter, James and John saw Jesus on a daily basis, but they all had encounters with God on mountain tops that made them tremble in reverence. On that basis we could ask – have we ever been afraid in His holy presence? If we have not, have we ever truly been in His presence? (Proverbs 1:7, 9:10).

When we are baptised in the Spirit, we are introduced to the

Person of the Holy Spirit. But many are content never to progress beyond that introduction and to learn to know the voice, guidance and ways of the Spirit. Learning to hear from the Holy Spirit begins by sensing when He is grieved and responding to change our ways. If we close our hearts to hear when He says, "No," we shall never hear Him say, "Yes." If we respond to His rebuke and correction, He will honour our obedience with clear direction. Some may believe the Holy Spirit gives direction on an hour-by-hour basis, but Samuel found that the Lord dealt with him over time, giving him space to ponder His Words and grow in character. The Holy Spirit may speak to us on many occasions, but the bigger purposes in one's life are outworked over time. For Samuel, this was often over years or decades. Satan always plays the short confidence trick. He offers us our fleshly hearts desires and if we respond, he takes all (Luke 4:5-8). Discerning the voice of the Holy Spirit can take time, as the intercessor learns to know the ways of the Lord, as well as His leadings. Meanwhile, there are three 'leadings' that can influence us. 1. Human thoughts. 2. Divine thoughts. 3. Demonic thoughts. Human thoughts are those produced by man's good ideas. Divine thoughts are the guidance the Holy Spirit places in our spirit, through a direct word, Scripture, prophecy or inspirational idea. Demonic thoughts are those inspired and often controlled by Satan. The negative, critical and even false leadings as Satan comes as an angel of light to deceive and take advantage of believers (2 Corinthians 11:14). These ideas from dark demonic beings are 'dropped' into the minds of Christians to belittle them and their faith, or to lead them to a false step of faith, which results in rejection and doubt of God's faithfulness. It takes time to distinguish between the three influences, but the Bible states that the peace of God should be our guide to discern His will (Colossians 3:15).

"Ebenezer" on the courtyard wall of Derwen Fawr Estate
'Hitherto hath the Lord helped us' (1 Samuel 7:12)

Over the decades, when a year of study at BCW came to a close, Dr. Priddy also warned the students never to trust in themselves, but to trust solely in the Holy Spirit's direction, to guide them into the Lord's perfect will. "If you should have a feeling within you that because of my training and my gifts, I believe I am going to be able to cope with the ministry that is ahead of me, then I feel very sad for you," warned Dr. Priddy. "For if that is how you feel, then all you will ever do is what a man can do in his own natural state. The realm of the possible is the realm of the natural man." In this scenario, "You can do what your gifts and training have made possible, but the things of God that matter for His eternal Kingdom are in the realm of the impossible and the natural man cannot do anything in that realm." Paul testified that he had a great education, a high standing and a place of great authority as a Pharisee, but he learnt to 'have no confidence in the flesh' (Philippians 3:1-10). "Independence is false," said Norman Grubb at the College. "You think you're independent, but you're not really independent; you're in the power of the spirit of the flesh and you don't know that."

These messages to students were always a challenge: If we claim to serve the God of the impossible, why is everything that we pray and do within the realm of the human possible? Only when we step out of the possible do we enter into God's realm. That is the realm where Moses, Elijah and Daniel exercised / exerted influence in intercession. Why aren't we? Samuel would always remind people that we can only move into the realm of the impossible by following the direction of the Spirit. Samuel wanted all to know that we are not called to build a work for God; we are called to allow the Holy Spirit to build His Kingdom through us. He does not need our good ideas and intentions; He needs our obedience and empty vessels.

Samuel realised that messages on full surrender to the Lord are desperately needed in the Church. Often congregations are seeking sermons of encouragement only, and ministers are reluctant to preach on Scriptures which challenge. However, these do not feed the soul and spirit, producing a feeling of inner dissatisfaction in the hearts of believers. The flesh is an all-consuming black hole. It cries out endlessly for more and when it gets what it wants, it is not happy. The flesh does not know what the spirit and soul needs to have true peace and joy. The flesh is self-obsessed. When it is fed constantly, it drags the soul into a dark abyss, leading to self destruction. There is only one antidote for the flesh – crucifixion, death to self, to take up one's cross daily and follow the Master (Matthew 10:38, Luke 9:23).

Chapter Fifty-Five

Fifty Years as Director

As the decades passed Samuel greatly appreciated the new young staff members, mostly former students, who were seeking to work alongside him during difficult days. When one of these young people made a mistake, Samuel showed his inner peace by saying, "Don't worry! I've given up worrying about anything. All I have is my Bible and the quietness of my room and that is enough."

It was not always easy for new students arriving at the College to identify immediately everyone on the campus, particularly as the older members only seemed to appear in the evening and Sunday morning services in the prayer room of Derwen Fawr. Many, by this time preferred a particular seat, earmarked with a cushion so that newcomers were cautioned not to occupy those prime positions!

The Howells family in 1947 next to the "Jehovah Jireh" plinth at Derwen Fawr. On the reverse side is "Faith is Substance"

In February 2000, Samuel looked back over his shoulder for a brief moment and could trace the good hand of the Lord upon his fifty years of ministry as Director. He would have been ashamed, just as Ezra had been, to ask for any protection other than that provided by God (Ezra 8:22). Those years had certainly not proved plain sailing, but God had remained faithful to His promises in a big way. For many this would be an ideal time for a biblical Jubilee away from the onerous responsibilities that he still carried at the age of eighty-seven years, but he settled for a modest celebration in the prayer room, where staff and students gathered.

During this latter period, Samuel's physical health was showing the impact of long years on the 'spiritual battleground.' Summer months intensified his hay fever and a fresh irritant, eczema, on his pale skin found him often without a tie and wearing an open necked shirt, quite uncharacteristic! Even shoes became unbearable sometimes. Some students puzzled why Samuel was always wearing his slippers throughout the day, except on Sundays or when in the prayer meetings. Few people ever realised that his suffering was quite acute at times. Never a hint of complaint ever passed his lips, just adoration and praise for his wonderful Saviour and Lord.

Samuel Rees Howells, age 86 with George Oakes in 1998 on the edge of the Italian Gardens at Derwen Fawr. George as a BCW student had become friends with Samuel in the mid 1930s.

Age was now catching up with Samuel and a series of falls produced by sudden shifts in his blood pressure caused him to black out, often with dangerous consequences as he struck his head. In one meeting, he collapsed whilst preaching and seeking stability from the pulpit pulled it down upon himself. After that incident, the pulpit was screwed to the floor, and after some months, Samuel began to preach from a seated position instead. It was obvious that realistic preparations were required for the future and new trustees were being appointed.

Chapter Fifty-Six

Vulnerabilities

In Western culture, any vulnerable part of a person's character can be known as their 'Achilles heel.' In any individual's walk with God, particularly someone vitally involved in affairs and interests of the Kingdom of God, Satan will always snidely search out and seek to penetrate vulnerable areas in that person's life (Luke 22:31). It was certainly so in Samuel's life, as we shall endeavour to illustrate.

Throughout his years, Samuel had always remained very reserved, and the various added personal attacks upon his character and the work he represented, familiar to all Christian leaders, made him extremely cautious (Galatians 5:15). He rarely contributed in round the table business discussions or expressed his opinions, but preferred to speak to people on an individual basis in private. This perceived secrecy in some aspects of his ministry provoked much speculation among his critics. Sometimes false accusations were made against him and it often took some damaging years before they could be conclusively disproved. A seemingly reclusive nature and the difficulties with sharing with others was his Achilles heel.

Throughout Samuel's lifetime, there were many controversial issues at the College. Concerns were represented to him about repairing and modernising existing facilities, the need of suitable care for elderly staff members, the provision of School equipment and many other issues. All ministries have their own difficult challenges to face. In his role as Director, it was suggested to Samuel that he should share the responsibilities more with other members of staff. As was his custom when faced with complicated issues, his only response when presented with well prepared and carefully planned ideas (which had taken long hours to think through) was, "We'll see!" This was Samuel's way of saying, "I am not really keen on the idea, but I will consider it prayerfully."

Samuel's leadership style was complex, but he always had reasons for his decisions. As an example, for over a thousand years in Europe, Christians built 'palaces' for God to be worshipped in, whilst ignoring the Lord's command to make disciples of all nations! These buildings consumed the wealth of the Church and in foreign lands were often confiscated by rogue governments. This would affect Samuel's feeling about buildings considerably and determined his apparent reluctance to invest too heavily in repairing properties, or in a building programme, often rousing the passions of many. He felt it a wiser policy to invest in providing the Scriptures, knowing that these would touch lives, while buildings would crumble or fall into the wrong hands. The living Church is not a building, but a fellowship of believers and Samuel wanted to invest in the spread of the Gospel (and His Word), which would last for eternity. Even so, perhaps some of his reluctance was tempered by the fact that he just did not like change, particularly if it involved the demolition of buildings or cutting down trees, so his caution did provide a buffer against the more ambitious members of the College fellowship.

There was also a significant age difference between Samuel's contemporaries and following generations. As the ageing staff became unable to continue their work, finding people to match their calibre of surrender, in an age where the Church gets distracted by temporal pleasure was hard. Samuel's ageing body certainly affected his ability to be 'seen' at the College, and he was possibly endeavouring to avoid the trap of becoming a popular figure. His father had been outgoing and forthright in his public statements and drew together a band of followers, not all of whom could appreciate the nature of his walk of faith. As with Jesus when He rode into Jerusalem on His final entry, the fickle crowd wanted a hero.

Maybe it could be argued that Samuel in his elderly years shared similarities with the aged King David. He was Israel's greatest king, his exploits were exceptional and Israel owed much to his faith and obedience; but he still exhibited vulnerabilities which caused many problems. In his last years, his frailties led to many crises, including the failure to establish an orderly succession (1 Kings 1:5-53).

As with every ministry, mistakes were made at the College, but they should not overshadow its fruit. Sometimes Christians have the misapprehension of believing that men and women used by God can never be at fault! On the other hand, there is a danger of dismissing all the achievements of Christian leaders when they err. If this was biblical, Abraham, Isaac, Jacob, Moses, David, Solomon, Peter, Paul and nearly all the people in the Bible would have to be written off as no good! In Scripture, many of the people chosen by God erred and in the life of every Christian ministry, the same is true. Jesus forgave Peter after his denial and re-commissioned him (John 21:7-19), and Paul corrected and forgave him too (Galatians 2:11-16). Doubting Thomas was also given a second chance.

Perhaps some of the difficulties at the College were due to the fluctuations between apostolic leadership and the calling to hidden intercession. Samuel had found that the ministry of intercession does require protection from 'tares' (Matt. 13:24-30), and he learnt that it was unwise to share too much with those who had not walked the same path. The awkward balance between the need to protect the ministry of intercession and the desire for apostolic leadership put him in a difficult position. An intercessor can arise from any of the roles of Ephesians 4:11-16, but as they must know the purposes of God and declare His living Word for today (during and after an intercession), the prophetic element is often strong. The intercessor must be able to find God's authority for a world situation and only then can he or she speak His Word. It is not man's word that they speak, but God's Word, with God's power behind it!

Meanwhile, in the face of mounting pressures in the home camp, and feeling his own physical weakness, Samuel fixed his spiritual eyes on Jesus in the intercessions God had laid upon him and pressed forward. In situations like these his true spiritual stature shone through. With dogged determination (often misconstrued as stubbornness) his concentration and focus was in the prayers upon him, being fully persuaded that the Lord meant every promise that He uttered while He was on earth. In concluding his letters, Samuel would often add: 'We are proving the reality of those words of the Lord, "Except a corn of wheat fall into the ground and die, it abideth alone; but if it die, it bringeth forth much fruit" ' (John 12:24).

Life was not easy for Samuel, because over many years Satan unleashed a series of schemes in a determined effort to destroy the Lord's work as it had developed through the ministry. To undermine him, the enemy had tried to paint a convincing, but false picture of what Samuel had been doing. It was not a case of trying to frustrate the progress of this Bible teaching facility, because there were other similar colleges providing training for students worldwide. These attacks were designed to block the ministry of intercession and practical support directed towards Christians working in countries around the world. Some were former students, others were nationals in difficult areas hostile to the Gospel, and many were nationals involved with agencies distributing the Scriptures.

The College was 'a house of prayer for all nations' and Satan resists prevailing prayer. However, the strength of Samuel's position in these tests lay in the fact that he had already relinquished every hold he had on the ministry. Everything was totally in God's hands and nothing could touch it. It is always a very important lesson for Christians to learn that until everything is totally surrendered into God's hands, there is always room for Satan to work. He is no gentleman and will trample over everything to obtain his ends.

During troubled times at the College, Samuel often found strength in some of Rees' potent sayings, "The Holy Spirit does not know doubt, misery or worry, these are of self...Unless we believe in a test we have never believed...If I only take a thought that the devil is stronger than the Holy Spirit I can close this Book (the Bible) once and for all." Satan has no new tricks and is no match for the Holy Spirit who is the Master every time.

Chapter Fifty-Seven

God's Word Available for All

One of Samuel's lifelong burdens was that every person in all nations would have access to the Word of God (the Bible). In British and European history, Satan has often fought viciously to stop God's Word being readily available to all. In the fifteenth century, many were martyred for translating and printing the Bible in English, but the intercessors of other generations had prevailed so that it can be read by all. Now Samuel felt the same burden for the world and was prepared to make sacrifices to gain a position of intercession for the nations, so that all could have access to the Bible.

Many Christians in the West want a personal prophecy from God, but how many have stopped to realise that God is already trying to speak to them through the Bible? Samuel never took the Bible for granted. He never became familiar with the idea that God Himself has already revealed the past, present and future of all history in the sacred pages of Scripture. The answer to every question is found in His written Word and the full revelation of the ministry of Christ and the Holy Spirit from before time began, to the fullness of time, has been printed for all in the West to read!

In his anointed ministry sessions, Samuel continually stressed the importance of the Word of God and pointed out how one of Satan's strategies is to deprive people of the privilege of access to the Scriptures, as had been the case in Eastern Europe under Communism. When the storms are raging around us God's Word becomes a rock, leading us to the Saviour. The importance of committing Scriptures to memory, especially early in life, cannot be overestimated. It is the ministry of the Holy Spirit to bring revelation and understanding. Samuel was confident that what people needed most in the world was the Word of God, not sermons, so he pressed forward, despite his real frailty and the buffetings that he was experiencing on every hand, to send many gifts to agencies and individuals around the world who were involved in taking the Scriptures to the people. Writing of the work he stated: 'In addition to the work of the College, the Lord has also given us a worldwide ministry and we endeavour to help missionaries and national workers in the various countries, particularly in the provision and distribution of the Scriptures.' In each year he received news back. In 1995 a letter arrived. 'May I thank you for your recent gift for helping in the distribution of God's Word among these needy people, especially refugees. The situation in our country and in Bosnia-Herzegovina is still very distressing.'

Now, as Samuel was reaching the last few years of his life, he felt a heavy responsibility to prevail for the finances required for the Every Creature Vision to be completed and for a copy of the Bible to be provided to all who desire it. After the war years, Samuel's father became increasingly concerned about the need for intercession to prevail to release the finances needed to reach every creature with the Gospel. The Gospel is free, but the cost of sending it is not. If the last command of the Lord was to be obeyed by the Church, every believer would have to deny self to release the money needed to support God's appointed and anointed work around the world.

In his final intercession, Rees had the assurance that victory was complete. Some weeks before his death, Rees asked his son Samuel to promise to make a practical demonstration of his faith, by releasing a large gift in fulfilment of this intercession. Samuel was to give away £100,000 (worth £2,700,000 / $4,320,000 in 2012!) with no strings attached. "There is one thing I want you to promise me," said Rees. "That you will see that the £100,000 will be given away to the countries of the world as I have believed and desired to do, because the intercession for world blessing is wrapped up in that sign. You will not let it go, will you?" Samuel reminded his father that he did not have the faith for such a large sum, nor even a much smaller one, but he promised that he would not let it go, whatever happened." Samuel had been thrown in at the deep end!

Under Samuel's leadership, few of the young intercessors had anticipated the struggles Satan would unleash against Gospel liberty around the world, and the intercessions for each crisis kept them engaged for long periods. These spiritual battles from the 1950s and beyond became so intense, that Samuel often had to put aside the financial concerns of the Bible College to focus exclusively upon them. Afterward, he would need to put the same amount of prayer into seeking God for the release of money for the College bills. With all this in mind, the burden to pray for the £100,000 was very heavy and though Samuel gave away more than this in many smaller gifts, the full amount was not available for two decades and charity law itself was a hindrance to its release.

As the College drew into its latter days, Samuel still remembered his promise to Rees and he raised his faith to believe the College would now release a vast sum, as a gift to seal the Vision. However, the younger trustees could not understand why Samuel was holding College money back from the urgent renovations needed for the properties, but Samuel wanted a large gift to be given away to purchase Bibles, so that the emerging Church would have complete access to God's Word. Samuel became increasingly aware that the Church in the developing world was living through great revivals, yet they had very few resources. In the same period, the Western Church enjoyed material benefits but lacked Heaven-sent revival. This conundrum and the solution to it seemed to be identified in the Bible. 'That now at this time your abundance may supply their lack, that their abundance also may supply your lack' (2 Cor. 8:14).

Almost fifty years to the day after Rees Howells' death, Samuel said, "We believe that it is the Lord's will to give these large deliverances for the dissemination of the Word (the Bible) throughout the world. We believe that. There may be delays and disappointments at times, but our faith is not shaken in any way. We know that these matters are to be fulfilled and that these large sums of money will be forthcoming. For the Lord to give us the grace and strength to continue until everything has been completed. And we want to thank Him this evening for the way He has been with us. For the way He has helped us. We could have given in often, but His grace has been more than sufficient" (2 Corinthians 12:9-10).

To release these large sums of money, Samuel knew that he could not, in the words of Rees Howells, "prevail upon God to move others to give larger sums of money towards God's work than he himself has either given, or proved that he is willing to give, if it were in his power to do so." With this in mind, he decided to make an enormous personal sacrifice to sell Glynderwen Estate. It was a bitter decision for everyone concerned, especially the residents of Glynderwen House, when it was realised that Samuel was prepared to sell not only the grounds and playing fields of this 6.67 acres estate, which had stood as a monument of faith for seventy-five years and had been the home for many generations of missionaries' children. Was that great landmark of faith to be sold? It was clear however, that the old buildings required very large sums of money to be upgraded and maintained. Also, Samuel's vision encompassed a whole world and not just a College and he was already preparing his heart to lay the entire College on the altar.

Negotiations for the sale of Glynderwen took place over many years and the burden upon Samuel's shoulders to fulfil his promise to Rees rested heavily upon him; but when the sale was completed, the donation from the College would be increased from £100,000 to millions; perhaps now the decades of delays in giving away the seal of the Vision would be worth it. To maximise the sale price, he was advised to set up a new Christian Trust, which would be responsible for all three College estates and he did so with expert advice from a former head of the Charity Commission's legal department.

Due to Samuel's retiring personality, it was difficult for many at the College to appreciate his true aim in making this choice. However, Samuel tried to explain his objectives to the staff in one meeting.

Chapter Fifty-Eight

The Final Intercession

A solemn hush rested over the prayer room in an evening meeting as Samuel finished reading the story of Abraham's steady climb up Mt. Moriah, and Samuel saw himself walking the same path. With perspiration pouring from his brow Abraham raised the knife ready to plunge it into his only son's breast. To believe the resurrection in truth is a very costly process. "Today," Samuel pronounced in the College prayer room, "I have placed the whole of the properties and the work here, on the altar. It is all entirely in God's hands now."

Samuel had now transferred all the BCW estates into the new Christian Trust and the eventual sale of Glynderwen would release millions into the Kingdom. Instead of keeping the money for the ministry, Samuel wanted to give the money to buy millions of Bibles for the poor in the developing world. For Samuel, this gift was tied irrevocably to the intercession for every creature to hear the Gospel. If every creature was to hear the Gospel, someone would need to gain the place of intercession for the financing of the endeavour. Samuel believed his last gift, or the willingness to give, would break open the treasury of Heaven, as he claimed the hundredfold not for himself but for the world (Genesis 26:12, Mark 10:28-31, Luke 8:8).

Samuel measured this proposal very prayerfully and in the light of the cross. He was facing laying fifty years of costly ministry on the altar just as his father had done, when in May 1939, he was prepared to sell Glynderwen, Derwen Fawr and Sketty Isaf Estates to save and house at least 1,000 Jews at the Penllergaer Estate. He was totally convinced that God would bless the world ministry and his present transactions with Him would one day release much for the Kingdom. The door to Heaven's treasury was open for financing the Vision to complete the Matthew 28 Great Commission.

Samuel had often ministered from the passage of Scripture concerning Abraham's willingness to sacrifice Isaac (Genesis 22). Sacrifice and the truth of Abraham's willingness to lay down everything is a truth easily discussed among Christians, but often a problem when we are asked to lay aside important sections of our lives – our family and friends, health, homes, possessions, gifts and our ambitions etc. To us it is the end! Samuel spoke with great solemnity, pointing out that true worship must always carry with it the element of costly sacrifice. He would point out that lip-service does not impress God at all, but rather what is going on in our lives. He would remind the College that the Saviour laid down the conditions for service very clearly. "If any man will come after Me, let him deny himself and take up his cross and follow Me" (Matt. 16:24).

Samuel had laid the College estates on the altar and by doing so, he showed the willingness to give up everything his family had ever worked and prayed for. Samuel had learnt that the work of intercession often needs to be protected and private; but the secretive manner in which events unfolded created tension in the College. However, Samuel would not relent and he was prepared to sacrifice his own legacy and stare death in the face, as his reputation was shattered. He embraced death to the fullest, even alienating himself from some of his own staff, who because of misunderstandings, could not appreciate what he was hoping to do.

Samuel had laid all on an altar and the equivalent of death was experienced. Like Abraham, he had laid his Isaac down, with the knowledge that the promise of world blessing was tied into his life (Genesis 17:19, 21, 22:2-19). That very sacred transaction marked a pinnacle in Samuel's walk with his God; a position which very few have ever achieved (Genesis 22:16-17). It was Samuel's belief that this gift would not only provide Bibles for millions, but would also gain him a new position of intercession concerning the heavenly treasury, so that the need for world evangelisation would be met.

Before transferring the College properties to the new Christian Trust, Samuel wrote to his legal advisor (an expert in Charity Law, a former head of the Charity Commission's legal department) along these lines: 'I want to know that I am legally correct and beyond reproach, before taking this step.' He received a positive response. Another senior lawyer also examined the process. They could see no reason for the transfer not to be made. However, last minute objections reversed the plans. Samuel, now entering his ninetieth year was advised to retire and transfer his leadership to Alan Scotland, who would take the College forward into the twenty-first century. It was a sad and difficult period for Samuel. In addition, negotiations for the sale of Glynderwen had to begin again.

Sometimes when we place a sacrifice on the altar, the Lord takes it and we watch it go up in flames; at other times the Lord gives back the offering we gave to Him. Samuel had laid the College on the altar, but the complicated rules of the Charity Commission meant that his sacrifice could not be received. Like Abraham, Samuel received back his Isaac, but his willingness to lay everything down secured the future of the essential ministry to the world, in line with the Every Creature Vision; just as Abraham's obedience secured the blessing of the world through the Promised Seed. 'By faith Abraham offered up Isaac...concluding that God was able to raise him up, even from the dead...' (Hebrews 11:17-19).

Chapter Fifty-Nine

A Living Legacy

Throughout the years, many new trustees were brought in to assist and help at the College. One of them was Alan Scotland, whom the Lord had used on many occasions to help churches and ministries. Alan was a BCW student from 1969-71 and then married Betty. He became a member of staff and undertook private study with Ieaun Jones whilst his wife was a student. They both share vivid memories of the faith of Samuel Howells. One of Alan's duties during that era was to be on security around the Bible College and in his own words, Alan would often see "Mr Samuel walking around on the top of the building (Derwen Fawr House) at three in the morning, praying and interceding. He wouldn't sleep much and he ate very little food. He gave himself constantly to prayer for the nations."

After leaving the Bible College, Alan Scotland held two pastorates before Alan and Betty founded Lifelink International, which comprises an international group of churches and ministries involved in strengthening churches and training leaders. With over twenty-five years of ministry experience behind him and travelling extensively throughout the world, preaching and teaching in local fellowships and conferences, Alan gained a reputation as being a respected pastor to pastors. Throughout the years, Alan returned to the Bible College to teach and on one of these visits the Holy Spirit spoke to him saying, "One day I will entrust you with this legacy." The sobering effect of what those words meant frightened Alan. For many years, he pondered what the Holy Spirit had said, keeping those precious words in his heart. Then one day, the College sent a letter to Alan asking if he would consider becoming a trustee.

Alan often visited the College to preach, which led to his ministry team deepening their relationship with the College, and their assistance in all matters secured the immediate future of the work. Samuel was greatly blessed by Alan's advice and on one visit Alan and Samuel took a private trip to the bridge where Rees had stepped out into the life of faith. Returning to the location where it all began, Samuel asked Alan what the Lord was saying to him regarding the future of the College. "That's when I shared with him how the Holy Spirit had spoken to me (years before) and the two of us kept that in our hearts for a while," he said.

In the past, Samuel had conveyed to Alan, as he had to so many of the young men and women who sat under his ministry, the burden to see the Vision completed, given to Rees Howells on 26 December 1934. The College was to remain a House of Prayer for all nations. Samuel Rees Howells, almost ninety, handed the leadership to Alan Scotland and his apostolic team. Samuel was assured in his spirit that Alan was God's choice to be the appointed person to take the work forward into the twenty-first century and there was no doubt in Samuel's mind. The elderly staff were now able to hand over many responsibilities and Alan brought many younger skilled men and women to the Bible College to prepare it for the mission ahead. The future of the ministry to the world was already secured as Samuel placed his total confidence, not in man's efforts but upon the Person of the Holy Spirit, whom Jesus had sent into the world to complete the work and there was no doubting that.

Now that Samuel was relieved of the burden of the ministry, many were able to view with deep respect the achievements of this quiet man of faith. For over fifty years, Samuel Howells was responsible to pray in the enormous sums needed for the ministry, but he had almost nothing to his name. Inside his bedroom, his personal possessions included a collection of old books and a few suits. The bed he slept in, the chair he sat on, the desk and the roof over his head belonged to the Charity of the Bible College of Wales.

Throughout the years, many young students struggling with the disciplines of College life had questioned Samuel's leadership style and faith achievements. Yet they forgot that Samuel's faith was subsidising their fees by two-thirds, providing them with a full year's accommodation, food and schooling, with no extra charges, all for the unbelievable price of £2,400 ($3,800) in the year 2000!

After graduation, many tried to build ministries themselves and they soon learnt to appreciate the staggering achievements that Samuel accomplished alongside the cooperation of staff members who had 'sold all' and followed the Lord. As Samuel once said, "Jesus fed 5,000 men, plus women and children. Moses fed two million people, so God must have been dwelling in him. If God is in you, what have you done?" The burden on Samuel was also very heavy at times, for he once said, "No one knows what liability is unless he has to walk it." It is one thing to sing that 'all things are possible;' it's another to prevail in prayer and to be able to write a cheque (check) for thousands knowing that the funds will clear!

Looking back at Samuel's ministry Alan Scotland said, "Mr Samuel has always been my unspoken hero. He was deeply dedicated to prayer, a shy man, but given to prayer and intercession and I used to say the greatest miracle in the Bible College of Wales was not the founding of it, but the sustaining of it for fifty years. Mr Samuel was a deep, humble man. He didn't like the big platforms, but he was forever calling upon God, whether it was for the needs of the College, or the needs of the nations. He had a real apostolic mandate to reach the nations" (Mark 16:15, Matthew 28:18-20).

During Samuel's era, thousands of pupils received an excellent education at Emmanuel School and at the same time students graduated from the Bible College every year to reach the nations. Some students went on to see revival and many have had very fruitful ministries. "People who come from every era of the College life will tell you of incredible experiences of God's presence on the campus, in the meetings and in the times of prayer," said Alan.

Throughout Samuel's years of leadership he sent substantial financial assistance to missions and missionaries abroad and his own travels took him to the world. Numerous missionaries were supported and unknown quantities of Scriptures found their way into the hands of believers from poor nations, as Samuel quietly interceded for the finances for them. Samuel was also very forward thinking in his ministries abroad; many organisations try to build an empire around the world with them in the centre, but Samuel released the works the College founded abroad, enabling local people to take full spiritual responsibility for the endeavours.

Many compared Samuel's achievements to his father's, as the faith of Rees Howells was visibly seen in the buildings he erected by faith; whilst Samuel's legacy was written in the hearts of countless numbers of souls saved through missionaries he supported, or in the Bibles that he purchased by faith (Luke 17:20-21, 2 Corinthians 3:2-3). 'You are the seal of my apostleship in the Lord' (1 Cor. 9:2). Peter and Paul did not build buildings, they left the living Church!

It was also Samuel who gave Norman Grubb access to the Bible College archives and worked to get the legacy of Rees Howells' intercession out to the global Church. How many millions have been blessed and taught by Rees' life of faith? In addition, the prayers and intercessions of the Bible College team continued for many years and had a role to play, with others, in shaping world events.

The Lord has also blessed the intercessions in line with the Every Creature Vision. When Rees Howells began his life of faith in the early 1900s, the numbers of Christians outside the Western world was relatively low. But for eighty-five years at the College, including fifty-two of them under Samuel's leadership, the College staff prayed for Gospel liberty and for the evangelisation of the world. These remnant intercessors dedicated their lives to believe for the Gospel to go to every creature, and as we evaluate global statistics today, we learn that the Church worldwide, through missionary endeavour and intercession, has radically transformed the world!

In 1900, there were 7.5 million Christians in Africa, today there are 505 million! In South America in 1900, there were only 700,000 Bible believing Christians, today there are 93 million! In Asia in

1900, believers numbered 22 million, today they consist of almost 400 million! In the Pacific and Caribbean many unreached people groups converted to Christianity and in the Western world judgement has begun in God's house (1 Peter 4:17). In Europe, there has been a substantial decline in formal Christian observance through the result of liberal teaching as opposed to steady growth in Bible-believing Spirit-filled ministry. Truly the Lord has been pruning the Laodicean Western Church and has sent revival elsewhere!

Samuel spent his life interceding and witnessing these tremendous changes in the world. After receiving news from missionaries that he was supporting in India and China, Samuel said, "It thrills one's heart to read how God is working all over the world. How refreshing it is in the days, heavy laden with bad news in the media, to lift one's mind and heart to praise God that He is in control!"

George Verwer, founder of Operation Mobilization and friend of Samuel spoke of all staff when he said, "They've had a phenomenal vision for prayer, for training students and sending them out to the mission field and a great vision to reach everybody in the world with the Gospel and they've maintained that vision all these years."

Samuel Howells proved a point throughout his life, which is often witnessed by those chosen by God for a special work. The greatest ministries are often hidden. True intercessors will always be found in the unlikeliest of places. They will often be dismissed, overlooked or disdained by believers whose walk of faith is less than it should be. Their hidden ministry of deep intercession can only be understood through spiritual revelation, therefore it is rarely comprehended. This is the life of crucifixion, as the Holy Spirit sets intercessors aside in prayer, withdrawing them into a life of abiding under sacred guardianship. To protect them from pride, the Lord allows them to be misunderstood, maligned and belittled. The hidden nature of intercession will frequently be misinterpreted and some will ask, "What do you do?" and "What is the point of all this prayer?" All these disparaging comments are a part of Satan's strategy to bombard the minds of intercessors and that of the greater Church, with doubt and confusion concerning the usefulness of prayer. After decades of intercession which led to a complete transformation in Eastern Europe, Samuel said, "It seemed to be an impossible prayer and how often the evil one taunted us and said that we were praying in vain." The intercessor must overcome the fierce darts of the enemy and live above the doubts of others in the Church. Then, to achieve a greater victory (before God), after a prayer is answered the intercessor's victory may be called into question by those who cannot comprehend the connection between intercession and a transformation in the world (Mark 11:22).

Samuel learnt that the call to hidden intercession is a life of intimate fellowship with the Holy Spirit, as He guards His Bride in holy jealousy. The intercessor learns that the Holy Spirit only shares His secrets with those who will listen and never reveal His word unless He directs. Samuel walked this obscure pathway to its end and discovered that every 'public death,' gave him authority in Christ to claim and witness the greater resurrection of the Lord in private. Samuel, as with all intercessors, chose to identify with Christ who 'made himself of no reputation...He humbled Himself and became obedient to the point of death, even death on the cross' (Philippians 2:7-8). "We are not seeking popularity are we?" asked Samuel at the College. "It was a cross that was given to our Lord. The popularity of the religious, of the evangelical world – what does that mean? To a true man of God, a man that has been to the cross and is broken at the cross – what does it mean?" (Galatians 2:20).

In the final years of his life and during testing times at the College Samuel said, "May the Lord bless us and may these days be sacred ones in His Presence. May we be careful of the way that we walk in Him day-by-day, hour by hour; realising that we are not in the presence of one another, but in the presence of the Almighty, the One who gave His Son to die on that cross for the salvation of the world. The Lord means more to us now than He has ever done before and our sole desire is to see His Son glorified and for Him to see of the travail of His soul and to be satisfied. May the Lord bless us and take us on until the work is finalised and completed."

Samuel loved the Lord and never simplified the cost to Jesus of Calvary. When speaking of the Lord's death he would often draw the College into a silent atmosphere of awe. With strained emotions breaking through he asked, "Have you thanked Him today for what He has done? Have you spent some time alone with Him, just to thank Him for His great love, inexpressible love that was demonstrated on the cross? That is the foundation of everything."

In February 1950, before Rees Howells passed into glory, he said to his son, "Whatever you do, you stand and maintain the intercessions." Now fifty-two years later, Samuel, with deep conviction knew that he had been faithful to this apostolic mandate. "But you couldn't do it yourself," said Samuel, "only the Holy Spirit could do it. If anything is precious to us, it is the intercession of the Holy Spirit. It's become a part of us...these intercessions. They are my life" (Romans 8:18-39, 2 Corinthians 5:1-7).

When his father died the Holy Spirit asked Samuel to take on the role as Director saying, "The gap is there. Will you fill it?" It was this commission from God that prepared Samuel for a lifetime of intercessory ministry which had a substantial impact on the world!

Chapter Sixty

Samuel's Last Few Years

The new Director, Alan Scotland, showed a deep respect for Samuel and as long as he had the strength to do so, Samuel would continue to appear at the pulpit, although his delivery was much slower and with fewer additional comments, he would read the Scriptures under the Holy Spirit's anointing. Probably his last public service was on the morning of 26 December 2002. It was sixty-eight years to the day since Rees Howells had received the Every Creature Vision and Samuel commemorated this day by recalling the Vision, the cost and the commission that had shaped his life. Jesus said, "Go ye into all the world and preach the Gospel to every creature" (Mark 16:15). Then, with a final public declaration of faith he closed, "We believe in the fulfilment of this Great Commission more than we have ever done. The Holy Spirit will be poured out on all flesh. There may have been unexpected delays, but there is not a shadow of doubt in our minds; God will intervene."

Sketty Isaf House on the Sketty Isaf Estate, 2011

Samuel never lost that passion which, by the strength of the Holy Spirit, had brought him through the severest of trials to a place of unassailable faith and confidence in God's revealed will for the future. At the College there would be outward changes as there had been since the foundation of the work, and differences of opinion led some to leave. It was also time to reassess the educational programme at BCW to meet the ever changing demands even within the Church. It was agreed by Samuel, that an appropriate aim would be to work in partnership with centres of study and prayer overseas.

Alan Scotland already had experience with Bible College ministry, and could immediately draw upon qualified lecturers from all over the world to assist in a similar proven teaching programme. Samuel was assured that there would be as smooth a development of the course as possible. The new staff who joined the work came in, from various corners of the United Kingdom, with very deep commitments and a close walk with the Lord. There was also a depth of experience and gifting. The seeding of the nations was their goal, and a warm spirit of love and unity prevailed.

Samuel, in his retirement at ninety years of age, was cared for most admirably. He was given a large room in Sketty Isaf House. Late at night, other residents in the building would hear him parading the large landing outside, on his nightly prayer vigil, sometimes with his lately acquired Zimmer frame. He enjoyed the early morning bird song, and the changing colours of the trees in each season, and he spoke often of the Lord to his many visitors, one of whom was George Verwer. Samuel had known George and supported him since the 1960s and through his regular visits to see his son, who was a boarder in Emmanuel School.

Physically, life became gradually more wearisome for Samuel, but he remained very alert mentally and with complete understanding of all that he discussed. Samuel's health gradually deteriorated in March 2004, so he was admitted to hospital where he stayed for several days, seeing close friends before finally falling into a deep coma from which he never recovered. He finally fell asleep in Christ early on 18 March 2004, aged ninety-one. As Richard Maton sat there quietly in the room for some time, recalling all those years of privilege sitting under his ministry, Samuel's last personal words came to mind, "Richard, they need you."

Richard and Kristine Maton, June 2012

On Wednesday afternoon of the 31 March 2004, a simple service of Thanksgiving was held in the Conference Hall. The College welcomed two hundred friends, who felt the loss, and sang two of Samuel's favourite hymns, including 'Jesus the Sinner's Friend.'

Alan Scotland, spoke briefly from the Scriptures, although he was emotionally moved by the loss of such a special friend and role model. His thoughts are expressed in his tribute printed in the Order of Service booklet: 'Mr Howells stood out to me as one who cultivated a profound prayer ministry of intercession. His journey throughout ninety-one years was not walked out on great platforms of this world. However, from a little room in the Bible College of Wales, he reached and touched the lives of many across the globe. His responsibility in bringing leadership to the College and its family of intercessors was greatly challenging, yet he remained true to the Vision to reach every creature with the Gospel of the Kingdom. He went beyond the superficial; when he said, "I will be praying for you," he really did intercede. Intercession was not just another word for prayer – it was his life. There are many memories I cherish of Mr Howells and his example is a continuing provocation to us all today. He was a very gracious and humble man and often reminded us that if we do err, let it be on the side of mercy, not judgement. His life was rich in spirit and in word, and though often preferring to withdraw from the crowd, he was a deeply affectionate man and knowledgeable of world affairs. There were times that Mr Howells felt his own weaknesses, yet he continued to pursue the purpose to the very end. He was truly a man of God and it is our great privilege to have known him and to have worked with him. The world did not deserve him (Hebrews 11:38). His was a life of purpose undergirded by prayer; such a powerful combination has changed the lives of many. His life has deeply influenced, motivated and inspired many. We mourn his passing.'

George Verwer speaking after Samuel's funeral said, "I was with him even as he came out of hospital a few months ago and when he turned over the leadership. Mr Samuel was a man of prayer; he was also a man of vision. He made prayer the priority of his life, which is so unusual in these past decades when there's been a decrease in the prayer emphasis. Here's a man who's an icon of spiritual reality, still a human being and it was just a privilege to know him."

The interment was with Samuel's parents in the family grave at St. David's Church, Penllergaer, Wales, U.K., which is marked by a stone engraved with: Samuel Rees Howells, Born August 31ST 1912, Glorified March 18TH 2004, Honorary Director of the Bible College of Wales, From 1950 to 2004. "With Christ which is far better" Phil 1:23. "Well done, good and faithful servant" Matt 25:21.

SAMUEL REES HOWELLS

BORN AUGUST 31ST 1912
GLORIFIED MARCH 18TH 2004

HONORARY DIRECTOR OF THE
BIBLE COLLEGE OF WALES
FROM 1950 TO 2004

"WITH CHRIST WHICH IS FAR BETTER"
PHIL 1 23

"WELL DONE, GOOD AND FAITHFUL SERVANT"
MATT 25 21

Memorial stone of Samuel Rees Howells (1912-2004)

Samuel's pathway to victory had been by the way of the cross all the way and this had made his ministry so very powerful. Such memories of Samuel's ministry linger long in our minds. Throughout his years Samuel always felt, as did his father, that people are too easily satisfied with little time spent with God and much activity to influence a few, rather than much time spent alone in the Divine Presence to see the wicked strongholds of evil broken and millions released from spiritual darkness and bondage. As a wise sage once aptly said, "Before we speak to men about God we must learn to speak to God about men." So as was his custom, he had prayed for 'young Alan bach' whom he loved with fond affection, appreciating to the full what it would cost his successor to ensure that the Vision of Rees and Samuel Howells was perpetuated into the twenty-first century and inculcated into the daily life at the College.

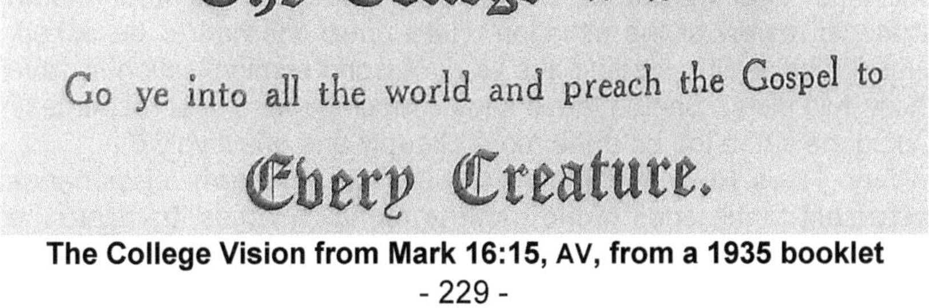

The College Vision.

Go ye into all the world and preach the Gospel to

Every Creature.

The College Vision from Mark 16:15, AV, from a 1935 booklet

Chapter Sixty-One

The Vision in a New Wineskin

Alan Scotland's personal history at the College gave him a deep insight into the legacy of both Rees and Samuel Howells and when he became Director, the Vision burned within him. "We want to maintain the ethos of prayer, intercession, believing God," he said. There was a new expectancy around the College and the work of renovations and reinvigoration began. Every year new students arrived and others graduated, and the new staff worked hard to transform the Bible College. With a new team of experts invited in, architectural plans were commissioned to find the cost of fixing the substantial structural issues of the properties and to prepare them for another century of training and ministry.

Samuel had already prepared the College for the sale of the Glynderwen Estate, and it was a sad day when bulldozers entered the site, but this was Samuel's will and this enabled the new trustees to make substantial investments into the College. In the past, Samuel had decided to invest in the Kingdom around the world, instead of in the College buildings. This sacrificial choice was deeply honourable, but now for BCW, the ramifications of them came crashing home. Experts examining the Bible College had to condemn parts of it and the costs of fixing the very old buildings were escalating. The two remaining estates of Derwen Fawr and Sketty Isaf were in a decrepit state and after years of development, the deficiencies of the buildings remained severe.

According to Matthew 25:21, God gives greater responsibility to those who have been proved faithful in the small things and the Lord found his new servants to take the work forward. Many friends of BCW from the past had romantic notions of what they hoped would happen, but as Samuel (and now the new team) found, there is a huge difference between having a human desire for an outcome and being entirely responsible for it, financially and spiritually! After several years of hard work and investment, Alan Scotland called a leadership meeting to address the serious structural issues of the buildings and the team began an exhaustive eighteen-month strategic review of the situation. Hard questions had to be asked. Was it God's will to neglect the work of world evangelisation to save these two sites? Should these sites consume these vast resources? Could the same job be done more cheaply and effectively?

When Rees Howells founded the College, Western missionaries were sent to the ends of the earth to found churches, translate the Bible and open schools and hospitals. Only the West had the money, means and Christian legacy to do so. Now eighty-three years on, the global Church had changed dramatically. The Church in the developing world already contains hundreds of millions of believers, who already know the local language and culture, and the Bible is available in all major languages; however, the work continues to translate the Word of God into every known language. The mission field is still crying out for labourers, but the work of a missionary is often different. Alan and his team understood that the young Church in the developing world needs training, assistance, financial aid and apostolic leadership. With this in mind, the trustees began to question if it would be wiser to have a smaller training facility in Britain and invest more in training Christians overseas.

Emotionally, there was a deep sentimental attachment to the old College grounds, but was it really God's will to take money away from world evangelisation, to save two mansions that were falling apart? These troubling questions are not unprecedented in Christian organisations. A. C. Stanley Smith, probing into the question of an out-of-date facility in *Road to Revival* (1946) wrote: 'The mission was faced with a problem here. Was it to maintain an old time-honoured institution, whose essential usefulness was passing, or was it to husband all its resources for more fruitful fields of endeavour? There is little doubt that the latter was the right alternative; but how often have the wheels of advance been clogged by the burden of an institution that has had its day.'

When the architects presented the plans for the College renovation to the new trustees, the possibilities were beautiful, but the cost of fixing the dilapidated sites would be millions! Therefore, after much prayer and with the eighteen-month strategic review at its end, the difficult decision was made to relocate the College to England, and sell the old properties. As the Bible College of Wales could not be located in England, a new name had to be found and it would be called Trinity School of Ministry. This facility would be established with the twenty-first century in mind and finances released would be ploughed into Christian projects and training all over the world!

The future was very exciting, for they could now focus on training and evangelisation on a global scale, instead of maintenance; but others wept at the thought of BCW possibly being demolished and turned into homes. Was all lost? Where now was the legacy of Rees Howells? In July 2009, eighty-five years after Rees Howells opened the College, the last student graduation took place in Swansea as observers declared, "The Bible College of Wales is dead." But faith stated that this was just the beginning! The words of Jesus became a comfort to many, "Most assuredly, I say to you, unless a grain of wheat falls into the ground and dies, it remains alone; but if it dies it produces much fruit' (John 12:24). As some were mourning this decision, others realised that the greatest death in the Rees and Samuel Howells story – that of BCW itself, could now become a prerequisite for a worldwide resurrection of the ministry!

In the 1930s, Rees Howells had a vision of training centres all over the world, and Trinity School of Ministry in England, became the first part of the post BCW resurrection, where students with British and European passports only (due to immigration problems) could study. In other parts of the world, Global Horizons, through a variety of partnerships, enables students to be trained within the worldwide Church. This is just the beginning of a new era of training and expansion, as the successors of the Howells' reach out around the world in the task of world evangelisation and discipleship.

Alan Scotland also treasured the legacy of intercession from Rees and Samuel Howells. One of his first decisions was to get the College archives catalogued and systematically checked. He also commissioned the publication of a biography of Samuel Howells and this second book concentrates on the particular intercessions in which the College were involved. In this way the many spiritual lessons, which resulted in the great victories that helped shape twentieth century history could be shared with the Church worldwide. Many other suffering Christians played a vital part too.

The author also prays that those who read of the legacy will respond, not just with a nod of approval, but by committing their lives unreservedly to the Holy Spirit's leading. The original BCW staff and students who responded in this way in 1935 and later, are mostly in glory now. They completed their mission; the calling of God continues. Throughout the world now, there is need, as never before, to see the satanic strongholds which have controlled sections of the world for centuries, broken. There is only one way this can happen; through Holy Spirit led intercession (Eph. 3:10-11).

"The Holy Spirit will take everyone as far as they'll let Him," said Doris Ruscoe. "There's a price to pay in intercession and the price doesn't get less. There are times when there are agonies in it. When there is deprivation in it and only the Holy Spirit can give the strength to go through, ultimately there must be the faith to believe that the victory is coming. You wouldn't hold out in the path of intercession if you didn't believe that the Holy Spirit would give the faith to believe through you that God's purpose in the intercession would be completed. There must be faith equal to the intercession."

Samuel often reminded students at the College, that the Holy Spirit is always seeking empty vessels through whom He can intercede. The need for intercession and intercessors will persist until Christ returns to fulfil all things. Until that time, the Lord seeks those who are willing to lose their reputation and to follow Him into a path of costly obedience. Those who obey may find the Holy Spirit leading them into a prayer that beautifully transforms into a life of costly intercession. Intercessors are not born, for they are called as they respond to the revelation given to Ezekiel: 'So I sought for a man among them who would make a wall and stand in the gap before Me on behalf of the land…' (Ezekiel 22:30).

"There are not many intercessors," said Samuel once, "and I was very much impressed by that statement in the fifty-ninth chapter of Isaiah, when God wondered of all those religious people, there was no intercessor. God was amazed that there wasn't a single person. There wasn't an intercessor in Jerusalem!" In the days of Isaiah, there were many religious people performing religious rituals and private devotions, but all of them were in the shallows. None was prepared to be called out into the deep into a ministry of intercessory prayer. Could the same be true today? "That's been the challenge today," said Samuel. "He's asked us as individuals to be intercessors. That's what He asked us many decades ago. He said, 'Are you prepared then, not to be a hireling, but an under-shepherd?' The hireling will flee in danger. But the under-shepherd will not flee. He will remain on the field until the victory is obtained. He must challenge us personally otherwise the thing is general. It must be in the particular. He speaks to us – 'What are you going to do then? Are you going to be responsible for an intercession?' "

Samuel often reminded his silent listeners, that the Holy Spirit is ever looking for a person to stand in the gap. The need was great, the labourers few, but God can do much through one surrendered individual. It was uncharacteristic of Samuel to make appeals for intercessors, but when he did, he reminded them to consider carefully all the implications and changes in their lives that this would mean, before they did so (Lamentations 2:11, 19, 3:28, 49). The Holy Spirit searches to and fro across the earth to find His man or woman. He found the man in Ezekiel and Daniel's days. He found them in the twentieth century. He will find them again in the twenty-first century. Perhaps you, dear reader, will be one too.

'He wondered that there was no intercessor…then I heard the voice of the Lord saying, "Whom shall I send and who will go for Us?" Then I said, "Here am I. Send me!" (Isaiah 59:16a, Isaiah 6:8).

Trinity School of Ministry

The Bible College of Wales of Swansea, South Wales, U.K. was founded in 1924 by Rees Howells and became a registered Charity in 1955. In 2003, it became the Rees Howells Trust and is now, Global Horizons. Rees Howells' Vision was to 'seed the nations' with the Christian message as was the vision of his son and successor, Samuel Rees Howells, in their obedience to the Great Commission (Matthew 28:18-20, Mark 16:15).

Trinity School of Ministry (TSM) formerly known as the Bible College of Wales is a non-denominational, non-residential Bible Training Centre based in Warwickshire, England. At the centre in Rugby, TSM seeks to train the whole person for ministry and outreach through a blend of sound Bible teaching and practical ministry training. TSM offers a variety of courses, with built in flexibility to cater for individual circumstances.

For more details, please visit www.TrinitySchoolOfMinistry.org.

Global Horizons

Global Horizons, under the leadership of Alan Scotland continues the work begun by Rees Howells who had a Vision that Every Creature needs to hear the Gospel. Today, many of the world's seven billion people, which includes every tribe, nation and tongue, have not yet heard the Good News of Jesus Christ. Jesus told His disciples that the harvest fields were vast and ready, white unto harvest (John 4:34-38). He urged them to pray that the 'Lord of the harvest would send labourers into the harvest fields' (Matthew 9:38).

Global Horizons, an apostolic company of believers (Ephesians 4) is at the heart of Lifelink churches, and is committed to training such workers with the necessary skills for the twenty-first century. This is made possible by the provision of theological training delivered through a variety of partnerships with the worldwide Church. Global Horizons Lifelink represents a group of churches across the U.K., the USA, and on mainland Europe, with further church relationships into South America, southern Africa, India and China, all of whom have chosen to work together in different ways for the advancement of God's Kingdom. Each church that affiliates with Lifelink is unique and has its own character and mission.

For more details, please visit www.Global-Horizons.org.

ByFaith Media Books

The following ByFaith Media books are available as paperback and eBooks, whilst some are also available as hardbacks.

Christian Teaching and Inspirational
The Baptism of Fire, Personal Revival, Renewal and the Anointing for Supernatural Living by Paul Backholer. The author unveils the life and ministry of the Holy Spirit, shows how He can transform your life and what supernatural living in Christ means. Filled with biblical references, testimonies from heroes of the faith and the experiences of everyday Christians, you will learn that the baptism of fire is real and how you can receive it!

Tares and Weeds in Your Church: Trouble & Deception in God's House, the End Time Overcomers by R. B. Watchman. Is there a battle taking place in your house, church or ministry, leading to division? Tares and weeds are counterfeit Christians used to sabotage Kingdom work; learn how to recognise them and neutralise them in the power of the Holy Spirit.

Holy Spirit Power: Knowing the Voice, Guidance and Person of the Holy Spirit by Paul Backholer. Power for Christian living; drawing from the powerful influences of many Christian leaders, including: Rees Howells, Evan Roberts, D. L. Moody and Duncan Campbell.

Jesus Today, Daily Devotional: 100 Days with Jesus Christ by Paul Backholer. Two minutes a day to encourage and inspire; 100 days of daily Christian Bible inspiration to draw you closer to God. *Jesus Today* is a concise daily devotional defined by the teaching of Jesus and how His life can change yours.

Samuel Rees Howells: A Life of Intercession by Richard Maton is an in-depth look at the intercessions of Samuel Rees Howells alongside the faith principles that he learnt from his father, Rees Howells, and under the guidance of the Holy Spirit. With 39 black and white photos in the paperback and hardback editions.

Biography and Autobiography
The Holy Spirit in a Man: Spiritual Warfare, Intercession, Faith, Healings and Miracles by R. B. Watchman. One man's compelling journey of faith and intercession – a gripping true-life story. Raised in a dysfunctional family and called for a Divine purpose. Sent out by God, he left employment to claim the ground for Christ, witnessing signs and wonders, spiritual warfare and deliverance.

Samuel, Son and Successor of Rees Howells: Director of the Bible College of Wales – A Biography by Richard Maton. The author invites us on a lifelong journey with Samuel, to unveil his ministry at the College and the support he received from numerous staff, students and visitors, as the history of BCW unfolds alongside the Vision to reach Every Creature with the Gospel. With 113 black and white photos in the paperback and hardback editions!

Revivals and Spiritual Awakenings

Global Revival, Worldwide Outpourings, Forty-Three Visitations of the Holy Spirit: The Great Commission by Mathew Backholer. With forty-three revivals from more than thirty countries on six continents, the author reveals the fascinating links between pioneering missionaries and the revivals that they saw as they worked towards the Great Commission.

Revival Fire, 150 Years of Revivals, Spiritual Awakenings and Moves of the Holy Spirit by Mathew Backholer, documents in detail, twelve revivals from ten countries on five continents. Through the use of detailed research, eye-witness accounts and interviews, *Revival Fire* presents some of the most potent revivals that the world has seen in the past one hundred and fifty years.

Revival Answers, True and False Revivals, Genuine or Counterfeit Do not be Deceived by Mathew Backholer. What is genuine revival and how can we tell the true from the spurious? Drawing from Scripture with examples across Church history, this book will sharpen your senses and take you on a journey of discovery.

Reformation to Revival, 500 Years of God's Glory by Mathew Backholer. For the past five hundred years God has been pouring out His Spirit, to reform and to revive His Church. *Reformation to Revival* traces the Divine thread of God's power from Martin Luther of 1517, through to the Charismatic Movement and into the twenty-first century, featuring sixty great revivals from twenty nations.

Revival Fires and Awakenings, Thirty-Six Visitations of the Holy Spirit: A Call to Holiness, Prayer and Intercession for the Nations by Mathew Backholer. With 36 fascinating accounts of revivals in nineteen countries from six continents, plus biblical teaching on revival, prayer and intercession. Also available as a hardback.

Understanding Revival and Addressing the Issues it Provokes by Mathew Backholer. Many who have prayed for revival have rejected it when it came because they misunderstood the workings of the

Holy Spirit. Learn how to intelligently cooperate with the Holy Spirit during times of revivals and Heaven-sent spiritual awakenings.

Supernatural and Spiritual

Glimpses of Glory, Revelations in the Realms of God Beyond the Veil in the Heavenly Abode: The New Jerusalem and the Eternal Kingdom of God by Paul Backholer. In this narrative receive biblical glimpses and revelations into life in paradise, which is filled with references to Scripture to confirm its veracity. A gripping read!

Prophecy Now, Prophetic Words and Divine Revelations for You, the Church and the Nations by Michael Backholer. An enlightening end-time prophetic journal of visions, words and prophecies.

Heaven, A Journey to Paradise and the Heavenly City by Paul Backholer. Join one person's exploration of paradise, guided by an angel and a glorified man, to witness the thrilling promise of eternity, and to provide answers to many questions about Heaven. Anchored in the Word of God, discover what Heaven will be like!

Christian Discipleship

Discipleship For Everyday Living, Christian Growth: Following Jesus Christ and Making Disciples of All Nations by Mathew Backholer. Engaging biblical teaching to aid believers in maturity, to help make strong disciples with solid biblical foundations.

Extreme Faith, On Fire Christianity: Hearing from God and Moving in His Grace, Strength & Power – Living in Victory by Mathew Backholer. Discover the powerful biblical foundations for on fire faith in Christ! God has given us powerful weapons to defeat the enemy, to take back the spiritual land in our lives and to walk in His glory through the power of the Holy Spirit.

Historical and Adventure

Britain, A Christian Country, A Nation Defined by Christianity and the Bible & the Social Changes that Challenge this Biblical Heritage by Paul Backholer. For more than 1,000 years Britain was defined by Christianity, discover this continuing legacy, how faith defined its nationhood and the challenges from the 1960s onwards.

How Christianity Made the Modern World by Paul Backholer. Christianity is the greatest reforming force that the world has ever known, yet its legacy is seldom comprehended. See how Christianity helped create the path that led to Western liberty and laid the foundations of the modern world.

Celtic Christianity & the First Christian Kings in Britain: From St. Patrick and St. Columba, to King Ethelbert and King Alfred by Paul Backholer. Celtic Christians ignited a Celtic Golden Age of faith and light which spread into Europe. Discover this striking history and what we can learn from the heroes of Celtic Christianity.

Lost Treasures of the Bible: Exploration and Pictorial Travel Adventure of Biblical Archaeology by Paul Backholer. Join a photographic quest in search of the lost treasures of the Bible. Unveil ancient mysteries as you discover the evidence for Israel's exodus from Egypt, and travel into lost civilisations in search of the Ark of the Covenant. Explore lost worlds with over 160 colour pictures and photos in the paperback edition.

The Exodus Evidence In Pictures – The Bible's Exodus: The Hunt for Ancient Israel in Egypt, the Red Sea, the Exodus Route and Mount Sinai by Paul Backholer. Brothers, Paul and Mathew Backholer search for archaeological data to validate the biblical account of Joseph, Moses and the Hebrew Exodus from ancient Egypt. With more than 100 full colour photographs and graphics!

The Ark of the Covenant – Investigating the Ten Leading Claims by Paul Backholer. The mystery of the Bible's lost Ark of the Covenant has led to many myths, theories and claims. Join two explorers as they investigate the ten major theories concerning the location of antiquities greatest relic. 80+ colour photographs.

Short-Term Missions (Christian Travel with a Purpose)
Short-Term Missions, A Christian Guide to STMs by Mathew Backholer. *For Leaders, Pastors, Churches, Students, STM Teams and Mission Organizations – Survive and Thrive!* What you need to know about planning a STM, or joining a STM team.

How to Plan, Prepare and Successfully Complete Your Short-Term Mission by Mathew Backholer. *For Churches, Independent STM Teams and Mission Organizations*. The books includes: mission statistics, quotes and more than 140 real-life STM testimonies.

Budget Travel – Holiday/Vacations
Budget Travel, a Guide to Travelling on a Shoestring, Explore the World, a Discount Overseas Adventure Trip: Gap Year, Backpacking, Volunteer-Vacation and Overlander by Mathew Backholer. A practical and concise guide to travelling the world and exploring new destinations with fascinating opportunities.

ByFaith Media DVDs

Revivals and Spiritual Awakenings
Great Christian Revivals on 1 DVD is an inspirational and uplifting account of some of the greatest revivals in Church history. Filmed on location across Britain and drawing upon archive information, the stories of the Welsh Revival (1904-1905), the Hebridean Revival (1949-1952) and the Evangelical Revival (1739-1791) are brought to life in this moving 72-minute documentary. Using computer animation, historic photos and depictions, the events of the past are weaved into the present, to bring these Heaven-sent revivals to life.

Christian Travel (Backpacking Style Short-Term Mission)
ByFaith – World Mission on 1 DVD is a Christian reality TV show that reveals the real experience of a backpacking style short-term mission in Asia, Europe and North Africa. Two brothers, Paul and Mathew Backholer shoot through fourteen nations, in an 85-minute real-life documentary. Filmed over three years, *ByFaith – World Mission* is the very best of ByFaith TV season one.

Historical and Adventure
Israel in Egypt – The Exodus Mystery on 1 DVD. A four year quest searching for Joseph, Moses and the Hebrew slaves in Egypt. Join Paul and Mathew Backholer as they hunt through ancient relics and explore the mystery of the biblical exodus, hunt for the Red Sea and climb Mount Sinai. Discover the first reference to Israel outside of the Bible, uncover depictions of people with multicoloured coats, encounter the Egyptian records of slaves making bricks and find lost cities. 110 minutes. The very best of *ByFaith – In Search of the Exodus.*

ByFaith – Quest for the Ark of the Covenant on 1 DVD, 100+ minutes. Join two adventurers on their quest for the Ark, beginning at Mount Sinai where it was made, to Pharaoh Tutankhamun's tomb, where Egyptian treasures evoke the majesty of the Ark. The quest proceeds onto the trail of Pharaoh Shishak, who raided Jerusalem. The mission continues up the River Nile to find a lost temple, with clues to a mysterious civilization. Crossing through the Sahara Desert, the investigators enter the underground rock churches of Ethiopia, find a forgotten civilization and examine the enigma of the final resting place of the Ark.

www.ByFaithDVDs.co.uk

Social Media
www.facebook.com/ByFaithMedia
www.instagram.com/ByFaithMedia
www.youtube.com/ByFaithMedia
www.twitter.com/ByFaithMedia

Lightning Source UK Ltd.
Milton Keynes UK
UKHW02f1828081217
314106UK00009B/451/P

9 781907 066139